WILLIAM GARRISON

SIMON & SCHUSTER

New York London Toronto

Sydney Tokyo Singapore

SMALL BARGAINS

Children in Crisis
and the Meaning
of Parental Love

SIMON & SCHUSTER

SIMON & SCHUSTER BUILDING
ROCKEFELLER CENTER
1230 AVENUE OF THE AMERICAS
NEW YORK, NEW YORK 10020

DESIGNED BY PEI LOI KOAY
MANUFACTURED IN THE UNITED STATES OF AMERICA

1 3 5 7 9 10 8 6 4 2

LIBRARY OF CONGRESS CATALOGING-IN-PUBLICATION DATA
GARRISON, WILLIAM T.
SMALL BARGAINS: CHILDREN IN CRISIS AND THE MEANING OF
PARENTAL LOVE / WILLIAM GARRISON.
P.   CM.
1. PARENT AND CHILD—CASE STUDIES. 2. CRITICALLY ILL
CHILDREN—FAMILY RELATIONSHIPS—CASE STUDIES. 3. EXCEPTIONAL
CHILDREN—FAMILY RELATIONSHIPS—CASE STUDIES. 4. PARENTS OF
EXCEPTIONAL CHILDREN. 5. PARENTAL ACCEPTANCE. I. TITLE.
RJ47.5.G37   1993
155.45—DC20   93-18779 CIP
ISBN 0-671-78680-6

DISCLAIMER

All names and identifying characteristics of the persons and places portrayed in this book have been altered to protect the confidentiality of my patients. This collection of cases reflects my experience across a number of professional settings and is not solely representative of any one university, hospital or medical center with which I have been affiliated. And, due to the fact that this book was written *prior* to my arrival at the Children's Hospital National Medical Center, any perceived similarities between persons, places or situations described here and the patients or staff of Children's Hospital is purely coincidental.

ACKNOWLEDGMENTS

I would like to thank my editors at Simon & Schuster, Sheridan Hay and Bob Bender, for believing in the potential value these stories hold for parents and for others who reflect on the meaning of the child in the psychological world of their parents. They helped shape a rough first manuscript into a more focused and fluid form. I also thank my literary agent, Nancy Love, for her earnest support of the project and her efforts on my behalf. Also my gratitude is extended to Peter Davison, who offered kind encouragement and advice to me at the outset of this project.

It is clear to me that this book would not have been written at all if not for the inspiration and ongoing education that both extraordinary and ordinary children offer me within the context of my work, and I acknowledge the fact that having children of my own has provided a major part of the impetus to my attempts to understand and relate these fascinating yet haunting clinical tales. These are the children who began both my professional and personal journeys toward a better understanding of the child's place in adult life.

For my own children.

For other people's children.

For the child who might have been.

CONTENTS

SMALL BARGAINS

PROLOGUE

EACH DAY BEFORE I BEGIN MY WORK I see my own reflection in the faces of my children.

On a wall in my office there is a photograph of two of my children, taken years ago when they were quite young. They are tan and relaxed, sitting close to one another after a long day at the beach, their mutual affection for each other easily apparent. It is one of those photographs that a parent holds dear, even though the children have changed so very much, perhaps because it captures a feeling we cherish; or because it somehow reminds us of a time or place we hope to reclaim. It is difficult to say why this particular photograph holds such value for me, just as it is no easy task to describe the role my children play in my psychological life, or to explain what it means to be their father.

Before I begin work, as I head out through the doorway from my office, I will sometimes pause to straighten my tie, using the reflective surface of my children's photograph as a makeshift mirror. Though the focus of my immediate attention begins with the loosened knot around my neck, it will often shift to the faces of my children and then back again to my own reflection on the glass surface. For this fleeting moment my face is superimposed upon that cherished image of my children, and I become aware of the work I am about to do.

What is the meaning of the child in the life of the adult?

I am a child psychologist attached to a large medical center, and because of the nature of my work, I often have the opportunity, and at times a pressing need, to consider and reflect upon this basic question about human relationships, which, more specifically, concerns the nature of the relationship between adults and the children in their lives.

This apparently simple question—like so many others that involve fundamental matters—is likely to have many different answers. It is evident to me now, for example, that the child will often become a catalyst for a change in parents' development, behavior and motivation. To paraphrase the writer Iris Murdoch, the entry of a child into any situation tends to change that situation entirely. Children *do* indeed have clear and powerful effects upon the lives of adults who encounter them, just as parents are a major influence in the development of their children.

Numerous psychological theorists have spent much time trying to explain both the normal and the abnormal in adult-child relations and have had much to say about the value and meaning of the child to parents. Few actually provide simple or satisfying answers, however. The most popular model of parent-child relations among the general public—a view that happens to hold the greatest appeal for parents themselves—is the sentimental version that suggests that altruism, selflessness and love are the foundation of the parents' bond to their child. An extension of this view to the larger society would suggest that *all* children are beloved and must be cared for, due to the child's special, almost sacred status.

A less romantic view—and one that attempts to reduce this bond to a simpler form—is provided by the behaviorist B. F. Skinner, whose theory of human behavior might suggest that children are valued by their parents largely because of the rewards the children provide to the adults in their lives. These rewards could include everything from the youngest infant's emotional responsivity and attachment to its mother or father, to the fully grown child's role in generation of the family line (i.e., producing grandchildren), thus ensuring a sense of psychological completeness in the parents.

More complicated notions about parent-child relations have been proposed as well—largely by writers and thinkers who seek to explain the very worst examples of this primary bond. Their ideas portray some parents as apt to use children to meet their own narcissistic or dependency needs. In more recent years, a few writers and professionals have suggested that adults seek to dominate and shape the child to enhance their own sense of self-worth and personal efficacy. Others have alluded to a pattern whereby the child's life serves to indirectly provide a parent with needed closure to his or her own unresolved psychological issues—as in the case of the parent who strives to make a child perfect or ideal; or the love-starved parent who has been unsuccessful in getting other adults to meet his or her emotional needs and who expects the child to provide the love that is missing in life.

Sociologists have performed large surveys that seek to capture knowledge about the essential nature of the parent-child relationship. First of all, the sociological surveys tell us that the vast majority of adults do have, or plan to have, a child or children in their lives. One large study from the University of Michigan, for example, went beyond this fact and asked a large sample of U.S. parents about the perceived advantages in their having children. Mothers and fathers in the United States indicated that the chief benefits of children have to do with the stimulation and fun their offspring are thought to bring into adult life, as well as the child's capacity to enhance family ties and feelings of affection. Parents in this country also speak of love, companionship, family and marital closeness. Mothers of children in America see their children as sources of joy, happiness and feelings of self-worth—and say that children are a distraction from life's worries.

The same survey asked parents about their *expectations* of their children—a question that might reveal reasons parents might value a child in their adult lives. By far, the most commonly endorsed item on the survey form was "being a good person." Given that the concept of *goodness* is quite broad, however, and open to individual interpretation, this finding doesn't shed much light on the true meaning of the child in the adult's psychological life—or of the wide range of expectations parents might actually hold.

The least romantic view of what a child means to a parent is likely to be one that combines biological and social processes. In such a perspective, children represent the future of the species itself. This view presumes a drive or instinct in adults that compels them to reproduce and nurture their offspring—and for reasons largely outside their conscious awareness, reasons that have more to do with survival of the species than with selfless parental love. Some studies in support of this decidedly biological view of parent-child relations have demonstrated that adults in nonindustrialized, or "primitive," cultures are apt to point out the very concrete value of children as a resource to the family and do not couch the child's meaning in terms of sentimental or abstract Western concepts such as "stimulation," "fun" or "joy."

In the final analysis, though, perhaps this question about the meaning of the child in the life of the adult is wholly inappropriate. Could it be that the bond between child and parent, for example, is *intended*, by its very nature, to be shrouded in romance and mystery—largely inaccessible to the scrutiny of poet or social scientist? If this is so, then there is much that may never be explained adequately, many difficult and disturbing things, such as child abuse and neglect, preventable starvation and sickness in perfectly innocent children—or the broad array of child victimization and misuse known to occur with regularity and frequency in modern times.

Can each of these things be dismissed, simply attributed to insanity or written off as alien to *normal* adult-child relations? And how do the horrible examples of the child as helpless victim reconcile with the special reverence our society-at-large purports to have for all children?

As a psychologist, I cannot accept a self-limiting view of the adult-child relationship, for this will inevitably hamper my ability to understand many of the people I seek to help in my work, namely, those parents and children whose problems derive from their relationship together, or from their primary bonds being tested through unusual or unexpected life events. Often these are families that must try to cope with life even as they endure the very worst it has to offer. And there is the fact that I have encountered certain clinical cases that, after I have had time to reflect upon them, challenge popular and sentimental notions about the meaning of the child in the adult's psychological world. It is my impression that many adults who are parents—and other adults who have contact with other people's children—have not reflected carefully on the value or the meaning of these children in their lives. A great deal appears to be presumed or left unquestioned when it comes to the adult's personal relationship to the child.

In an age that has become more secular in nature, the writer Joseph Epstein has referred to children as among the last of our sacred objects. But it seems that whenever we examine those symbols or rituals that a particular society holds sacred, we embark on a painful and ambiguous journey. Few answers may emerge, for it is often presumed that attempts to ascertain the meaning of our sacred symbols must be in vain. Many parents I have met interpret their relationships with their children as uniquely powerful and pure and, understandably, show a reluctance to delve much further than this. As with a religious leap of faith, the psychological meaning of children can be left largely undefined—palpable only at the emotional level. Most of the adults I have met, much like myself, find it difficult to express the special reverence they have for their children.

Perhaps it is precisely because of this essentially emotional reaction—the one that typically accompanies parents' thoughts about their children—that they find it so difficult to translate meaning into words that might provide a more exacting definition. But I have also witnessed parents caught up in attempts to balance personal impulses and desires with what appears to be a powerful, ingrained sense of sacredness they associate with their child. After a while, in counseling or perhaps following a period of self-reflection, some parents come to the startling realization that they cannot abide their child, the very object they feel obliged to hold as sacred. These parents may even go on to question whether or not they truly love their child.

When I encounter that sort of case it engenders difficult issues. It raises questions that challenge my comfortable assumptions about the ordinary, less examined aspects of other lives—not to mention my own. And the nature of my particular vocation, as a hospital psychologist, gives me frequent opportunity to play a role in the lives of children and parents *in extremis*, children and parents who have serious problems in their lives—problems that vary widely in type or severity. To be more specific, these children are the babies born with physical or mental defects. They are the children who contract life-threatening diseases or chronic conditions that can sometimes handicap them. They are the children who are labeled emotionally disturbed or mentally ill. They are the socially and behaviorally deviant.

I have come to recognize that the individual stories of these special children illuminate latent and unappreciated aspects of adult-child relations. The time I have spent amid the stressful events and extraordinary conditions that can occur in family life has provided me an opportunity to examine the limits and the boundaries that more typically remain unobserved and untested in the relationship between ordinary parents and their children. A dramatic or traumatic turn of events in any given family can shed light on all of human nature.

It is precisely during these more trying times in adult life that parents may be most likely, perhaps even predisposed, to reflect upon the meaning of the children in their lives. This will be especially true when it is *their* child who is the focus of extraordinary and unexpected events or conditions, rather than the child of a stranger or an acquaintance. It is often in these moments of trial and tribulation that parents are forced to examine the true nature and origin of the bond they have known with their children. For some, this can be a troubling and dispiriting process. For others, though, it can be an uplifting time of self-discovery, as they begin to grasp that parental love can be more complex and profound than any emotional attachment they have known before.

The stories of these remarkable children and their adults blend the details of clinical cases with personal observations and associations. I use some of my factual knowledge about the manner in which these children have been studied and seemingly understood to more broadly explore the ways adults intervene in the lives of children when things have somehow gone awry.

To protect the confidentiality of the children and their adults, their names and any other information that might identify them have been altered. The dialogue is reconstructed but it is based directly upon interactions with children and adults I have encountered in my work.

CHAPTER 1

SMALL BARGAINS

. . . with mine own hand [I] wrought to make it grow;
And this was all the Harvest that I reap'd—

—EDWARD FITZGERALD,
RUBAIYAT OF OMAR KHAYYAM

"WHAT DO YOU WANT TO BE when you grow up?" I asked the small boy.

"Now how *exactly* do you mean that?" Paul Dreiden responded instantly—and with a thinly veiled smile—after I'd posed one of my standard-questions-to-young patients. Then he began to chuckle in a silly and mischievous manner—and peered back at me intently, ready to challenge me again.

This little boy had asked me pointedly what it was I'd meant to say. What precisely *had* I meant by my very simple question?

"*Growing up* can be more than one thing, you know!" he admonished me gently. "So do you mean when I get older? Or do you mean when I become a man? Do you mean to say when I'm married and have children?" He went down the list one by one, pausing briefly before each item. "Do you mean when I begin to grow as a person"— he gestured to his heart— "in the *psychological* sense of the word?" He paused and smiled knowingly—even triumphantly.

"Or maybe you're talking about when I *finally* start to grow!" he suggested with mild irritation.

He looked mercilessly at me again, waiting for my answer—knowing full well he'd caught his new child psychologist off guard.

I didn't anticipate the effect of such a simple question on that particular boy, so I was naturally surprised by Paul's ability to appreciate subtle differences in semantic meaning—and within such a seemingly straightforward question. In fact, it had been deliberately worded to seem simple and straightforward to *him*.

Adults will often reword their questions to children—in order to make them more understandable. They probably do this in an attempt to bridge the gap between the child's level of understanding and their own. And perhaps because I am a peculiar sort of adult—one who's been specially schooled in the ways of the child—I've been led to believe that my simple questions can often tell me more than the child himself will understand. But Paul Dreiden's response had forced me to stop and wonder if I hadn't taken much more for granted than I'd realized—taken for granted that I somehow knew children better than they could know themselves.

I'd underestimated Paul, but he'd quickly reminded me he was no ordinary little boy. Indeed, he was almost a young man. And the distinctions he was forcing me to make were bringing me back into *his* world—and away from my abstract conceptions about the life of the child; away from the misleading and concrete cues of my adult perception.

I could tell he'd done this before—probably to other unsuspecting adults who'd asked him such a question. Perhaps to a teacher or a relative. I realized he must have rehearsed his quick response to my standard question.

But his reply made me wonder how I could be so utterly insensitive to *his* particular problem. After all, I *was* aware of his special situation. It was as though I couldn't keep the words from coming out just that way—the way they always had before—despite the subtle pain they might inflict on little Paul Dreiden.

"Well, I suppose I meant when you get *older*," I finally said, mildly flustered by my mistake. "When you get out of school and go looking for a job," I continued. "What would you like to do when you're, well, when you're finished with school?"

This had been a better wording of the question—more exact and to the point. Paul smiled, as though he'd taught another grown-up a lesson about thinking before speaking.

"I know *exactly* what I want to do," he said immediately. "I want to be a businessman—just like my father. But I want my *own* business—you know, a store where *I'm* the boss. The guy in charge, not somebody who answers to a higher-up. You know, the one who calls the shots."

He smiled broadly at the thought of this prospect, his legs dangling over the edge of the large couch, his feet pedaling excitedly up and down, several inches from the floor below him.

"And what will you sell?" I asked. "What kinds of things will you have to offer in your store?" He perked up again as I allowed him to expand upon his plan for the future.

"Lots of things—lots of different things," he said, pausing to give my question even more careful consideration. "But it'll be high-quality merchandise. Sold at discount prices," he quickly added. "Small bargains," he said proudly, gesturing "a little bit", by holding the tip of his index finger a short distance from his thumb.

"So you'll sell well-made things at a lower cost. Kind of like a bargain basement store?" I asked.

"Yeah . . . something like that," he responded. "I like a good bargain, don't you?"

I nodded that indeed I did.

"Yeah, most grown-ups I know love a good bargain," he mused. "They love to get something really good for next to nothing."

He remained silent briefly, contemplating his remark. And then he continued.

"But you know what I look forward to most?" he asked me. "I mean, when I get older and I'm a man."

"What's that?" I inquired.

"When I'm an adult I won't always have to be around lots of people. I can find a job where I can be a success, but I won't have to stand in lines or go to gym twice a week. I won't have to be in groups all the time," he added. "And I won't have to take the bus!"

Paul was fifteen years old when I first met him, and from the very start, something just didn't seem right about that number. My mental image of the boy—created quickly as I read through his fact sheet at the front of his chart—was much different. As I went to greet him in the waiting room, though, that image had dissipated in an instant.

He stood straight against the wall and seemed to be quite lost there—just staring along the walkway, drumming his fingers nervously against the cold concrete surface behind him. He reminded me of a convict attempting his escape from prison in the middle of the night—inching his way slowly along the walls, hoping the searching spotlights wouldn't find him.

As I turned into the office, I met two secretaries standing just inside the threshold. They were peering out and through the doorway, smiling at the little boy. But he made believe they weren't even there, gazing off into the distance and in the opposite direction. His miniature size, and the incongruent appearance of maturity in his face and manner, had exerted an enchanting effect on those secretaries, who giggled and chatted about the boy.

"What a little doll," one exclaimed to the other.

"Oh, he's just so adorable," her friend whispered back—just loud enough for the boy to hear. "He is just the cutest little thing! I could pick him up and give him a big hug."

He *was* so tiny, making me think at first he might be six or seven years old at most. But his face was strangely older than that. And his eyes flashed pain as he looked at me—another man—and realized I'd witnessed this embarrassing scene with these women.

The incongruence between his stated age and the child I met that first day was entirely due to the fact that he was only a few inches over four feet in height. He had been diagnosed several years before with *genetic short stature*. After I'd come to know him better, though, he seemed even *more* mature than his chronological age would suggest. He also had a better sense—a realistic sense—of what his life might really be about. At least, more so than any other fifteen-year-old I'd ever met.

The medical label he'd been given—genetic short stature—meant only that smallness was a characteristic shared in his family with at least one of his parents—and perhaps with one or two of his siblings, if he had any. Probably with a grandparent or two, as well. He'd inherited a tendency toward being short—and not because of any identifiable failure in his body hormones or any other problems in his life known to cause such shortness in children, such as parental abuse, neglect or severe malnutrition.

He'd been referred to me by Lisa Redmond, an endocrinologist who specialized in the disorders of children's growth. She felt that counseling about the psychological effects of his unusual shortness might be in order just now, as he began to negotiate the issues of what might easily become a difficult adolescence. And perhaps a few words with his parents would be helpful as well, she reasoned.

I knew that Paul and his parents had decided—almost a year and a half before—to start him on a daily regimen of biosynthetic growth hormone injections, in an attempt to make him grow more rapidly and dramatically. This relatively new substance, made available through recombinant-DNA technology, would boost the amount of naturally occurring hormone in his body and perhaps stimulate his physical growth.

This hormone was thought to have distinct advantages over an earlier treatment because it had been developed synthetically in a laboratory and therefore was more pure. It wasn't derived from the pituitary glands of cadavers, as had been the case previously; a technique that carried some remote but certain risks. While fewer dangers were thought to be associated with this new synthetic substance, only time would really tell. It had been available for a relatively short period, so no one knew what the longer term effects might be.

In fact, for children like Paul, the emphasis was on short-term practical and psychological benefits, such as bringing an unusually short child closer to the normal range in physical height. There were no guarantees that this would happen, though. And the treatments, even if successful in accelerating growth during childhood, might have a relatively insignificant impact on eventual adult size.

Paul's parents had been told of the risks and potential benefits and that it was uncertain how much height their child might gain. They'd decided it was worth a try, despite the unknown risk. And they were even optimistic it might make a major difference. It seemed a worthwhile treatment to pursue, even though it would cost them more than ten thousand dollars a year.

More than eighteen months later, the boy had gained a total of a little over an inch in height. It was difficult for his doctor to say for certain how much of that additional inch had been due to his medical treatment and how much was the result of his natural physical maturation during the past eighteen months. His growth chart suggested that the *trajectory* of his growth curve, or the velocity at which he appeared to be growing, had increased during the time he was prescribed the hormone. So it seemed the treatment had helped in that it had speeded up the process just a bit. But the result was well below the mark that had been set in the minds of Paul's concerned parents, for they'd read articles about children who had gained almost a foot in height with this treatment.

Since their son hadn't made the strides his parents hoped for, there was some upset and disappointment within the family. Part of the reason Dr. Redmond had sent Paul to me in the first place was to see if Paul wanted to continue the treatments. She didn't know for certain, since he always seemed so nervous when he came for his evaluations.

I'd also been told that Paul's case was different from that of most other children treated for growth retardation or delay. He'd previously shown a relatively normal growth trajectory for much of his life, until he was about ten or eleven years of age. Beginning then, the other boys he played with began to grow more rapidly, from two to four inches per year, on average. But Paul had lagged steadily behind, with the difference becoming more evident, and more easily noticed. By the time he was twelve years old, he was dwarfed by most of his friends who'd been in school with him since their kindergarten days together. So Paul became the short boy in his crowd. His parents then took him to a major university hospital to be evaluated for his troubling short stature.

It was interesting to me that very little research had been done on Paul Dreiden's problem, although some studies of children with various physical conditions known to be associated with short stature were available. *Hypopituitary disorder*, for example, where a deficiency in the body's ability to produce natural growth hormone had been detected. There were a number of studies on dwarfs and midgets, but these were largely concerned with the individuals' adult development and adjustment. There were even studies of children who didn't grow simply because they lived in abusive or neglectful households. *Psychosocial dwarfism*, it was called, and it was a pattern that laid blame upon a general deprivation by the child's parents or caretakers, although the phenomenon wasn't understood well enough to justify such generalizations.

Hardly any information was available about children with genetic short stature. This was because their size had not been thought of as a *medical* problem—at least not until the development of an apparent "cure" for the condition. But some endocrinologists had speculated that even these children might have a physical problem, a problem with being able to fully utilize their own growth hormone. The science of this remained to be worked out, however, but it left open the possibility that the treatment could be justified on medical grounds.

Conceivably, genetically short children might have it somewhat better, though, one psychologically oriented article had suggested. They would be reared in an environment where at least some of the first-degree blood relatives would be smaller in size and perhaps more accepting. Other studies, the ones that lumped together children who were short due to a variety of reasons, concluded that all types of short children had their own peculiar psychological issues; issues directly related to their short stature. No child spends his or her entire life in the comfort of home and family. Even these physically healthy children might show a pattern to their problems.

In several of the studies of short children, and especially the ones that focused on smaller boys, such children were reported to show less emotional maturity. This was thought to manifest itself through poor social judgment. The child might behave like a "class clown" or in a way that suggested he was much younger than his actual chronological age. Some of the short boys were described as having problems with moodiness and with the inappropriate use of physical or verbal aggression in social situations. The child might either appear overly submissive and conforming to the peer group or, conversely, hostile and dominating.

One study suggested that later in childhood, and usually beginning in early adolescence, short children can show an abrupt pattern of serious social withdrawal and a reduction in their interest in team sports or scholastic pursuits, a loss in their sense of competitiveness and level of interest in the outside world.

In general, many of these children were thought to be at risk for developing anxiety symptoms associated with group activities and social events. These small adolescents would begin to avoid situations where they might be singled out and then teased, taunted or bullied. They might even stay away from everyday situations where they could be made a spectacle for others, such as in school or at community events. This avoidance hadn't struck me as all that unreasonable, however unfortunate it seemed.

Synthetic growth hormone was seen by some as a breakthrough in the treatment of many problems in children's physical growth, regardless of the particular reason for short stature in a given child. Indeed, recent medical trials of the hormone had suggested that just about any child stood a moderate chance to gain some additional height from use of the substance. But the exact gains, and the children who might respond, could not be estimated well. Some children had shown major spurts, growing from four to six inches within a year or two, while others had shown no increase at all. These differences occurred despite identical medical protocols in terms of dosage and frequency of administration of the hormone. The average gains in height were between two and five inches, achieved over a course of from one to five years, depending on the age of the child when the treatments began.

As with many advances in medical technology, the development and use of synthetic growth hormone on children had been accompanied by its own thorny ethical issues. For example, it wasn't clear that the treatment should be used for children like Paul Dreiden, who were physically healthy in every respect. For a boy like Paul, what would be the medical *disorder* the physician would be treating? He just happened to be short, as his father and grandfather had been. Was *shortness* to be defined as a handicapping condition, or as a disorder of childhood? Was this, in turn, a statement about short people in the society at large? What *were* the origins of this concern about the height of our children, of ourselves? After all, how short was *too* short? How tall was tall enough? And were there real advantages to being taller in this world?

Additionally, there were the many cases of anabolic steroids and growth hormone being used to improve the chances that a boy might have a successful athletic career. These potent metabolic substances had been prescribed specifically to increase height and muscular bulk and not for medical reasons, since many of the boys were of average build and height. Rather, the problem seemed to be they just weren't big enough, not strong enough, not fast enough. At least not enough for someone's liking. This was a practice some physicians would allow and supervise if the parents gave their permission. Or if the parents had somehow insisted the doctor make their son much larger than he was.

These cases had raised the question of whether or not *any* child, short or not, should have access to treatment in order to gain additional physical height. If it could be justified for the constitutionally small child, some critics had argued, then why deny the substance to others, to the children who had their own psychological or practical reasons for wanting to be bigger. It was an issue that challenged existing definitions of medicine's role in altering human development. And what, after all, was our conception of the normal child? Was it any child found within the full range of variation that we knew naturally existed? Or was it the *superior* child certain parents seemed so intent on having in their lives.

Paul Dreiden only knew it might be better to be a little taller. I don't think he ever fully understood what the fuss was all about.

The first thing I noticed about Mr. and Mrs. Dreiden was the stark difference in their height. I really didn't have an appreciation of it until they both stood up to greet me in the waiting area outside my office. Mr. Dreiden was a compact man with a muscular build, approximately five feet in height. His wife, on the other hand, was at least four or five inches taller than her husband, a dramatic difference made more apparent as she cast her long shadow in his direction.

Geneticists have a term—*assortative mating*—a rather unromantic scientific term that refers to the fact that we humans, like many other species, tend to be attracted to and seek out mates who are very much like ourselves. There is a pattern to our behavior that suggests we actually *prefer* people who are quite similar to us. Perhaps someone who is like us in behavioral habits or personality, or someone with a similar range of interests. We are attracted to others who are at the same levels as we are in terms of things like social class, intelligence and schooling. There is even a tendency for average-sized people to be attracted to and marry other average-sized people; for tall women to marry tall men, and for short men to marry short women.

The geneticists regard this as a kind of convenient matching-up process that they don't completely understand. They do suspect that it has to do with biological evolution, and with the intricate relations between our genetics and our overt behavior, and perhaps with the psychological observation that we often seek out other people with whom we can be ourselves.

While there are certainly exceptions to this overall trend, they *are* the exceptions. So Mr. and Mrs. Dreiden seemed an unusual pair right from the start. After seating ourselves in my office, Mr. Dreiden got right to the point.

"I want to tell you a little story, Doctor," he said seriously. "I've given this some thought, and it's how I'd like to introduce myself to you." He had a smooth quality to him, like a salesman or a successful banker. But he also seemed sincere in his intentions.

"A few years ago—I was about thirty-five at the time—I was walking down a street in New York. Just walking down the street, minding my own business. Hundreds of people walking in front of me and behind me. You know how it is in the city, it's easy to just blend in on a busy sidewalk, to not even be noticed by the many, many people you might pass on any given day."

I noted that his story had somehow grabbed my interest, for he had a charismatic, entertaining style.

"So I'm walking along and all of a sudden I hear someone calling out from behind me." Mr. Dreiden sat up in his chair and placed his hands along the sides of his mouth, as if he were about to yodel across the Swiss Alps.

"Hey, Shorty! How the hell are ya?" he said, pretending to yell.

Mr. Dreiden's sense of timing in the telling of his story was exquisite, and he paused to readjust himself in his chair. Paused just long enough to achieve that critical moment needed to create the maximum effect.

"It was a guy I hadn't seen for twenty, maybe twenty-five years," he finally told me. "Just some dumb kid I grew up with back in the neighborhood. One of the schmucks I used to hang out with when I was living there." He shook his head back and forth slowly and incredulously.

"This guy from way back then . . . all he's got to say is 'Hey, Shorty!'; like I'm the same shrimpy kid he used to know."

Mrs. Dreiden looked to me in a way that said she'd heard this story many times during the past few years. It somehow served to sum up a vital aspect of her husband's life, as he himself had suggested at the beginning of his tale.

"*This* is what I want to protect Paul from," he added. "All my childhood I was called names like that—*Shorty, Midget, Squirt, Small-Man, Dink*—you name it, I was called it! But nobody ever knew how much that hurt me. I guess it hurts just about any guy that's made fun of in that way. Especially when you're a kid and you don't know what you're supposed to do. I still walk around wondering who's gonna yell it out next. And how many people are thinkin' it, too."

He paused again briefly to straighten his tie and readjust his suit coat. "Doctor, let me tell ya, being short is *hell on earth*," he said. "At least, as far as I'm concerned."

And with that simple but touching piece of showmanship, Mr. Dreiden sat back as if he were through. As though his rendition of that one moment would be enough to share the most painful part of his life with me, a total stranger.

At that point, as if they'd choreographed the whole event, Mrs. Dreiden produced a newspaper clipping from inside her handbag and carefully unfurled it in front of her. I could read the banner headline, although the paper had begun to yellow around its edges. TALLER MEN ARE MORE SUCCESSFUL, STUDY SHOWS, it said. I didn't have to read any more.

"*This* is my concern, Doctor," she said, knowing that I understood her point. "I've read so many things, and I think it's true—about how being taller gives a man certain, well, certain *advantages* in life. And this article says it can even mean they'll make more money, and people will respect them more and trust them," she said. "Doctor, did you know, for example, that over seventy-five percent of the presidential elections during the past hundred years were won by the *taller* of the two candidates?" she offered, glancing down to the faded clipping to make sure she'd gotten the details exactly right.

"She's always showing that clipping to someone," Mr. Dreiden interrupted. "If I get my hands on it I'm gonna burn it!"

I could sense he was quite serious, but something kept him from simply grabbing it away from her there and then, and probably had before. After all, it served some purpose in his life; and in a way, it was also a validation of the trials and tribulations of the short man.

"I don't really care about all of that," he added. "I just want to protect my kid from all the crap I went through. Now I'm in a position to pay for this hormone stuff, and if it'll make Paul taller, then I'll be happy. It's already given him an inch, I wish it were more, it's only a little bit," he said, holding his index finger a short distance above his thumb. "Of course, these aren't exactly *bargain* prices we're talking about here, you know," he added. "I mean, ten grand for a lousy inch! But we'll take what we can get, no matter what it costs."

The urge to ask a delicate question was suddenly upon me. It was there in the very front of my mind. It began to form even as I first met this odd couple. The Dreidens' opening comments had somehow ignited this curiosity, but I simply couldn't ask it. It wouldn't be appropriate. Not *now* anyway, not so early in our time together. But it was so *obvious* a question—there they were, just staring me in the face. My curiosity grew, and the question lingered at the threshold of my thoughts.

Mr. Dreiden knew what was pressing on my mind.

"You're probably wondering why she married me, aren't you?" he asked with a smile, gesturing toward his wife beside him.

As her husband motioned in her direction and began to chuckle, Mrs. Dreiden seemed to blush a bit.

"I just love the guy, that's all there is to it," she said, and her husband reached over and squeezed her hand gently. *This* was a scene they'd played before, I suspected, for all the others who'd been curious about their relationship. It seemed heartfelt and genuine just the same.

But then Mrs. Dreiden's mood altered, as did her expression. She slowly pulled her hand away from her husband's and then turned to face me more directly. Her tone of voice seemed to change, as well; it was now more forceful and determined.

"But *my son*," she said. "Now that's a different story!" And then she paused a second to gather her thoughts.

"I want only the best for him, no matter what it costs," she continued. "He's my baby boy and there's *nothing* I wouldn't do for him. I love his father very much, and his size was never a problem. Well, not a big one, anyway. But a *mother's* love is very different from a wife's, you know? I want only the best for him," she repeated. "If being taller is going to open up more opportunities for him, then he should be taller."

At last, it became my turn to speak—or so I assumed, because Mr. and Mrs. Dreiden sat back in their chairs and relaxed, cuing me to ask my questions. They seemed ready for anything I might say. But this beginning to our conversation had been almost too much for me to absorb in just one visit. I had a number of questions to ask them, but strangely, none came immediately to mind. So I asked for some clarification.

"Can you expand a bit on what you said before?" I asked Paul's mother. "The part about the love for a child being different from other kinds of love. Say, the love you feel for your husband?"

"Sure. Well, let me see. I guess what I meant to say was that what's good for me and his father isn't necessarily good for my son. I want him to have every advantage we can give him. And if that means he takes this hormone for three or four years, then that's fine. We hope he gets more out of it than just an inch or two. But we'll take what we can get, like my husband said before."

She paused to see if this was what I'd been after. I remained silent, thinking about what she'd just said. She interpreted this as a signal to go on.

"Love for a child is different from love for a husband or a relative. You have so many hopes and wishes wrapped up in your children. Sure, you want them to be *like* you, to believe the things you believe, to know what's wrong and right. You know, to behave, to be happy in life . . . to be a good person. But you don't necessarily want them to be *exactly* like you. A mother hopes her child will have it better than she did."

Mrs. Dreiden paused a moment to look toward her husband, who was nodding his head slowly in silent agreement.

"Like my husband said—we want our son to be spared what he went through when he was a teenager. And I don't want Paul to be discriminated against just because he's short," she added. "I see it happening already. With the other kids and with new people he meets, after they find out he's really fifteen years old. Before, they treat him like he's an adorable genius or something. And it doesn't hurt that he's such a cute boy. But afterwards, when they find out how old he really is, they treat him like he's a freak."

And then her husband spoke up again—but this time in a softer, less theatrical tone.

"He's our son, Doctor. We love him. He means everything in the world to us," he said, as his eyes misted over. It was clear his son *was* as important to him as he said. "If we can spare him the pain, then we'll do it."

"But what if he doesn't grow?" I asked them pointedly—having decided to confront them with the prospect that things might not go the way they'd planned. "What if he becomes a man much like yourself," I said to Mr. Dreiden directly. " A small-sized man who is successful—married, with children of his own. Is it possible that he can be quite happy despite his size?"

The Dreidens paused—and looked at one another, to determine who might want to respond to my question. Mrs. Dreiden looked back to me and then down to her lap, suggesting she had no answer. Mr. Dreiden stammered his reply, as his eyes misted over even more.

"I'm not really happy, Doctor," he said. "Despite the jokes and the stories . . . there's this feeling of, well, of emptiness in me." He drummed his fingers nervously on the side of the couch. "I don't think anyone who feels so different from other people is really very *happy*, you know?" And then he stopped, signaling me he was somehow finished.

"Is it possible that this unhappiness—or the emptiness you say you feel—has something to do with how you view Paul," I asked. "I mean, your desire to make him grow—and your worries about his future?"

"Yes . . . I would say it does," he answered confidently—although I had the feeling he didn't understand his attitude that fully. "But I can't think of any way to make it better for him—except to make him taller. When you're so different, the only real solution seems in somehow making the things that set you apart go away. You just wish it would go away."

His facial expression suggested he was puzzled by his own words and that these ideas might be new to his awareness. But his sense of helplessness was apparent as he grappled with exactly how he might ensure his son's happiness and perhaps, in some vicarious manner, his own.

Finally, Mrs. Dreiden chimed in.

"I suppose if Paul was taller we'd have some sense of relief," she said. "I mean, more than just knowing he would have an easier time in life."

"A sense of relief?" I echoed.

"Well, the sense that somehow everything was normal," she explained. "That the problem with his shortness was just a fluke somehow—and now we'd fixed it as best we could."

. . .

Paul Dreiden and I got along very well during our time together. He was verbal and friendly right from the start, and he had a special knack for ingratiating himself with the people in his world. This was especially true with strangers. In this respect, he was much like his father, who had captured my interest during those first few minutes after we'd met. It was a skill he'd worked on, or so he would tell me later. He said there was "survival value" in being liked by other people.

One day, after we'd known each other for several months, we had a rather wide-ranging and random conversation. It was memorable to me primarily because we seemed to cover so much ground in such a brief time. Paul was like that. On certain days *he* would predetermine, we could talk about the issues on his mind and the reasons why he was coming to see me. On other days, though, we might go through our entire time together and never say one word about why he was there or what was troubling him that day. In this way, Paul had subtly wrested control from me, which was something I could allow to happen.

"Dr. Redmond says it's up to me if I want to continue the hormone shots," Paul said one day, after he'd been to the clinic for his regular visit. "She said I didn't grow that much so far, but there was a chance I could get another few inches before I was eighteen or nineteen."

I knew that growth hormone had a limited period of effectiveness, and this had been what his physician had referred to. After puberty began and his body started to produce larger amounts of sex hormones, his bone matter would gradually fuse and harden. This was a normal process known to occur during middle to late adolescence, and it would gradually render growth hormone ineffective, for the hormone could no longer permeate the skeleton and promote additional height. So Paul's time on the hormone was running out.

"What do you think about that?" I asked. "I mean the idea you could get a few more inches?"

"I don't know. I guess it would be good," he said softly. "But you want to hear something *real* weird," he asked, beginning to giggle. "All the time she was talking to me, I mean Dr. Redmond, I just kept thinking how weird it was that she was so damn tall! You know, she's got to be over six feet tall!" He laughed and looked down to the floor, shaking his head back and forth at the thought of it. I noticed again that his toes seemed no closer to touching the carpet below him than they had several months before.

His offhand comment made me pause to recall the six or seven endocrinologists I'd known over the years. Based on that informal survey, the boy was right. There wasn't a small person among them.

"Why do you think that's weird?" I asked, although I smiled in a way that hinted I understood the irony in his comment.

"Well, maybe it's just too hard for a short person, I mean, like a short man especially. You know, to go into a job like that." He'd obviously given this some thought.

"People might think he wasn't very good at what he did," he added seriously, not aware of the humor in his comment. "I mean if he was short himself." And then his face changed expression, and I sensed he wanted to say something more personal. Something about himself.

"When I go see her it kind of reminds me of when I was younger . . . when I was just a little kid," he said. "I thought my father and mother were like giants, so big and tall. They could just pick me up and hold me like I was nothing. I used to think they could do anything, that they were superbeings or something. I was a little scared of them, especially my father. He can talk real tough, you know?" He paused.

"But now it's different, they don't seem so big and powerful after all. At least my father doesn't," he added quietly. "And now I know there's things they just can't do for me; there's things that nobody can do for me. I have to do them for myself. I guess that's part of getting older, huh?" He looked to me to respond.

"Maybe so," I said. "When you get older things *can* look very different from when you were a child." I was still curious about his earlier comment about his visit with the endocrinologist.

"What about when you meet with me?" I asked. "I'm about as tall as Dr. Redmond. Does it ever seem weird to talk with me about your size?"

"No, not really. I mean, I don't think you can understand completely what it's like, 'cause you're normal. But you don't stand over me the whole time, either, the way she does," he pointed out. "When we're sitting down it's more like we're. . . . well, like we're equals. I can look you in the eye."

We both became silent, to ponder this for a moment or two. Finally, he spoke up.

"You want to know the absolute *worst* thing about being small?" Paul asked me quickly, convinced he might convey the sum of his problems in one extreme example, much in the way his father had attempted to do.

"I'd like to hear about the absolute worst thing," I said, suggesting I'd believe just about anything he might say.

"Well, it's being on a bus ride! You know, being on a public bus," he said, pausing for effect in exactly the same way his father had when he'd told me *his* story about meeting his childhood acquaintance in New York City.

"Why do you say that," I asked. He had piqued my curiosity.

"Because on a public bus I'll run into old people and little kids," he said, playfully prolonging the sense of mystery his story had now created. "They are the *worst* of all!"

He rocked back and forth in his chair quickly, as an energetic fifteen-year-old boy is apt to do. He could see I was unsure of what he meant, which was exactly what he'd intended. Finally, he explained.

"You see, it's like this. The old ladies always make a big fuss about how 'cute' I am—I guess 'cause I'm small. And the little kids—you know, the real young ones, like three or four years old—they're the ones who want to know why I'm so small. And they'll come right out and ask me: 'Why are you so small?' You know, they make a big deal, right there in front of everybody. In front of my friends and in front of all those strangers." He paused and sighed out loud. "*That* is the absolute worst thing that could happen to me. I just want to crawl in a hole and hide. But I can't. I have to stay on the bus until I get to my stop. And I have to just put up with it, you know, put up with it 'cause I'm stuck there on that bus."

"But what about at school," I asked. "You told me once that some kids there make fun and tease you. They tease you about your size."

"Yeah, but that's easier to take," he said confidently. "First of all, most of the kids like me, so they don't really mean to be cruel when they let something slip out. I can see in their faces they're sorry, and so it doesn't bother me as much. I've gotten used to the slip of the tongue. And the kids who *aren't* my friends, they've learned I'll get my revenge if they keep it up. So most of them will stop it after a while."

"Revenge?"

"Yeah . . . I have my ways. Sometimes I just punch 'em in the face real sudden, when they don't expect it at all. My father calls it *sucker-punching*. No matter what they might do to me after that, they'll think twice before mouthing off again. I'm kind of tough, you know, even for my size. I don't really want to be, but if I'm not, then I'm in big trouble. And I have to be ready with a comeback. You know, I have to be quicker and nastier than they are, or they'll tease me all the time," he said.

"And sometimes, when that doesn't work, I'll get some of my friends to rough up the asshole. I've got some powerful friends," he added with pride. "They like me 'cause I'm funny and I don't take any nonsense from the jerks," he added proudly. "I've worked on that for a *long* time. I mean, keeping my powerful friends."

"How do you do that exactly?" I asked.

"Well, mostly, I try to hang on to my friends from when I was younger. They're all big now," he said. "But a lot of the time I just keep 'em all laughing. That seems to work pretty well most of the time. I'm a pretty funny guy, you know!"

"So you feel more comfortable at school now?" I asked. "It's not like being on the bus."

"Well, it took some time to make it that way. At first it wasn't so great. But I sort of got it worked out now. I mean, I have a *plan* for getting revenge if I have to. And that's made a difference. And I have a reputation for not putting up with any crap. It's the *new* kids I get trouble from. The ones who haven't learned yet."

I nodded in understanding, remembering the articles I'd read about small-sized children adapting to frequent teasing in a variety of ways. It made some sense to me that the research had noted emotional immaturity and inappropriate use of aggression in some of these children. Others remarked it was common for short boys to assume the role of the class clown, or of a kind of "mascot" to other children, as a way of ingratiating themselves with their peer group.

But what had seemed unusual and atypical behavior as I'd read those studies, now seemed perfectly logical to me. Some children apparently adapted better to the daily torture than others. And if they were at all successful, they would carve out a more comfortable and protected niche for themselves. A niche within the harsh world they were forced to endure each day.

Paul's next comment made me think he'd read my mind, for it was parallel to my own train of thought.

"But you know, Doctor, the thing I look forward to the most is when I get older and I don't have to go to school anymore," he said seriously. This comment also made me anxious, for I knew what it might mean. Several studies had suggested that academic performance and school attendance could suffer badly during the short child's early adolescent period, so I pursued his statement further.

"What do you mean? I thought you liked school?" I said. "And you're doing so well in your classes now."

"I know. But when I'm older, *I* can call the shots. *I* can pick out where I'll go and where I'll stay. I'll be the master of my own fate," he said with a flourish. "I read that somewhere," he quickly added.

"When I'm older and out of school I won't have to be one of the gang, you know, hang out with kids I don't really want to be with. I won't even have to ride the bus when I can drive my own car!" he said happily.

Just then he became unusually silent for a second, and I could see his face begin to tremble slightly, as if he were about to weep openly. But he quickly gained control and asked me another one of his questions.

"Hey, Doctor," he said. "Did you ever hear that song on the radio, the one by Randy Newman? You know, the one that says 'Short People Got No Reason to Live'?" He asked me this and then repeated the title of the song, this time in a singsong fashion and a remarkably true approximation to the original melody.

I nodded that I had, but I didn't smile. Paul was smiling at me, although he didn't seem happy in the least.

"Yeah, I've heard it," I said, recalling I'd laughed heartily the first time I'd paid attention to the lyrics. Only *later* did it seem to be in poor taste.

"The other kids get a real kick out of that song, you know," he said. "They just *love* singing that song over and over and over."

We both paused to reflect on his words. Then I asked him a question that had been on my mind for several sessions.

"What about the growth hormone shots?" I asked. "What do you think about continuing them? I've talked about it with your parents, but I'm not really sure how you feel about it."

He smiled and tilted his head slightly—as if to say he wasn't really sure how he felt. He giggled nervously.

"Well, I suppose I don't really like getting them—especially since I don't seem to be getting very much out of it. But it's pretty important to my parents—especially my mom." He paused. "They think it's in my best interest." As he said this last phrase, I realized it was something I very seldom heard a child or adolescent say—unless they were mimicking an adult in their life.

"But what if it were up to you and you alone," I inquired. "What would you do about the hormone injections?"

"I don't suppose I'd get them—I mean, if it was up to me. They hurt, you know? But it's not just my decision. They're my parents and they only want what's best for me," he added dutifully. "Besides, I can't take the stuff for much longer anyway—Dr. Redmond said there'd be no point to it."

We sat there in silence, uncertain what might come up next. After a moment or two, Paul said his final words on the subject.

"I figure I'm just going to be short—I mean, smaller than other guys my age. I can live with that," he shrugged. "I just wish everyone else would leave me alone."

■

Paul remained well below the average height for his age. Perhaps the growth hormone treatments contributed an inch or so to his eventual size. He went on to college, where he studied hard and did quite well. He was popular, as before, and had little need of someone like me, having managed to become more independent and autonomous than he could be in his teenage years.

As I am reminded of Paul Dreiden and our conversations together, I think back to the special respect and friendship I'd felt for him—and the important lesson he'd taught me. A lesson about a child's coping with daily pain—pain that other people knowingly or inad-

vertently caused—and his ability to overcome other people's expectations about what was and wasn't normal. He'd given me a momentary glimpse into an extraordinary child's view of the world—and the
meaning of his own imagined future.

"What do you want to be when you grow up?" I had asked him. He
told me much more than I ever expected to learn from such a simple
question.

CHAPTER 2

THE QUIET PLACE

She was not really bad at heart,
But only rather rude and wild;
She was an aggravating child.

—H. BELLOC, *REBECCA*

AT THE SAME MOMENT I TURNED down the long hospital corridor, I almost collided with my first child patient. A little boy was moving very quickly toward me—almost running—edging along the wall as he did. He didn't look directly at me, apparently more concerned about the two large men who were following close behind him. He was talking loudly—screaming, really—in an angry, desperate voice, as he hurried down the hall.

"Fuck you . . . and fuck this place," that little boy was saying, in a barely controlled voice that was guttural and intense. It was clear he was about to make a run for it, but he had to have known that he could only go as far as the end of the hall, for the massive metal door was locked and would be impassable to him. This didn't dissuade him from a desperate dash for freedom, though—he was clearly much too angry to consider the reality of his current situation. Perhaps this was part of the reason he was there to begin with.

The two staff members—young men who worked in the hospital for low pay—were former football players from a local college. I would later discover that they were there to get some experience before moving on to something better. The smaller of the two staff members called to the boy to stop where he was, but he kept on bolting toward me at the other end of the corridor.

In the next instant, and just moments before he was upon me, he was somehow in their grasp. Because he was relatively small in size, they handled him easily and got him under their physical control with a swift and powerful motion. Although his resistance was intense, especially for one as small as he, the outcome was inevitable. Down he went with surprising speed and gentleness, despite his energetic protestations.

The sight of two large men bending over the tiny frame of a forty-five-pound screaming child, his arms pinned and his face reddening from the weight above him, produced a sense of drama, and other staff members had been attracted to the scene, having heard this little boy's screams. It appeared to have had an electrifying effect on everyone nearby. Even some of the other patients watched from their doorways, although not one of them dared to set foot outside.

Although I was aware that those were just responsible people doing their jobs—work that can require dire measures with such difficult and disturbed children—things that smack of violence are typically unsettling, especially when encountered in the reality of everyday life. "You get used to it after a while," one of the male staff members would say to me later, almost like a veteran of many battles. "Sometimes it's the only thing we can do. If we lose control of them, even for a minute, they'll chew us up. They have to know who's boss, or they take charge."

"We're going to take you to the QR, Jim," one of the staff workers had said to the little boy—as he picked him up and cradled him tightly in his massive arms. "When you settle down you can go back to class." The boy continued to resist, though halfheartedly by then, his screams transformed into pathetic cries, like the whining of an injured animal.

He appeared to be holding on to his supposed opponent, rather than fighting him off, as he was carried down the hall. I followed along after them to a small room with no furniture or windows, through a door that had only one knob—located on the outside. I saw a tattered carpet on the floor, scratched through to the concrete by previous occupants of the room. This, I learned later, was intended to be a solitary place where the child was encouraged to reflect, or simply to regain composure. It was a place that saw regular use and was referred to, somewhat paradoxically, as the "Quiet Room," the QR. But I would soon learn it was hardly ever a calm or silent place.

As I was forced to inhale the intrusive odor of disinfectant that permeated the long hospital hallway, I was reminded abruptly that this place, intended to be a temporary home for children with emotional problems, was designed to be a kind of scientific laboratory as well. It was a place dedicated to the care and psychological study of children with serious psychiatric disorders. Some might have felt that those children had the most serious problems a child could have. Known more formally as a *child mental health unit,* it was one small part of a much larger hospital.

I was there to begin to learn about disturbed children firsthand. I was a psychologist-in-training, my experience no longer limited solely to reading academic journals and textbooks, or to following the dry lectures and abstract discussions of my learned professors. As I walked down the hall, farther into the center of the unit, I wondered about the little boy I'd seen restrained and then placed in the room with padded walls. Might he be clinically depressed? Or was he autistic; in a world all his own? Would he be psychotic, or exhibit any one of a thousand possible phobias or irrational fears, each a riddle to be deciphered? These disorders, although rare and exotic, were the initial reason for my interest in childhood psychopathology.

I would come to find out later that these were not the run-of-the-mill child psychiatric cases. Those would be something very different. I was destined to have an altogether unexpected first glimpse of my chosen field, which, until then, had remained quite apart from the more sheltered world of the university. I was also about to learn about the life of a psychiatrically disordered child—and I was not at all prepared for the lesson.

Many children in psychiatric hospitals will be somewhat reluctant to be cured or helped. As a result of this reluctance, there were thick steel bars on the windows—and the metal door behind me would click audibly as it automatically locked on closing. The majority of the children were not there by choice; they were there because their parents or a doctor had requested it. Sometimes they were there simply because there was nowhere else for them to go.

Their situation was unlike that of the patients found in the adult psychiatric wards, which were located only a few hundred yards away.

Nearly all of the patients in the adult units had been admitted of their own volition and would remain only if they wished to. Most of the adult patients were very depressed or highly anxious; some had serious problems with drugs or alcohol. Most of the children in the psychiatric unit, I would learn, displayed the same symptom—aggression of some sort against the adults in their world. Many of them were known to fight with words and deeds, and they would fight most fiercely against the important adults in their lives—the parents and teachers who tried to tell them what to do. While the children were in residence, the doctors, nurses and other staff members would quickly take the place of the adults these children left behind, outside those locked doors, and the ferocious battle would continue.

Ahead of me, farther down the hall, several people were sitting behind a wall of Plexiglas. That space, reserved for staff only, was called the nurses' station, and its doors were also locked. The jingling of the keys in my pocket reassured me that I would be able to enter. I remember thinking that this was one of the two ways you could tell the staff from the patients—the staff seemed to jingle as they walked along the corridors.

The other way to tell them apart, of course, was that all of the patients were children. If you were a child, you were immediately recognizable as a resident there. Even the most casual observer would know that and wonder what type of problem you might have, since psychiatric problems were the common denominator for the children in that place.

Jimmy Parkman—the boy I'd encountered on my way in that first day—would be my first patient in the child psychiatric unit. I discovered he was eight years old—a child of biracial origins who had been adopted at the age of three months by a middle-class Caucasian couple, the Parkmans. He had gradually revealed certain behavioral symptoms that were troublesome for his adoptive parents. They described him during the initial admitting interview as an increasingly aggressive child—difficult to manage, short of temper and eventually quick with his fists. His mother told the interviewer that Jimmy had been colicky as an infant, a fussy eater, needing to be held all the time. At least, that was how it seemed to her.

Jimmy had slept poorly throughout his early years and had problems with toilet training. In fact, at eight, he still had "accidents" from time to time, and this was especially upsetting to his parents. "The smell of him can be just awful," his mother told the admitting psychiatrist.

Jimmy had been evaluated, prior to being admitted to the hospital, by other mental health professionals, all of whom remarked on his tendencies to "regress," or to seem younger than his years, especially in the face of any type of stress. At times he might talk like a baby, or laugh and become silly somewhat inexplicably. At other times he could behave very much like the eight-year-old he was.

As Jimmy's behavior became more and more troublesome, his adoptive parents had increasing concern that perhaps he was displaying traits inherited from his biological parents. "His *real* parents," Mrs. Parkman had said, during the admitting interview. As a result of this suspicion, she and her husband became more curious about his background, much more so than they had been at the time of his adoption. That had been a time when he seemed the perfect baby—young and whole and healthy.

He had always been a handsome child—with chiseled features, a tan complexion and thick dark hair. "You're going to be a Latin lover," his mother had told him long ago. "You're going to set the girls' hearts on fire." Soon after Jimmy's fifth birthday, the Parkmans were finally successful in conceiving a child of their own—another son—quite unexpectedly. They named him Karl—and the fire in their hearts for young Jimmy had suddenly grown cold.

All of this was in his medical chart. As I read through it that first day, it occurred to me that his chart was a biography of sorts—unlike more traditional medical charts with their test results and brief descriptions of physical complaints. I was expected to formulate a theory about little Jimmy Parkman's problems—a theory about his life. My educated intuitions, in turn, would help me devise a treatment plan. Jimmy had been a patient in the unit for only a week, so we were both relatively new to the place, and each of us had much to learn.

I made my way through reports and letters from teachers and psychologists. There was a note from a child psychiatrist who had seen Jimmy, to consider psychotropic medications. A long letter written by his adoptive mother, describing in some detail the first eight years of his life, had also been included in his chart. It was a letter that took me through a litany of his adoptive parents' trials and tribulations. The narrative portrayed a life that seemed to be going quickly downhill. It told of failure after failure, problem upon problem, and no relief in sight. It revealed the story of a mother and father who seemed at a loss for what could be done, or for any ideas as to how all of this might have come to pass—except to hypothesize that perhaps his particular genetic inheritance was ultimately to blame.

Jimmy had been given an official psychiatric diagnosis by the admitting physician, taken from a standard manual of such things. It was entered in his chart as *oppositional-defiant disorder of childhood*. It even had a number code, for use in confidential reports or insurance claims: 313.81. This would be the number used on all the reports about Jimmy Parkman from that point on.

I looked it up in my handbook to review the specific symptoms that merited that psychiatric classification.

> . . . a disturbance of at least six months during which at least five of the following are present: often loses temper, often argues with adults, often actively defies or refuses adult requests or rules, often deliberately does things that annoy people, often blames others for his or her own mistakes, is often touchy or easily annoyed by others, is often angry and resentful, is often spiteful or vindictive, or often swears or uses obscene language.

I knew there had been some professional controversy over this diagnosis, especially in those circles of the mental health field that preferred empirical research as a basis for psychiatric labels. One British psychiatrist, writing in an influential professional journal, had likened the diagnosis to "spitting into the wind," implying that mental health professionals might be doing themselves a disservice by adopting diagnoses with little foundation in research studies. This had been a recurrent problem with American psychiatry, he said— our predilection for creating elaborate systems to name psychological disorders. He went on to point out that these were taxonomic systems that, by and large, no one else in the world would use. The rest of civilization used another, more abbreviated and practical method for naming psychiatric disorders.

There had also been some discussion about that particular diagnosis being much too loosely defined, thereby allowing too many children to be inaccurately called psychiatrically disordered when their main problem was simpler than that. For example, how often was "often"? This was left to individual, imperfect human judgment. Many children, for whatever reasons, just didn't get along with the adults in their worlds. While there were other diagnostic codes designed to be more equitable in assigning blame—and to capture things such as *parent-child conflict,* or problems in relationships—medical insurance companies were apt to refuse reimbursement for such seemingly frivolous "social or interaction diagnoses." So *oppositional-defiant disorder* had been eagerly embraced by many mental health professionals for largely practical reasons, that is, to have a means of capturing the many cases of children who opposed the authority of their parents or teachers. And, to some degree, to facilitate insurance reimbursements for problems that fell short of traditional notions about child psychiatric disorders.

Jimmy *did* seem to have a history of many of the behaviors mentioned in the handbook, but I wasn't concerned that he had been misdiagnosed so much as I suspected his diagnosis might be missing the point.

I chose not to introduce myself to Jimmy on that particular occasion, especially since he would be spending a good amount of time going in and out of the Quiet Room, and his level of upset was apparent. Instead, I watched him, and the staff, as the cycle repeated itself again and again that day. To the QR, then back to his classroom. Another incident would occur, always seemingly instigated by Jimmy and directed at his teacher or some other staff member who was convenient. This would be followed by some screaming and then chasing and resistance, with physical restraint applied each time. The scene became almost comical in quality, like a pratfall or a punch line that announces itself ahead of time. It was as if an excerpt from a script of a play was being practiced over and over by its actors in the hope that eventually it might come out just right. Because of its tiresome repetitiveness, I, like the others there, found myself becoming inured to it and somewhat removed from my initial feelings of discomfort.

On my second day of work on the unit, I was determined to meet my new patient—perhaps to establish rapport with him, to become a friend in some manner. I wanted to be someone he could look to for support—a grown-up he could confide in and trust. I had been told many times by my professors how important this was in the psychological evaluation of children and adolescents. "Gain their trust," they would say to me. "Establish rapport." And so I set out to do just that.

I tried to select a moment when Jimmy seemed approachable and not disposed to a fit of rage, as he had appeared the day before. But since he didn't share my agenda, he greeted me coldly, even ignoring me as I attempted to begin a brief conversation with him. In the course of these things, I noticed his clothes were all damp—his shoes made a kind of squishing noise as he paced back and forth in the room he shared with another little boy. I asked him what had happened.

"I don't know . . . nothing," he said, rather matter-of-factly.

This would be his response to all my other questions that day. Questions about what had happened to his clothes, about why he was in the hospital, about home and school. In the end, I learned from a nurse that the other children, as they are wont to do in such settings, had indoctrinated Jimmy in a way reserved for the newest children on the unit—or for those who were considered exceptionally weird or nonconforming, the ones who had no chance of ever fitting in, even in a community of atypical children.

Jimmy had been thrown into the shower with his clothes on. In addition, a tube of toothpaste had been squirted into his battered, dirty sneakers. Washing them by hand in the sink had only partially removed the sticky sweet gel and had left the shoes soaked through. The squishing sound he made as he walked about the place meant the teasing would only continue. It also meant that the memory of this hazing by the others would remain fixed in his thoughts.

"Can't we get him to change his clothes?" I said to the nurse.

"He doesn't have any other clothes with him. And those are the only shoes he came with," the nurse told me with a peculiar grin she probably reserved for "green" trainees like myself.

"What? Why didn't he bring more with him? They knew he was going to be here a while." At least I knew he would be there four or five weeks, because that was how long his parents' medical insurance would pay the daily charges. It had said so right on the first page of Jimmy's medical chart, along with the most essential information about his case.

"Why don't you ask his parents?" the nurse suggested—in a manner that wasn't friendly.

My first phone call to the parents of my one and only patient was memorable. Up until then these two people had been only faceless characters in a drama—the drama contained in this child's medical chart and in the lore of the unit, the half-rumors, half-truths that accompany each child admitted there. I needed to speak with the parents anyway, to interview them about Jimmy's behavior and perhaps explore the origins of his problems. So I called to set up a time for them to come and visit.

His mother answered the phone, and I began my speech exactly as I had rehearsed it. Although I anticipated an eventual first contact, I had no idea that it would begin with such a practical issue as the need for Jimmy's parents to bring additional clothing. But at least this would create the opportunity to make myself known to them and to set up an appointment to start things off.

"This is Dr. Garrison, at the hospital. Your son has been assigned to my clinical team for evaluation and treatment. I'm calling, though, about a little problem here."

"My son . . . what kind of problem?" she inquired cautiously, as if the worst had happened.

"Yes, well, you see, Jimmy's clothes have gotten wet. Some of the other children were teasing him, you see—it's very common here—and his shoes are a mess as well. Would it be possible for you, or for someone, to bring by a suitcase with some more clothes for him? And an extra pair of shoes?" I added. "We're having his sneakers cleaned and dried out tonight."

There was a pause at the other end. Perhaps she hadn't heard me clearly. I waited a moment or two and then I broke the silence.

"Do you think you or your husband could bring some extra clothes by today?"

In an icy tone—as cold and calm as ever I would hear a mother speak in reference to her child—Mrs. Parkman finally responded.

"He has *all* of his clothes with him, Doctor. And we don't plan to bring any more to the hospital."

Now it was my turn to be silent, but only for a moment, as I attempted to compose my next sentence. I began to comprehend what was happening, though I didn't completely believe it could be true.

"Uh . . . you mean to say . . . uh, he has all of his clothes here?" No answer. "Well . . . uh, maybe they've been misplaced. Did he have a suitcase we've overlooked?"

"No, he didn't have a suitcase. We didn't have an extra one to give him. Besides, he has all of his clothes with him—his blue shirt and his brown pants, his sneakers and his raincoat." Again, there was a silent pause. I decided to take another approach—to see Jimmy's parents face to face. I secretly suspected this might be a more difficult task than I had originally imagined.

Quickly dropping the issue of Jimmy's clothes, I asked, "Could we set up a time for you and your husband to come in and discuss Jimmy with me? Just about any time this week would be good for me. I'd like to make it convenient for both of you."

"We won't be coming to the hospital," she replied—much more directly than I had expected.

"Uh . . . you . . . you *won't* be coming in . . . " I echoed, more a repetition of her statement than a question. She sensed I was at a total loss. It was as though we were speaking two different languages, and I was the one who was having the harder time of it. I think she took pity on me, though, by not making me ask her why.

"We haven't really told anyone this yet, I mean you people wouldn't have taken Jimmy into the hospital if we had. You see, we are leaving Jimmy with you. It's best this way; he can get the specialized care he needs, from people who know what must be done. Jim and I just aren't prepared to offer him anything more. It's been a long eight years, and we are, well, we're just worn out from all of this."

Again my only response was silence, as I reflected upon the meaning of the basic message I was only now beginning to receive. For some strange reason my next question was exceedingly concrete—a tendency I have when the more abstract completely fails me. "So he doesn't have any other clothes or shoes?" I asked to get it straight.

"Yes, that's right," she said. "You see, we had to give the clothes he used to wear to Karl. They're a little big on him, but he'll grow into them in time. Clothes are really very expensive these days, you know, and it seemed silly to just throw them away, they're all in pretty good shape." Her controlled tone of voice, her self-confidence, somehow reassured me—as though her words and her reasoning made sense.

But something was terribly wrong here—something that no one had warned me about. That nurse's grin—had she suspected something and not let me in on it? My simple case had suddenly turned into a confusing mess. This conversation had not been what I had expected. The whole experience was quite unnerving. In fact, it was so new and foreign to me that I was busily constructing some sort of explanation. Even in the silent pauses of my dialogue with Jimmy's mother, I was trying to build a frame of reference that might help me make some sense of what I thought I was hearing. And so I said, "Goodbye."

"Doctor, are you still there?" Mrs. Parkman said, and loudly, since I could hear her even as I began to hang up. "You mustn't think we are terrible parents. We really aren't, you know." I brought the receiver up to my ear.

"Some things just aren't meant to be. Jimmy didn't fit in very well in our family—I don't think he ever would have. When we came to that realization there was nothing left to do but put him in a place where he could get the professional help he needs—the help he deserves."

"Uh-huh," was all I seemed able to say.

"Believe me, we agonized over this decision." She began to lose the icy cool her voice had had only moments before. "We loved Jimmy very much—he was a *beautiful* baby. There were times when he could be so charming, so perfect. We were very proud. But then he just started to be more and more difficult; he became like a . . . like an animal. He has a terrible temper, you know! I'll bet you've seen it there, haven't you?" she asked me, but failed to give me a chance to answer. "Well, believe me, this was not an easy decision for us to make, but we think it's best for everyone."

She sounded almost rehearsed—as though this was what she had written down somewhere. Just then, a man's voice came over the phone. He introduced himself as Jim Parkman, Jimmy's adoptive father.

"Doctor, this has been hard for all of us. We're sorry about having to do it this way, but our attorney advised us it was the only thing we could do. The kid is just damaged goods, Doc, it's as simple as that. He was never right to begin with. At least, I never thought he was. Never really wired right, you know what I mean?" I sensed no real emotion in his voice, only an air of certainty—a sense of being sure that what he was saying was logically correct and the only alternative.

"But he can't stay here for very long. You know that. Someone will have to take responsibility for him," I offered feebly.

"Let the rest of the world take care of him for a while. We're through trying to change him. I don't think anyone can change him. He's just not my child, you know, and that's all there is to it, Doctor," he said with finality. "I've got to take care of my own kid now."

Minutes later, after I had said goodbye to Jimmy's father, as I sat stunned and confused by this turn of events, I looked over at the nurse—the one who had first suggested I call Jimmy's parents. She looked at me in a way that told me she might be kinder to me now. She had gotten the gist of my conversation with my patient's parents and understood my befuddlement.

"It's a *dump*, right?" she asked knowingly and simply.

"A *dump*?" I puzzled over this word, yet another technical term I hadn't been prepared for.

"They're dumping him here, right?" She could see that I was having trouble with her question. "It happens now and then. They're real cagey sometimes. Usually we can spot them a mile away, there are usually signs. But these folks were real smart. Boy, wait until Dr. Marshfield hears about this." Dr. Marshfield was the director of the unit, and he was soon to hear about my patient. And therefore, he would also hear about me—an inauspicious beginning to my career.

"People sure do funny things, don't they?" she asked me, just before she left to inform the head of psychiatric nursing.

As I sat there, speechless, I could hear Jimmy's piercing screams once more, as he was carried past the nurses' station for what must have been the tenth time that day. Down the hall to the QR, to sit for ten or fifteen minutes in a room with padded walls where he was free to yell and bounce and fight and kick—at liberty to battle his foes, real or imagined. He was left to vent his anger in that quiet place, which was invariably what he chose to do. Unfortunately, his emotional outbursts would only prolong his time in the QR. But he also had the option to begin to get the message.

The message was that he must try to fit in here—to behave himself, or there would be consequences, clear and firm consequences that would be meted out with a systematic regularity. But since he was a child who acted as though he had very little to lose, he took away some of the power the staff appeared to wield. Both of us, that angry little boy and his new psychologist, had much to learn. On my third day I set out to try.

■

None of us was persuaded by Jimmy Parkman's formal diagnosis: oppositional-defiant disorder. In some ways, however, it did fit his particular personality; he would invariably do or say the opposite of whatever an adult might request or expect of him. If he was asked to pick up his room, he wouldn't just refuse, he would trash it even further. If he was given an assignment by his teacher in the unit school, he would tear it up, and in a way that ensured that everyone would see. For him, the display seemed as important as the act of defiance itself.

"He simply won't listen," his teacher said to me one day. "He makes it his business to test everybody's limits."

It was my task, although few thought I had much chance for success, to try to break this pattern. I set out to analyze the situation—and little Jimmy as well—using an array of known devices. My methods were both simple and complex: psychological tests—some quite valid, others that seemed clearly off the wall—and behavioral observation were to be my primary tools for the assessment. All of this was standard practice. I would sneak up on my patient and sort of open him up, so to speak, for everyone to see and understand. We would get to the root of his problem by going to the root of his psyche.

As I sorted through my materials, I noticed the inscription *18GF* on the back of an 8-by-11-inch card. It was one of a number of such cards that comprise the *thematic apperception test*, or TAT, a widely used technique that is more generally called a *projective* test. It is based on the notion that viewers or patients, unschooled in the devious ways of the psychological examiner, will unknowingly "project" their own individual thoughts, fantasies, wishes, or fears onto a collection of ambiguous drawings or photographs. Unlike the *Rorschach inkblot test,* another projective technique with which most adults are at least somewhat familiar, the TAT uses pictures that were assumed by the test's developers to draw certain kinds of things out of the patient.

Card 18GF showed a woman—or what appeared to be a woman—standing on a stairway, or what appeared to be a stairway, for you could never be quite certain whether you were seeing what was there or projecting what you imagined. The woman is situated close to another human figure, much smaller, less well defined in gender or shape, who is seemingly just below and under the power of the larger figure.

The common responses to this ambiguous drawing—at least the answers children give most of the time—are primarily of two types. The first is something along the lines of a mother who is tending to her child. The child has been hurt by falling down the stairs, the respondents will suggest—or is ill for some unknown reason. In this version, the mother is seen as helping and supportive of the child figure—she is perceived as a nurturing and caring parental figure. The second type of response—and one that is routinely given in child psychiatric settings—is of a mother or some other female figure who is choking or strangling a child. Perhaps for some awful thing the child has just done, or because the mother is simply "crazy" and inexplicably out of control. Disturbed children have a tendency to describe their adults in this way.

When this technique is used with children (or adults), the stories that are told about the basic perception—or *apperception* of the cards—are recorded. These stories often have a beginning, a middle and an end—for that is the construction of even the simplest of children's stories. In this way, psychologists seek to examine relatively unseen forces within their patients, and without their complete awareness. Although somewhat controversial, the TAT is still considered by many as a useful means for psychological assessment.

I wrote down Jimmy Parkman's story, which he initially gave me with relish and delight, that day I showed him 18GF. He perked up quite a bit, I recall, even appearing happy. I had the feeling that *this* was something he could relate to in a direct and immediate way. And in a way that only young children and psychotic adults seem to show with that particular psychological test.

"That's *my* mother, isn't it!? And there I am," he said at first. "And there's our stairs . . . the ones in the living room. Where'd you get this picture? Did you take this picture at my house or something? Did my mother give it to you?"

As he said this, he became irritated with me. I suspected he was rather curious as to just how I had managed to enter his personal world, and with no permission from him whatsoever. I sensed this form of adult intrusion was annoying to him and that others had done this kind of thing before me.

Of course, in many ways his perception was accurate, for it *was* my purpose there with him to analyze and intrude—and not to truly become his friend, or to relate to him in a way he might wish some adult could or would. I was there merely to study him and to understand him better than the others had been able to do. My task was to learn about that child, with some tact and finesse, but to learn about him any way I could.

"So, Jimmy, can you tell me a story about what is happening in the picture?" I asked him with a growing sense of discomfort.

"What's happening?" he responded. His face told me he didn't really comprehend my instructions.

"Well, some kids make up stories about these pictures, you know, with a beginning, a middle and an end. Just like in the books you read at school." These were standard instructions for the child who didn't understand.

"I can tell you what my mommy is saying," he offered. "She's saying: '*You're a bad boy, Jimmy . . .*'" he added with a flourish.

"Why is she saying that to the boy?" I asked, pleased that we were finally off and running.

"She always says that." He was losing interest in the "game" and began to look around the room, then back to the table at the other pictures turned face-down in front of me.

"Do you have any other pictures?" he asked.

"We'll look at the rest of the pictures when we finish with this one," I said. "Can you tell me why the mommy is saying 'You're bad' to the boy?"

"She's saying it to me, stupid," he admonished me. "She's my mommy, you know!" He seemed even more irritated with me and with my failure to see him there in the picture with his mother.

"I'm sorry, Jimmy," I said. "Well, why would your mommy say something like that to you?"

"Because there's something wrong with me. I never listen, I'm too loud. I never do anything the way Mommy wants me to." He began to move forward as if about to grab one of the other cards, and then he looked at me as though he was calculating the odds I would do something to prevent it.

I tried to distract him from his plan to disrupt our session, by commenting on his new shoes.

"Hey, Jimmy, I really like your shoes," I said with false enthusiasm—something younger children find difficult to discern in adults.

He paused, sat back in his chair and looked casually down toward his high-top sneakers. He began to smile as he examined them closely.

"My parents got them for me," he said softly—and then he looked back up at me. I knew that it was actually the staff who had chipped in to buy his shoes—and several sets of new clothes for him to wear at the hospital. But Jimmy hadn't been told this.

"So let's get this over with," he barked at me, having forgotten about grabbing the test away from his psychological examiner.

"Well, how does your story end, Jimmy? A good story has to have an ending, doesn't it" I asked.

"You know how it ends! They lock him up and throw away the key. That's what happens when you're a bad kid, isn't it?" he said, as he peered angrily at me. "That's what my daddy said would happen to me someday."

■

"PPP!" our supervisor had said in the initial case conference on little Jimmy Parkman—with a broad, self-satisfied grin. As I looked around the room to the other professionals in training, I realized that not one of us had the slightest idea what he was talking about. Was this some abbreviated psychiatric diagnosis? A term we *should* know, but one that had somehow been left out of our academic preparation? Apparently aware of our confusion, the supervisor said it again—and this time with gusto for even greater effect.

"*PPP*," he repeated. "It's the cause of most of the problems in this place," he added, increasing our collective sense of inferiority. We sat there quietly, no one able even to offer an educated guess. Finally, he announced the answer.

"*Piss-poor protoplasm!*" he said—and then he waited a second or two to gauge our reaction to his humorous remark. "That's where it all begins, with the genes. And this kid's got some *great* ones," he added sarcastically.

A few of us chuckled over our own temporary confusion, and I suppose we were relieved that somehow we hadn't been as uninformed as we thought. But then some of our group realized how cruel and unenlightened his comment seemed—and several groaned in disapproval. He was, in his own peculiar manner, calling our attention to the "nature" side of the origins-of-psychiatric-illness debate. He was attributing the bulk of Jimmy's problems with his temper and aggressive tendencies to his constitutional makeup. To some fateful predisposition within him all along—a legacy, perhaps, of his equally troubled biologic parents.

And so, "PPP" was to be Jimmy's informal diagnosis—with built-in features of explanation and prediction. Of course, you couldn't find that particular diagnosis in any textbook or manual of child psychiatry or psychology. But I would suspect that it signifies a working hypothesis for a more recent generation of mental health practitioners who have been schooled in biologic orientations to the causes of mental illness.

In earlier times—and for most of the professionals working in mental health today—the all-encompassing causes were thought to be primarily environmental, stemming from the complex interactions within family and the child's broader social world. There was a time when much of the blame would be laid almost solely upon the mother—for had she not been the prime influence during those early and vulnerable years? The father would be blamed as well, but usually in a more indirect way—accused of the lesser charge of being absent, physically or psychologically, from the world of his children.

Even after I got the gist of what my supervisor was saying, it still struck me as a rather odd way to refer to the problems of this eight-year-old boy. Indeed, his general attitude had seemed hauntingly similar to that of Jimmy's adoptive father. *Damaged goods,* he'd said to me on the telephone. That phrase came back again, and it stayed with me for months. Both of these overlapping explanations held out little hope for improvement, since our ability to "rewire" such children—or to make the goods like new, the way they should be—was very limited. It seemed to me that this thing my supervisor had called PPP was as much an epitaph for a life as a diagnosis for a child's psychological condition.

This particular man had seemed rather burned out to some of us, even during those early months of clinical training. His tendency to use sarcasm in response to the human tragedy he encountered daily was interpreted by some of my fellow trainees as both a primary symptom of his burned-out status and as a coping mechanism that got him through the long days. We all felt this man had much to offer us, for he evidenced a keen mind and a vast amount of knowledge about his subspecialty. His sardonic sense of the more tragic side to his work, and his quips and seemingly insensitive remarks, actually served a helpful and educational function for us.

I suppose to interpret it otherwise would have left us viewing him as some kind of arrogant fool—mean spirited and even cruel. But we all agreed that there was something special about this man.

One day later that year, as I sat down with him in a corner of the cafeteria, there was a moment or two of silence; a common problem in supervisor-student meetings. He attempted to provoke some sort of reaction in me—to startle me into a lively debate. He was always likely to say something I didn't expect.

"Do you know what the two least contented medical specialties are?" he asked me. The way he asked his question made me think of a hunter, lying in wait for his unsuspecting prey. But he also asked it in a manner that made me think he was about to share some seemingly odd piece of information that might speak volumes of wisdom. I really hadn't ever considered his question, and so I hesitated for several seconds before I spoke.

"Uh . . . pathology . . . and, uh, . . . oh, I don't know what the other one might be," I had responded, curious about where his question would lead. In saying "pathology," I had reasoned that it couldn't be all that cheerful cutting up the dead bodies of people. There was a part of me that didn't really care what the answer was.

"Nope . . . wrong! Pediatrics and psychiatry!" he announced proudly.

"Now, how do you know that?" I retorted, as though this was some half-baked hypothesis—yet another symptom of his fatalistic outlook on the world.

"I read a survey of a large, random sample of physicians all over the United States. Each of the major specialties in medicine was represented. Along with a bunch of other questions, they asked them how happy they were with what they were doing. You know, how contented they were in their work and with their lives in general." He took a bite of his sandwich, giving me time to contemplate this tantalizing "fact."

"You see, pediatricians tend to be unhappy because they're the lowest paid and because the health problems of kids can be so, well . . . so boring. You know what I mean, very routine. Earaches, low-grade fevers, the sniffles and all those well-baby visits. Then there's the fact that pediatricians work with kids, and you know how much money insurance companies are willing to spend on kids—almost zero. They won't pay for checkups, so only the middle-class-and-up kids get seen regularly. Christ, they won't even pay for immunizations against infectious diseases! And take a look at the schools. Teachers get paid about the same as the guy over there making the hamburgers. Nope, we really don't value kids all that much, although we like to act like we do, don't we!"

"And *psychiatrists?*" I wondered aloud. "Why are they so unhappy?"

"Psychiatrists don't get paid so much either," he added. "They're just a little above the pediatricians. I mean, compared with a cardiac surgeon, or even a radiologist."

"Is *that* the only reason they're so unhappy?" was my next question. "I'm sure most of them had some idea beforehand that their specialty might not pay as well. Some of them must have gone into it for the type of work they would be doing, or because it was interesting. Or maybe they just liked helping children."

"Yeah, I guess so. But it's hard being someone who takes care of kids because there are so many, well, so many obstacles put in front of us." His frustration from so many years was readily apparent now, and he became much more serious than before.

"No one wants to pay for the preventive things we can do, you know, to work with the kids when they're much younger, or when the problems first begin. And the field is so focused on illness and pathology, we forget about the parent-child relationship. In so many cases *that's* the place to be if you want to have a decent chance to make a major difference. But the whole system is geared up to pay attention only when the situation is way out of hand. When the kid's so symptomatic it's going to be an uphill battle."

"I know what you mean,"I replied. My brief time in the hospital had taught me that our attempts at prevention or at early intervention with children's psychological problems often led to much better outcomes.

"But I think the bottom line here is that we work with children, and that's not *really* appreciated in this country—at least not enough that I can tell. And, we make a lot less money than, say, the guy doing the tummytucks, or the breast and hair implants. And then you work in a place like this, where every case is pretty much just like the one that came before. I mean, here's this kid who is a menace to society—at least according to his parents, who want him in here really bad. And you must know by now that we get these kids when it's too late." He paused to reflect on this last statement.

"Come to think of it, a lot of these kids *do* seem to have pretty much the same basic problem, don't they?" he repeated, as though he had landed upon some new insight.

"What's that?" I asked. I really didn't have any idea what he meant.

"Well, when you reduce it to the basic issue, I mean the heart of the matter—a lot of them just don't get along with their parents," he explained. "And trying to change that can get to you after a while."

"And what about PPP?" I hazarded to inquire, feeling confident he'd shown at least some appreciation for my sense of humor.

As I uttered the question, he began to laugh nervously—like a little boy caught in the act of pulling the cat's tail. "Oh, that's just something I say to get a rise out of some know-it-all trainee—or when one of you guys starts talking about the oedipus complex and little boys having the hots for their mothers."

We both laughed.

"I guess I also bring up the PPP diagnosis when I want to impress one of my younger colleagues, you know, the *new breed*," he added, referring to the growing emphasis in mental health on the biological origins of psychological disorders. Then he became much more serious about the topic at hand.

"Of course, someday, they probably *will* come up with a diagnosis like that! I mean, when they really get moving on the genetics research. And then the genetic counselors will take our place, I suppose."

I knew he was alluding to new developments in medicine that foretold the day when prospective parents could be advised of the probabilities they might conceive disordered or defective children. It was thought that such information in the hands of expectant parents would lead to more frequent elective abortions—and a reduction of children born with various defects that could be detected during pregnancy.

"And you know, this idea that children are born with these problems—and that it doesn't have anything to do with the way they're brought up—this idea's been around a long time," he added.

"Yeah, but it's sort of a chicken-and-egg thing, isn't it? We may never really figure out what comes first," I responded. "Take that case I had a few months ago, Jimmy Parkman, you remember him. You gave him the PPP diagnosis that first day. Remember how upset everybody got with you?"

"Oh yes, yes! But I do that every year. It's good for you to hear that kind of thinking. More and more people are thinking that way these days," he answered. "It's one of the reasons we're using so many drugs on these kids now. Also it's a convenient excuse for not doing anything about poverty—or things like child abuse and neglect. I guess it lets a lot of parents off the hook, too."

"I know, but I remember even Jimmy's father used that kind of thinking. He put it all back on the kid, on his real parents' having a history of criminality and substance abuse. He told me he thought the kid was 'wired' wrong." I paused a moment, but he didn't say a word. I went on.

"It's kind of a depressing situation when you . . . well, when you sort of give up on a kid like that. And that's what happened. They gave up on him, and we gave up on him. We couldn't change him and so we just shipped him off to the state hospital when he ran out of insurance coverage. We stopped trying. And now he's in a place that's, well, you know what that will mean for him. Eight years old, and a permanent resident of an institution for kids who can't be placed anywhere else." My voice cracked a bit, but only very little. I cleared my throat quietly, in an attempt to divert his attention from my unprofessional display of emotion.

I could tell, as he slowly nodded his head and gazed at me, that he had easily sensed my personal feelings about the boy. He had probably wrestled with these same issues himself. But his particular manner of dealing with such things, as I had found in the past, would be indirect. After a moment of reflection, he changed the subject. At least, that is what I thought.

"You know, the basis for this whole thing—this place, what we do, the way we think about these kids—the basis for the whole thing is as old as the hills," he said. "It's the 'good-and-evil' thing all over."

"What do you mean, the 'good-and-evil' thing?"

"In the Dark Ages the wisest men—the physicians or the scholars or the clerics—they would look at insanity or nonconformist behavior and call it 'evil' and 'wicked.' They'd chalk it up to the Devil, or to some Original Sin that needed to be cleansed. Those ideas evolved into theories about substances or fluids in the body—*humors* they were called. Dark ones and clear ones; thick ones and thin ones." He looked at me to ask a question. "You can probably guess which ones got you into trouble and which ones didn't."

"The dark, thick ones were bad for you, right?" I answered. He nodded.

"And look at the history of child mental health—even in this century. You have big-name guys like the eminent Dr. Maudsley in England—using phrases like 'the inherent viciousness' of children. And

the 'hereditary taint' in the misbehaving children he met in the re-
form schools.

"The priests were in charge of the early forms of what we now call
child psychiatric hospitals. Their job was to punish and discipline the
wayward children—to cleanse the souls of the 'wicked incorrigibles'
who were sent there by their parents, or by someone who found them
on the doorstep. The priests' approach was based entirely on the
concepts of good and evil and of keeping the 'badness' in check. The
kid's cure, or his salvation, was through acceptance of God. The alternative was nothing less than Hell!"

He paused to savor the moment, for I suspected he felt he had
landed upon some simple truth.

"What about now?" I asked. "What's that got to do with you and
me—and this place?"

"Now we live in a time where science gives us another kind of explanation—at least it does for the kids whose parents can afford to
pay for it." He smiled a knowing smile. "The good-and-evil thing has
just changed a little bit, but it's still there—there at the core of everything we do. The new religion is all about health. So when something goes wrong with practically anything, we blame it on stress and
genetic predispositions. Do you know how many things we chalk up
to stress and genetic predispositions these days? Take your pick,
there's a million of them." He paused to sip the final portion of his
iced tea.

"So now that blaming it all on Mommy isn't too popular, we blame
it all on genes or the broken brain. It's more comfortable for everyone
involved," he added, "except maybe for the kid." And then he quickly
brought us back to my earlier remark.

"Don't be so bothered by Jimmy Parkman, either. His parents probably seemed pretty bad to you, didn't they?" I nodded that they did.

"Did you ever stop to think how many parents out there would like
to turn their kids back in? You know, just return 'em to the store—
the used-kid store. How many parents threaten their kids with that?
You know that kind of thing, or something a lot like it. It's said as a
joke, but think about it. Some of them really mean it!"

"Do you really think that's true?" I asked skeptically.

"The only thing that keeps them from doing it is that it's not popular these days. But it's still not against the law, you know. I mean, abandoning your kids just because you can't stand them anymore—or because you can't hack being their parent. People do that all the time. But for most of 'em, having a kid is like a lottery: they're stuck with the results—good or bad. And when they find out it isn't exactly what they expected—the kid's a big disappointment, or too much for them to handle—there aren't too many ways out."

"You really think there are more parents like that out there?" I asked incredulously.

"Look . . . the Parkmans got away with it because they had the kid on a kind of *trial* basis. For a lot of unhappy parents—I mean the ones with their own kids, the ones they conceived—all they can do is make the kid as miserable as they are, or abandon the whole thing by just getting out. You know, blame it on the marriage, or on a mid-life crisis. Or whatever. They come up with lots of excuses, but sometimes it's just that they want to get away from the kids."

Our time together was almost finished, and he began to stand up, holding onto his cafeteria tray. He stood still at the edge of the table for a moment, reflecting, and then he spoke.

"Of course, we can't give these kids what they really need, you know," he said.

"What's that?" I answered, anxious to know what he felt our failed attempts boiled down to.

"We *can't* be their parents. We *can't* love them like they're our own." He seemed sad at this realization. "It just isn't the same if they're not your own."

■

In the morning hours of each day, at least for the seven or eight weeks I knew Jimmy Parkman, he would be chased and held and carried off to the Quiet Room for some infraction or another. Sometimes it was a relatively small thing. At other times, it was a major crisis. But this ritual, performed routinely with certain staff members, all male, seemed resistant to alteration. Again, it was very much like a well-rehearsed play, with its own precision and a certain predictability to the script.

"When are my mother and father going to get me out of here?" Jimmy had asked one of the nurses early on. *I* would be the one who eventually told him what was to happen, when it became clear that he could not go home again. But he didn't get *that* message right away. How does a child accept or hope to understand that his parents have left him for good?

His first question, after I told him of his parents' decision, had been: "Will I ever get to see my brother, Karl, again?"

After a while, he stopped asking about his brother and his parents. He stopped talking about his home, so close to that hospital. For him, it could have been a million miles away.

Jimmy's favorite words were obscenities, and he would often say he hated just about everyone and everything around him. The staff, although they commiserated with his situation, had little patience for him. It became evident that this child, for reasons we couldn't easily identify, was eliciting the attention of the adults around him in such a way that just about any encounter with him would lead to his temporary incarceration. The psychologist Fritz Redl had called patients such as Jimmy "children who hate."

Once placed in the QR, he would rant and rave for a while and then begin to cry and act as though he had not really meant it all to begin with. The staff, meanwhile, would simply shake their heads— as if no one could understand why this pattern would repeat itself so often.

"Why doesn't he get the message?" one of the child-care workers had asked me one day. "All he has to do is behave, just do what we ask him to do, and then he won't have to spend all day in there. He just doesn't get the message. What is he, just a bad kid, or what?"

A nurse, overhearing our conversation, offered her appraisal of the situation, in the form of a rhetorical question.

"Why do you think they call them 'disturbed' kids?" she said simply.

But the young child-care worker persisted—perhaps because he was one of the two male staff members designated to chase Jimmy Parkman down during the day and carry him off to the Quiet Room. I could sense that the initial thrill associated with his new job, whatever its origin, was now subsiding rapidly.

"Look at him in there," he said, pointing through the tiny Plexiglas window in the door of the QR. "He's like an animal, screaming, out of control, pacing back and forth in there. He's like a caged animal."

The official rationale for using seclusion and restraint came from the need for safety on the unit. But in many situations, when children would not at all seem to be threatening someone else, or about to break the furniture, we were told that isolation provided time and space for a fragile "ego" to adjust. It was explained that the QR was an external support for a child who knew only aggression as a means for expressing a sort of primal rage. And forcing Jimmy to take "time out" also conformed with a major theory of behavior. By providing undesirable consequences for his inappropriate behaviors, we reasoned, we should decrease the likelihood he would continue to act in that way. This was a basic tenet of the science of human behavior. But Jimmy's persistence in the face of such punishment—which is what it was really intended to be, although we never called it that— defied our simplistic theory of how he might react.

Perhaps our daily ritual with Jimmy eventually gave us another kind of insight into the situation with his former parents. Had they gone through this sort of thing with him for months, or even years? Had they experienced the frustration we now felt, as we attempted to forcibly change his behavior? How different was our approach from what his former parents had attempted?

And so, out of desperation, one day we tried something different. We instructed the staff not to chase him down following his predictable oppositional displays, as had always been done before. We planned to contain him where he was, in a corner or a room—or perhaps at the end of the long corridor of the unit. We would not carry him off to the QR, as we'd done so many times before. His behavior would have no real consequences—unless he chose to physically attack a staff member or another child.

Several of the adults there—teachers, child-care workers and doctors alike—felt this just wouldn't work and that it would be a breach of security to simply let the boy misbehave. But we'd tried everything else up till then—punishment, solitary confinement and talking to him about his behavior. So, at long last, we chose only to ignore him.

His reaction was utter confusion—the rules of the game had dramatically changed overnight. He seemed pathetically uncertain for a while, as he walked the halls freely—with no real obstruction from his adult foes—trying to figure out why everything was suddenly different.

"Can't catch me . . . .can't catch me," he'd taunt the staff who usually chased him. "Fuck you," he'd say for an added touch, as he signified his feelings with a flip of his middle finger.

Soon thereafter he became a somewhat different child—much sadder and much less openly defiant.

"Isn't anyone going to hug me today?" he finally whimpered to a nurse, in the regressed speech of a much younger child that he would sometimes effect. "Isn't anyone going to hug me today?" he repeated in a baby's whine.

I recall one of the other nurses looked over to me that day Jimmy finally reached out to the adults in his institutional world. It was as if even *we* didn't know exactly what we should do. After a moment or two of indecision, a nurse approached Jimmy slowly, knelt down, her arms outstretched.

Jimmy leaned into her, stopping just short of allowing her to complete her embrace. He looked around at each of us, as if surveying the many grown-ups in this strange world of the psychiatric hospital. I could tell *this* manner of relating to others was largely foreign to him and that he failed to grasp that through submission to others he might find the love and attention he probably sought. His body finally stiffened, and he leaned backwards, stood upright. He seemed tragically proud.

"You're *not* my parents, you know," he said angrily, but with a scared little boy's tearfulness. Then he turned away, trudging slowly back down that long hall toward his room.

■

Many years have passed since my first encounter with Jimmy Parkman, but I do know that he spent most of his remaining childhood in a state hospital for psychiatrically disturbed children. Several attempts to place him in foster homes had failed miserably, as his aggression and anger apparently continued unabated on into his adolescent years. As is customary in situations like his, he would have been discharged when he came of age—on or about his eighteenth birthday—and sent out into the same world that had rejected him time and again from the very beginning of his life.

I wonder where Jimmy might be now—and whether any of the interventions had made a difference in his life. I fear he might be incarcerated—or perhaps might have become one of the growing number of the homeless who are actually mentally ill. Would he remember me, or any of the others who tried so hard to help him? Would he remember those adults with their good intentions—the ones who tried to offer him whatever it was he needed?

Anything, that is, but a parent's love.

CHAPTER 3

A QUESTION OF GENDER

> Oh! why did God,
> Creator wise, that people'd highest heaven
> With Spirits masculine, create at last
> This novelty on earth, this fair defect
> Of nature?

—MILTON, *PARADISE LOST*

SEVEN-YEAR-OLD FRANKIE ALBERSON first entered my office cautiously. He walked quietly, almost tiptoeing in—making very little sound as his small, sneakered feet carefully touched the ground. He smiled at me pleasantly, though with a hint of anxiety, as he sat down by the collection of toys I keep in one corner of my office.

He was an attractive little boy, with curly, jet-black hair and sparkling blue eyes. A lean child of normal height—he moved with a certain amount of grace—though he lacked the physical confidence a more assertive or athletic seven-year-old boy might typically display.

"You've got some neat stuff here," he said very softly, in a kind and cordial tone of voice. He gently prodded at the building blocks and then at the games and tiny toy soldiers. He briefly examined several fantasy creatures—"figures" the younger boys were apt to call them. They were the rage of the day. One was a menacing brute called Beastman, a frightening and powerful figure little boys tended to immediately gravitate toward only seconds after entering my office.

Frankie looked this fuzzy supervillain over quickly, offering a quizzical grin toward me—giving me the impression he didn't completely understand the fascination any other little boys might have shown for such a powerful and evil-looking creature. He gingerly placed the figure back on the floor and then picked up the Batman figure to examine it more closely. He focused on the flowing black cape that is a hallmark feature of that superhero. Soon, however, Frankie lost all interest in this imaginary character as well.

"These are awesome figures," he finally said, in a kind but unconvincing tone. "Have you got any girls?"

"Girls?" I echoed, uncertain of his meaning—and surprised by this unanticipated question.

"Yeah, do you have any girl figures? Like Shera . . . or Catwoman?" he specified, cleverly picking out the female counterparts to the all-male figures in my office collection.

"Or how 'bout a Barbie?" he asked hopefully, smiling in a way that told me *she* would somehow be the very best toy in all the world.

I looked around my office and located the stuffed doll I kept for younger girls who would sometimes visit. "All I have is this doll," I said feebly, motioning to the Raggedy Ann sitting happily on a shelf above him. Frankie shook his head no, to tell me that wouldn't do at all. But as he did, his face implied empathy, as though he realized I wouldn't be able to provide him with a suitable female figure.

He seemed to feel sorry for me—and for any problem he might have caused. I had the feeling that, if he'd known me a little better, he might have reached out and touched my arm, as if to say, "Don't worry, it will be alright."

For a seven-year-old boy, Frankie Alberson had an unusually gentle and caring manner.

"It's OK," he said sincerely. "These toys will be good to play with. Besides, I got Barbie at home . . . and I have clothes and furniture for her, too," he added proudly.

Frankie Alberson's particular problem—as it had been initially described to me by his parents—had something to do with his uncontrollable crying. That is, he cried too much for his parents' liking.

And too much for his teachers and classmates, since he was reportedly teased and taunted at school quite often. I was told his harsh treatment at the hands of his schoolmates was usually the result of Frankie's apparently uncontrollable emotions. Some of his peers had taken to calling him "crybaby" and "wimp." A few particularly cruel boys had begun to label him as "gay." The name-calling and ostracism by others would, in turn, just make the little boy cry all the more.

But I soon learned there was much more than this to Frankie Alberson's story.

"Do you know why your parents brought you here, Frankie?" I asked him, after he'd had a few minutes to explore my office and check things out.

Frankie lowered his head, as if in shame or embarrassment. He mumbled something to me—too low for me to decipher.

"I couldn't hear what you said, Frankie," I told him. "Could you speak up just a bit?"

Instead, he got up and sat closer to me—although he still maintained a comfortable distance between himself and this adult stranger. He looked up at me slowly, and I could see his eyes were now reddened, they began to mist over as tears welled up inside him.

His chin trembled ever so slightly, and he seemed disconsolate as he told me his unhappy tale.

"The kids at school don't like me," he stated simply. "They make fun of me and stuff like that." Frankie looked down to his lap, where his hands were resting. He seemed to study his slender fingertips for a moment or two.

I had heard this phrase many times before from children—though most typically from the very anxious or socially inept. Children who didn't have the slightest idea how to make friends. And sometimes I had even heard this complaint from highly aggressive kids—the ones who were too rough or out of touch with the needs of other children to ever successfully acquire genuine friends.

But *this* time, Frankie's words pierced me like a knife, as I glimpsed in his face some of the pain he felt as he struggled through the schoolday.

I would find out later that the ignominy did not end at school. A subtler, more sophisticated type of persecution and coercion was occurring in the context of his loving family.

"Why do they make fun of you, Frankie?" I asked him softly, lowering my head somewhat to see if I could see the pathetic look on his handsome, young face.

"'Cause they say I act like a girl . . . and I cry too much," he continued, pleading his case to a potentially sympathetic adult. "And 'cause I don't like to do the things the other boys like to do."

Frankie seemed more mature than his chronological age—although I would come to learn later from his parents that he was sometimes prone to overly silly and immature displays of behavior. But, just then, he seemed very adult in his manner—and even a bit weary of the world, in the way that middle-aged grown-ups can be. He impressed me as a child who might have been forced to grow up much too quickly. Indeed, when I compared him to the other seven-year-old boys I knew, he seemed altogether different.

"What kinds of things do you do exactly?" I asked him. "I mean, what are the things that make the other kids bother you?"

"Well, I don't really like sports that much," he explained. "And that's what the other boys always want to do. Or they want to wrestle and get rough. I don't like that." He shook his head in disapproval.

"Some kids like to just talk and tell stories about stuff . . . I like that. And I really like playing pretend. I like to use my imagination." He said this in a decidedly feminine way—as though he were emulating a TV actress, or perhaps a thoughtful woman teacher who had pointed out this positive trait.

"But the rough kids make fun when I won't even try their games at recess. They call me names and they just *never* leave me alone."

"What *do* you do during recess?" I asked him.

"Oh, I just sort of hang out," he replied simply. "I talk to different kids every day. I talk to the other kids who are by themselves . . . if there are any. Sometimes they're all playing with someone else." He paused briefly and looked away. "It's different ones every day."

It saddened me to imagine that lonely little boy roaming the playground at school each day in search of friends. I pictured him seeking out other children with whom he might have some social contact, but remaining vigilant for the bullies and cruel children who inevitably reside in that particular locale of childhood—a child's place that is set quite apart and away from the immediate awareness or protection of caring adults. A place where some children can be made to feel very much alone.

I had learned long before that only children truly know of the many dramas that actually unfold during recess time at any school on any given day. I have come to realize that most teachers or adult supervisors who might be on the scene as observers at children's recess are often out of touch with what actually goes on there.

Frankie went on to tell me that he secretly preferred to play with the girls in his class—they were nicer to him generally, and they did many of the things he happened to enjoy the most. He told me there were times when he thought it might be more fun to *be* a girl. But he'd been rejected more frequently in the recent past, both by girls and boys who he once thought of as his friends. His fellow classmates had evolved into what psychologists call a *peer group*—a powerful collective that now judged his cross-gender fraternization as unseemly and peculiar.

It hadn't always been that way, though, because Frankie could remember in kindergarten playing with girls and boys alike—and without criticism or consequences from other children. Now, in second grade, whenever he even casually stopped to talk to a girl at school, the act alone invited vicious attacks by certain children who seemed to delight in monitoring Frankie's behavior and then conveying his latest faux pas to everyone in the class.

"Frankie wants to be a girly . . ." they would taunt him cruelly. "Frankie wants to be a girly . . ."

And then Frankie would start to cry.

"I try not to be noticed at school," the little boy finally confided to me. "It's better that way."

We played and talked quietly for the rest of the session, as he told me about his troubles at school. Oddly, Frankie ended our first session together with his offer of a handshake. Since I seldom engage in such formalities with younger children—and it is only the occasional child who has been rehearsed to do such things by his or her parents—I suspected he'd learned this type of farewell from someone else. Perhaps his father, or an older brother.

As he left my office that first day, he seemed a bit relieved, as though he'd been allowed to unload a heavy burden. I knew that Frankie's problems were likely to continue. I knew that the power and influence of little Frankie's peer group was only just beginning and that more pain and persecution lay ahead for him—especially if he continued to display his cross-gender behavior.

Frankie Alberson's father and mother had come to my office for consultation about his problem, which had gradually become *their* problem as well. As is typical during a first or second session with many parents, the initial description of the *presenting problem*—the stated reason for seeking professional help—often moves quickly into other areas. Parents will often have in mind less obvious issues that comprise a *hidden agenda* when they come to see someone like me.

These issues will be the most pressing matters or anxieties, and not necessarily the problems that were previously stated. They are the things less delicately brought up with a perfect stranger on the telephone when making an appointment—or even during the first half hour or so after meeting. They are the secrets patients or parents will keep to themselves initially, since they are often uncertain what, and how much, they should disclose.

In our very first session together, the Albersons and I moved beyond reports of their son's heightened emotionality to what would become the crux of the matter, to the real reasons for their alarm. They told me of the long history of their son's problem—things that began as oddities in Frankie's behavior that, the parents hoped, would be short lived and unimportant in the long term. They told me of his early interest in and preference for certain toys and activities. Like playing with dolls, asking for girls' clothing and pretending to be a "mommy." They briefly mentioned that Frankie's only sibling, a brother, hadn't shown any behavior like this at all.

Assuming that Frankie's odd behaviors had been normal to begin with, they had not disappeared with passing time. While his older brother George watched "G.I. Joe" and "Looney toons" on television, Frankie preferred to watch a show about a teenaged girl. When allowed to watch the show—always only after some contention with his mother or father—he would tightly clutch his Barbie doll, suck his thumb and become hypnotized by the adventures of his favorite TV character. It was a television show that targeted the young girl, and Frankie had become fascinated with it when he was four or five years old.

"He was *addicted* to it," his mother told me.

Frankie's mother went on to describe her son's mildly effeminate behavior—which would become more pronounced when he was excited or overtired. As she told me, she glanced sideways toward her husband with a pained and frightened expression on her face.

She continued to explain that there could often be a girlish lilt in Frankie's voice, for example, and he occasionally displayed demonstrative and overly dramatic mannerisms. These quirks in his behavior were sometimes there for all the world to see and were especially disconcerting in public places. His taste in television shows and fantasy toys—now perceived as most peculiar and unnatural by his parents—spilled over into his preferences for games and books and records, and to other activities that girls were much more likely to pursue.

As Mr. and Mrs. Alberson sat in my office that first day, I remember with embarrassing clarity my own sense of professional ineptitude and anxiety when, at an altogether unexpected moment, Frankie's mother began to cry. Her tears seemed to well up within the depths of a mother's despair, from a place that might have been her love for her son. Or perhaps from elsewhere—from within some dark and awful fear.

She had started crying inconsolably after telling me a relative had called Frankie a little sissy. A sissy-boy!

After a few seconds of crying audibly, Mrs. Alberson looked about the room and then back to me again. Through her tears she spoke, managing a slight and trembling smile.

"What kind of psychologist are you, anyway?" she asked me. "You don't even have a box of tissues here for a crying mother."

We nervously chuckled over her comment, although she was unaware of the effects of her crying jag on my composure. As I fumbled about looking for paper towels—or anything that might stem the tide of raw emotion—I sensed a growing discomfort in myself. I wondered why I *didn't* have a box of tissues in my office, then, more slowly, I realized that her tears and sadness had touched upon some unknown anxiety in me, as well. This case had landed upon some ill-defined concerns about my own young sons—and parents' questions about their child's gender orientation.

I suspected that her remark—more telling than she knew—had been intended to mitigate the drama of the moment. She had come face to face with a painful realization about her unusual child and about her life as little Frankie's mother.

Mr. Alberson stared at us coolly. He wasn't tearful in the least. He seemed neither amused nor enlightened by our conversation. Rather, he was visibly irritated by this problem with Frankie through the years; and I think he suspected we might be taking it much too lightly. I also perceived he might be incredibly shamed and embarrassed by having to discuss the subject at all.

"I knew you'd bring it up!" he said nastily to his wife, and then he turned to me. Now that it was out in the open, I suspected, he could speak to me more honestly about his son.

"This is a big part of the problem, Doc; at least, that's my opinion," he said, gesturing to his wife, whose tearful outburst was by now winding down. "She's always crying at the drop of a hat. It's always something with her. If it's not the kids, it's our relationship. If it's not that, it's something she saw on television."

He mumbled a bit more in a low, gruff tone, and then he tried to sum things up.

"*Women drive me crazy!*" he announced bitterly. It was pretty clear by then just who was going to get the blame for Frankie's delicate condition.

Instead of contesting her husband's view, Mrs. Alberson began to nod her head slowly up and down, as if in agreement with her husband's blunt assessment of the situation. Her shoulders slouched down and forward, as she took on the burden of his words. And as she assumed personal responsibility for Frankie's situation.

"He's right, Doctor, I *am* a very emotional person. I really can't help it. I try to control myself, but I can't. George is much more controlled than I am. I guess it's just the difference between men and women."

Mrs. Alberson began to cry again, purportedly over some distinction between males and females that she was convinced must have something to do with her Frankie's problem.

Her husband, visibly annoyed with the continuing display of female emotion, turned away from her and adjusted himself in his seat to create a greater distance between them. Then he leaned sharply forward and stared at me intensely, almost aggressively. He stared at me in the way only fathers seem to manage when talking about a troubled child who needs my fixing.

But his eyes conveyed a kind of desperation, too, then seemed to show a less loving sense of frustration than his wife's. But he appeared desperate all the same. His prolonged gaze made me suspect that what he was about to say would be very important—essential, and to the point. He looked down for a moment and began to wring his hands. He did this with such force, that his large knuckles began to turn white. Then he looked up again, resolved to blurt out his deepest thoughts.

"I think our biggest fear of all, Doctor," Frankie's father said in a soft and deliberate voice—and as though he somehow knew *exactly* what his wife was feeling—". . . is that he will become . . . a . . . a homosexual."

Even as he uttered this final word, shame and shock resounded in his voice. It was as though his person was under some kind of vicious assault. The very thought of a son of his being gay was anathema to him.

"I don't think either one of us could take *that*," he said, again presuming to speak for both himself and his wife. But then he modified his stance somewhat. "Well, I know *I* couldn't."

Mr. Alberson sat back and seemed somehow relieved in the saying of it. He paused and then sat upright in his chair again.

"Now, *that*," he said, "would be just about the *worst* thing that could happen to us!"

Having said this, he turned back the other way, toward his wife, his body shifting closer to her. I thought he was finished, but he was the type of person prone to making declarative sentences that leave you with the false impression of finality. For, as soon as he'd made one dramatic remark, he was apt to launch right into another.

"If Frankie turned queer on us, that would be it." He announced firmly . . . again. And then he added, "*I'd disown him in a minute!*"

With that, Mrs. Alberson sobbed louder, as she registered her spouse's most threatening words, suggesting that her spouse's greatest fear had indeed been the actual cause of her earlier emotional outburst. She was afraid that somehow she might lose Frankie, because of her domineering husband's aversion to his son's problems.

"I just know it's all my fault, Doctor," sobbed Mrs. Alberson. "I mean, the way little Frankie is. Maybe I gave him too much love," she said, groping for any explanation. "Maybe I didn't let him be a man."

• • •

After it was in the open—the real reason the Albersons had come for guidance—I reviewed in my mind what I knew about these matters.

Frankie might be diagnosed with something called *gender identity disorder,* for he showed the two major features, or "symptoms," for that medical category. First, he expressed the wish to be the opposite sex. And second, he engaged regularly in cross-gender fantasy and role behavior. Moreover, Frankie didn't seem at all upset over this desire to be more feminine—a fact that is thought to be a hallmark sign of that particular and peculiar child psychiatric disorder. Of course, the implicit message in labeling such a pattern of child behavior a medical or psychiatric disorder was that the child was somehow defective, foreign to what was normal and expected.

But what all of this might really entail for young Frankie Alberson—both now and in the future—was not at all made clear through such a questionable psychiatric diagnosis.

The research literature on the subject of gender identity and gender confusion in children is fraught with speculation and personal opinion, and very little real knowledge exists. There are some scientific reports, however, suggesting certain identifiable trends among some of these children. For example, one study looked at "gender-disordered" boys who, like Frankie Alberson, behaved in an effeminate manner very early on, well before adolescence. These investigators noted that an unusually high number of the children they studied had chronically depressed mothers—and they even noted that these mothers often seemed "bisexual" in orientation. By this the researchers meant that the mothers tended to show both feminine and masculine characteristics, not that they were sexually attracted to women.

The study went on to suggest that these women had married relatively nonmasculine and "ineffectual" husbands—although how that particular trait was measured left much to be desired. But it was very clear that these conditions did *not* apply to every child they studied. The investigators concluded that the boys had somehow failed to achieve sufficient autonomy from their mothers and that this might have something to do with their cross-gender behavior. Frankie's case did not match up completely to this clinical profile, however.

The few studies that looked forward—the ones that followed these boys as they got older—suggested that homosexuality was indeed a common outcome. But in the years between their early display of feminine behavior and publicly becoming gay in adolescence or early adulthood, the boys gradually showed an ability to reduce outward signs of their cross-gender orientation. The researchers felt this was in response to the active and coercive disapproval of parents and others in their social worlds. While it became clear that many of the boys could modify their own public behavior, the cross-gender fantasies would actually continue, hidden away from the view of others who could not, or would not, understand.

Another study—one that examined the adolescence of a large group of gay men—found that the fathers of many more of these men than could be predicted by chance had died during their sons' teenage years. Initially, the investigators wondered whether or not this loss had somehow *caused* homosexuality in the boys—through the absence of a masculine influence during a period that was critical for gender identity.

But another interpretation of this study's findings was also possible.

Had the fathers' deaths during the boys' adolescence somehow *allowed* them greater freedom to emerge from an isolated and secretive world that had actually been created years before, when the urge to be like the opposite sex had first surfaced in their lives? This particular research article had ended with an interesting idea, namely, that the fathers of these boys performed a kind of braking force on the mother-son relationship and on the boys' overt tendencies toward feminine behavior.

When that was removed, these boys—and perhaps *all* boys—might be more likely to show another side of their personalities. They might begin to display and even develop certain feminine aspects of themselves that had been suppressed or denied in the presence of their fathers.

As is often the case, however, the specific patterns noted in the scientific or clinical research did not perfectly match the patterns in individual cases. But these studies did offer me avenues to explore, and hypotheses to test, as I went on with my initial evaluation of Frankie Alberson and his parents.

There was little else for me to do at that early point, except to listen and encourage the kind of dialogue that needed to go on between Frankie's mother and father—and perhaps between Frankie and his worried parents. I could try to bring the anxiety and concern out into the open, which I knew was likely to lead to some desirable change.

"Mr. Alberson," I said cautiously, for I could see he was becoming more agitated. "What might make this better for you? I mean, what would make all of this easier to deal with? Is there anything that would change the way you look at the situation with Frankie?"

He shifted nervously back and forth in his chair, avoiding looking at me or his wife directly. He sighed and shrugged and emitted various sounds that clearly communicated his frustration and a total lack of answers. I thought the rest of the session might go this way, with him unable to express himself. But then, with little warning, an unexpected thing happened.

Mr. Alberson began to cry.

Slowly, at first, he became misty-eyed, and the tip of his nose began to redden. A grimace came over his hardened face, as tears began to stream down his cheeks. He suddenly looked at me and saw my reaction—a look at least partly comprised of my honest shock at witnessing a grown man cry. Contrary to what people might suspect, this was hardly an everyday occurrence. Many mothers of the children I see will occasionally come to tears, but the fathers typically remain quite stoic. Even in the face of the worst catastrophes in their children's lives.

Mr. Alberson really began to blubber out loud, mouthing words that became incomprehensible. He was out of control, and he knew it. It was as though a huge, impenetrable wall had suddenly come falling down around him.

After a few seconds, he gathered himself together and spoke more clearly.

"This is my *son* we're talking about here," he cried softly, and yet with anger all the same. "My flesh and blood, for Christ's sake! He's the only thing that can make me cry. I got feelings too, ya' know?" His manly hands were locked together in one large fist, his body trembled from the sheer effort it took to maintain that anxious grip.

His wife sat frozen in fear and awe of what she saw before her. I could tell this was *not* an everyday occurrence for the Albersons either.

"Shit!, Shit!, Shit!" Mr. Alberson repeated angrily. "How can I love little Frankie if he up and turns queer?" His desperate eyes implored me, and I could see he was caught in an awful dilemma.

"I don't think I could even *look* at him again. I don't think I could call him my son."

He said these last words with a genuine and frightening sense of finality. His tone of voice told me he really believed this to be so. He'd let me know that he was prepared to divorce himself from a beloved son, Frankie—for the crime of acting like a girl.

With that, he angrily brushed the tears away from his eyes and rubbed his bulbous red nose with a large and powerful hand.

"So here we are," Mr. Alberson said at last. "We'll do whatever it takes, Doctor. Whatever it takes to make our little Frankie regular. Whatever it takes to make him a man."

■

Mr. Alberson's words that day reminded me that there were, indeed, approaches specifically designed to alter the eventual life course for effeminate boys—even though that future could seldom be known for certain. I knew psychological techniques *had* been developed, methods that sought to shape young boys' behavior toward greater masculinity and to promote their personal gender identity as heterosexual males.

These programs had been harshly criticized by many in the field of psychology as mindlessly reinforcing rather arbitrary cultural and sexual stereotypes, and with very little evidence that the long-term outcome for such children actually would be affected. There was a demand for such a treatment approach, perhaps from other parents like the Albersons who sought to transform their effeminate sons.

One program was founded on the notion of the "sissy-boy syndrome"—the very same term that had bothered Mrs. Alberson so much—and had been touted by some as a panacea for male homosexuality. The actual design of the "treatments" resembled a dogmatic kind of religious instruction or political brainwashing. It attempted to coerce boys into behaving opposite to the way they felt compelled to be. But it also incorporated modification techniques that were known to have success in shaping both animal and human behavior. Because of that, it was more than snake oil such practitioners were selling to the public, for their approach *did* have the potential for altering these little boys' natural inclinations.

In fact, such a strategy had already been tried by the Albersons, though not in any formal or professional way. Frankie's parents had sought to erase Frankie's undesirable behaviors through constantly pointing out his effeminate manner and day-to-day interests in their family life. And by repeatedly telling him to act like a little man. This had created a bind for Frankie, of course, for he loved and respected his father and mother very much. It was in his nature to try to please his parents and to spare them the pain he felt he gave them as their imperfect child.

I suspected that, in time, these pressure tactics would probably succeed in his parents' eyes, at least in a superficial manner. Research suggested that Frankie was likely to gradually learn to change his more feminine ways—at least in front of others. Or he might abandon them altogether, to please his peers and his parents. Or perhaps he'd change because *he* simply chose to do so.

What research there was suggested Frankie's eventual sexual orientation was likely to evolve relatively unaffected—and it was not at all certain that he would be gay. My ability to predict the future in a case like Frankie's was necessarily confined to a kind of guesswork that I could not share with the Albersons directly, since I couldn't be certain just how Frankie's story would turn out.

But his father's shame and his mother's self-blame—these were things I *could* deal with. I was in a position to soften the blows for the child by letting his parents live out their anxieties in my presence. Perhaps they might even come to another level of understanding. Could the Albersons find another way of looking at their unwanted situation that somehow redefined their perceived roles as Frankie's parents?

There was something else I needed to consider, and I thought it just might help the Albersons to navigate this storm. It was something to do with the way in which many parents deal with cross-gender behavior in *girls*, as compared with boys.

I could not recall one case in over fifteen years, for example, of a girl being brought to me for acting like a boy. I knew tomboyishness was a relatively common phenomenon, and girls were continually becoming more interested and capable in those pursuits or activities previously reserved for male children or adolescents.

On the other hand, I could recall over twenty little boys whom I had seen, or who had been seen by some other professional I knew, for a psychological or psychiatric evaluation related to their cross-gender behavior. Practically the entire research literature on the subject of cross-gender disorders dealt with boys exclusively. Even in the adult research literature, far more was known about the lives and psychology of gay men than those women who chose a gay or cross-gender orientation.

How much of Mr. Alberson's upset was actually due to some special valuing of his son—of *any* son? And how much of his worry and anger was really the result of a perceived likelihood his child might become gay? Would he have had the same intense reaction if he'd encountered this cross-gender pattern in a daughter?

The Albersons had no daughter, so I was forced to approach the issue in a much more hypothetical way. Mr. Alberson responded to my delicate attempts at inquiry quite honestly, though, and it helped me understand more about the situation he was in.

He told me that he had to admit that he *was* especially pleased when he thought about the fact that he had two sons, although he didn't necessarily have anything against a daughter. He'd been brought up in a large household in which the boys had been clearly valued over the girls—even to the point that his brothers were the ones who attended the best schools and received most of the attention and praise for their successes. His sisters, he told me, had been sent to short-term vocational training, or had been encouraged to get married.

Mr. Alberson's attitude toward having sons, in turn, reminded me of a common trend in some families—as well as in whole cultures—to prefer male children over females. This was thought to be based on many practical concerns found in nonindustrialized societies, where the child was seen as a very real resource to the family in terms of manual labor, or the income they might ultimately provide when older. In the most extreme cases, of course, we know of cultures in which female children are left to die or are even murdered by their parents, to make room or resources more available for male children.

I wonder how much of the upset and intolerance we see over male homosexuality in our culture actually has to do with things far more basic than simply sexual behavior the majority consider somehow abnormal. How much of it really has to do with the preferred status of the male and the expectation that men should be men—and why would they wish it to be any different?—and, that the masculine role or identity is primary, essential and good.

But here was Mr. Alberson, telling me about that special pride and place for sons in his view of the world. He made no apologies for his opinion, though I could tell he understood his preference for sons to be grounded in arbitrary and unfair assumptions.

Was this yet another factor I hadn't initially considered in this case? That Mr. Alberson's son's effeminate behavior actually threatened to rob the father of a male child he so proudly enjoyed possessing? That he stood to lose not only his Frankie—who was, aside from a question of gender, a very *real* child in his parental life—but he also might be diminished even more significantly, through the unanticipated loss of an inordinately valued son?

■

Frankie Alberson is only a few years older now, but his situation has changed somewhat for the better. He is not victimized quite so often as before. But this is almost entirely due to his increased ability to conceal his feminine preferences and proclivities, and *not* because of some major transformation in his young personality.

Frankie played soccer in an organized sports league the year after I saw him first, and he now has two relatively unassertive, nonaggressive boys he calls friends. His mother reported that he made a goal during his first season on the Peewee League—a triumph choreographed by a sympathetic coach, with the help of one or two of the better players on the team. I found irony in the fact that his coach was a student who played soccer at a local college—a young woman.

The Albersons have settled down quite a lot, although I think primarily because of welcome changes in Frankie's behavior rather than any increased sense of acceptance of his more feminine characteristics. I suspect the Albersons continue to be very concerned their son might eventually be gay, but the situation now seems less urgent to them than before, and denial can be a powerful defense.

Although I don't follow Frankie Alberson's case closely any longer, I still have my doubts that anyone could make an accurate prediction about how his life may evolve. And certainly not at the tender age of seven. I am reassured and comforted by his developing friendships with both boys and girls, for I know that these relationships—bonds that Frankie sought so desperately—will be essential to his eventual success as a well-adjusted person.

It appears Frankie may be learning how to carve out a more comfortable niche for himself, as all children who are different must eventually do. Unlike the adult's world, which offers a wide array of choices, children are typically put into situations in which they must perform each and every day. They are often expected to perform and achieve in the areas of their worst individual weaknesses as well as in those of their particular strengths. They are forced by life to contend almost daily with tasks or people they can't possibly avoid. Adults, on the other hand, conceivably have at least the choice to opt out of almost any given situation. And, of course, they often do.

I am also glad to know that Frankie has shown an ability to adapt to some of his more difficult situations, to alter the behavior that he has learned will cause him trouble. While it may be unfortunate that he must pretend to be something other than what he may know himself to be, it is a skill that will help him deal with a world that can be inhabited by the cruel and intolerant.

Even now, when I think back to Frankie Alberson, I also have unresolved concerns about myself and about the young children who happen to be in *my* care. Why had my own sons suddenly entered my mind in the midst of Frankie Alberson's story? Had *his* issues—and the thoughts and feelings revealed by his parents during our time together—touched upon some hidden fear in me? A relatively latent but powerful parental fear of the unexpected or unwanted?

Would *my* reaction to such a situation be at all like that of Mr. Alberson? Was I prepared to lose a beloved child because of a sense of shame or loss I might not fully comprehend? I must admit to an uncertainty about my reaction still—if I should encounter a child such as Frankie Alberson in my own life as a parent. I am not proud of these misgivings, nor of the possibility that I might behave as Mr. Alberson did upon experiencing the wholly symbolic loss of a valued son. Can any one of us be all that sure that we would behave in a certain manner when faced with the loss of an idealized child?

In my mind's eye, I can still see little Frankie on that very first day: a gentle and sensitive child who so cautiously entered my world and told me his sad tale. I worry for him even now, as I think of all the other Frankies who are scorned and rejected everyday for what they are.

CHAPTER 4

SYMMETRY AND BALANCE

... in our latitude miracles are not at hand
And one must learn to care for ordinary things:
The tufted sparrow, washed-out moon, or unlovely child.

— NORMAN WILLIAMS

"THIS IS CRAZY—absolutely crazy!" the young mother screamed desperately, as though she were about to lose all control. "Why in God's name do we even have children when something like *this* can happen?"

Natalie Carson's intense anger quickly gave way to despair, and she began to sob quietly, as she looked down at the floor of her hospital room.

"I wish *I* were dead! I wish the baby was dead!" she whispered bitterly, then looked up at me again. "Why couldn't we have just died together last night?"

She placed her hands over her face, as if to block the room and everyone there from view. Perhaps to block out the whole experience of the long night before and to erase the memory of her only child's birth.

I reached forward to touch her shoulder. It was all I could think to say or do at that moment. I was a stranger to her then, having walked into her life uninvited only moments before. The consultation request in my shirt pocket had a cryptic message scribbled by a doctor in the neonatal intensive care unit. *"Defective child . . ."* was the phrase the physician had written, along with the identification of the infant, and his mother's hospital room number.

"Baby Boy Carson," it said. *"Mother in room 302."*

• • •

Morning can often be a busy time for psychologists and social work-ers, psychiatrists and clerics—professionals in large hospitals, who are often called to counsel the parents of a baby born with a serious medical problem. Nearly one in every twenty babies is born with a defect of some kind—from spina bifida to congenital heart problems, or a variety of physically handicapping conditions and diseases. In a very large medical center, where the most unusual and difficult cases are often referred, children born with birth defects can be a common occurrence.

Many of us think of childbirth as a time of intense joy, and there are many parents who will recall the arrival of their children as some-thing akin to a peak experience or an epiphany. But this memory will often be a revised version of actual events, for even the birth of a normal child can cause considerable anxiety or pain to parents. A positive reframing of the child's birthing experience appeals to our more romantic and sentimental preferences and conforms with a kind of mythology that surrounds our understanding of the value and psychological meaning of children.

My work has taught me that childbirth can also begin a journey into the world of the unexpected and the uncertain. This can be true for those parents who have ordinary and normal children—infants who are healthy, intact, and thought to be perfect in almost every way. But the upset and changes that childbirth can bring are most immediately evident and dramatically charged with the birth of a physically imperfect child.

As I walked along the corridor that led to the obstetric ward, on my way to visit Mr. and Mrs. Carson and their new baby that wintry morning long ago, I happened to notice a young father. He was just finishing washing his hands before entering the neonatal intensive care unit, often called the NICU, for short—a place where babies with serious medical problems are given specialized care.

The entryway to that large series of connecting rooms was a small, dark and uninviting tunnel. Its primary purpose was not to welcome, but rather to ensure that all who entered would scrub their hands with stiff brushes and disinfecting soap—important precautions in-tended to reduce the chances of infection. It was also a kind of reminder that it was a solemn place, one for babies who had not come easily into this world and for those born much too soon.

I only briefly glimpsed that young father as he stood upright and began to place a scrub-green paper surgical mask across his face. As he did, he looked directly at me, his expression showing little emotion—at least not an emotion I could easily discern. Most new fathers will offer a smile of some kind, at the very least a hopeful, albeit halfhearted grin. Because his face was oddly uncommunicative, I suspected something was very wrong for him and for the baby he was there to visit.

Farther down the hallway, I prepared to meet the parents of Baby Boy Carson. I was greeted on the maternity ward by the silent stares of the nurses and doctors who worked there—stares that told me *this* birth was somehow out of the ordinary. The birth of Baby Boy Carson seemed to be especially upsetting to the staff, as well as to his parents. There was an atmosphere of mystery around that baby, although I knew that the staff had probably seen every possible birth defect before.

Natalie Carson's medical chart told me that during the early morning hours she had delivered her first child: a seven-pound, four-ounce baby boy. Reading on through the detailed notes written by her nurses and physicians, I learned that her husband had been with her throughout the hours of her labor and was present in the delivery room even as their child emerged from Natalie's womb.

I also read that something had gone wrong for their new son— something that she herself would later claim she had sensed all along, a shocking discovery she and her husband would experience in the first few moments, as their child gasped for his first breath. The baby's defect had been immediately self-evident—and along with it, came an overwhelming and accurate sense that their lives would never be the same.

As is my custom in such cases, when I finished reading Natalie's chart, I walked back down the hallway to the NICU to see this child for myself. The exact nature of any birth defect was important to my understanding of what the parents might be going through, although I knew I could never completely appreciate their pain or disappointment; after all, this was *their* child, and not my own.

I stopped at the nurses' station to read the baby's chart. I learned quickly that the Carsons' new son had been born with a highly unusual birth defect—he was missing the entire right half of his face, extending from forehead to chin.

It was as though his face had somehow been left unfinished. The formal diagnosis was written down in his hospital chart as "congenital hypoplasia of the right facial bones"—more a technical description of his defect than a meaningful medical diagnosis or an explanation of how things had gone awry.

I saw that as yet the child was left unnamed; he would remain so through the next few days. For a long time thereafter he would be known only as *Baby Boy Carson*, the routine words written on the blue card affixed to his hospital crib. Most of the newborn children would have their given names written in soon after birth, if not by a proud parent, then by a dutiful maternity nurse. It is a rule of thumb in such places that babies be given their first names as soon as possible, since this is felt to aid in a kind of bonding that goes on very early in the parent-child relationship. But not *this* child—born without a right ear and eye, and with badly deformed bone structure on the side of his face.

This child would go nameless, while his parents tried to recover from the shock of his arrival.

It may seem odd, but it is common for the staff in some intensive care nurseries to refer to their tiny patients as something other than persons—as subhuman creatures, or even objects of some kind. In that particular intensive care environment the terms were "frog" and "tadpole." It may be that this name derives from the observation— first made for me by a young physician-in-training—that very small newborns, usually born much too soon and weighing perhaps only a pound or so, do not appear wholly human. The peculiar posture of their bodies in their cribs, with their spindly legs tucked under them as their tiny backs arch upward, was a remnant of fetal positioning in their mothers' wombs. This position did render them oddly reminiscent of an amphibious creature. Indeed, nature had originally intended that these premature infants remain immersed in fluid a while longer. Instead, these tiny neonates would be surrounded by a high-tech morass of cathode-ray tubes and lights—lullabied to sleep by the clicks and beeps and assorted sounds of elaborate electronic monitoring devices.

Of course, the term "frog" or "tadpole" could not be used in front of parents or other outsiders who could not readily share in the special culture of the NICU. It was a sort of gallows humor—a peculiar language intended to ease the psychological strain on the people who cared for these sick and premature babies day in and day out. It was my psychological training that led me to interpret it as a kind of unconscious defense, a barrier against the emotional stress of bearing daily witness to those babies' suffering—the bulk of which was meted out by the medical staff themselves, as they went about difficult and often painful duties.

But there were no demeaning nicknames applied to Baby Boy Carson. I even noted fewer academic discussions among the doctors about his particular case. Such curbside conferences would typically be held for my benefit prior to a consultation. They would traditionally convene in open hallways for everyone to hear, for we were in a teaching hospital. But it was as if the freakish nature of his grossly deformed face had somehow precluded all of that. This event was somehow not comparable to the more usual hole in the spine seen in spina bifida—or more frequent cases of clubbed foot, cleft palate or missing limb. It seemed unlike any of the more typical assortment of physical anomalies that these professionals had seen before.

There was much less attention of *any* sort being paid to this particular baby, although everyone knew of his presence by the time I arrived. He didn't require all that much care from the nurses and doctors, at least not *medical* care. Surprisingly, he even appeared healthier, stronger and larger than the other infants there. But the nervous silence I had initially encountered, and the nervous glances of the staff, made me sense their uncertainty. Immense uncertainty, it occurred to me, about this child's future and his viability as a person.

As I approached the infant's *isolette*, a one-by-two-foot cubicle made of impact-resistant plastic, I became aware of my own growing discomfort with what I imagined I might see. From a distance, it was apparent that Baby Boy Carson was large by comparison with his premature roommates. So, even as I approached him, the baby appeared out of place. As I positioned myself to see him more clearly I quickly understood the silence and tension I sensed as I entered the unit. He was awake and quietly alert, and he stared up at me with his solitary eye, so blue and clear and bright. As I moved slowly around—to examine his face more fully—he tried to follow me with his gaze.

It was true—he was a child with half a face.

The right side appeared to be made of a sort of lifelike clay, stretched and fashioned in the strangest manner. I might place my cupped hand over his deformity, gently and with no real effort, or he might turn his head a little to his right, thus obscuring the missing side of his face. At that moment he would seem an altogether ordinary child, even quite beautiful. But as soon as I removed my hand, or his face readjusted to the left, he seemed so very different, even foreign. As I first glimpsed Baby Boy Carson, I realized I would need conscious reminders that *this* was a human being—that this creature was someone's child.

It was almost ten o'clock on that gray winter morning when I was finally prepared to walk into Natalie Carson's hospital room. I quickly introduced myself and described my purpose in being there. I sat down beside her, but she remained silent for a minute or so. As I entered her room and looked around, I realized no one was at Natalie's bedside. No husband, no relatives, no friends. She was conspicuously alone in that semiprivate room, while her happy roommate chatted busily with her husband and several relatives. Perhaps it was because I had assumed Natalie's husband would be with her that morning that he later became such a mysterious figure to me—a riddle to decipher.

As I searched for him that first morning, I suddenly wondered whether it might have been Bob Carson I'd seen just minutes before—that new father I glimpsed preparing to visit his baby in the NICU—for that would easily explain his absence. If it was, that was the only time I would ever see him. He wouldn't be present during any of my hospital visits with his wife. And he chose not to accompany his wife and their new son to my office for consultations during the subsequent years, despite my attempts to get him there.

It also occurred to me that he might have been quite alone just after the birth of his son, surrounded by the darkened rooms of sleeping mothers, ignored by the busy nurses who were constantly moving from room to room with very little time for husbands or fathers. There would have been the persistent cries of the newborn babies just down the hallway, from the nursery reserved for healthy, full-term infants. Perhaps he'd wondered which cry was that of his own new son—but only for a moment. He would quickly remember that it couldn't be, for his child was placed in the intensive care nursery, sequestered away from the normal and healthy newborns.

Natalie finally began our conversation, continuing a dialogue with herself that I felt she must have started long before I'd entered her room.

"I knew something was wrong from the very beginning. I was sick every day and I just never felt right. I told my doctor, but he said I was just overly worried about having my first baby. He asked me if everything was all right at home and was the child wanted and things like that. I told him of course it was wanted. We wanted a baby very much. And now this happens." Natalie began to cry.

"We had planned to call him Robert, Jr., if it was a boy, but I'm not sure that will happen now." Natalie then spoke about her husband and her apprehension over Bob's eventual arrival.

"He left last night after I fell asleep. I only slept for a few minutes, but when I woke up, the nurse told me she thought he'd gone home. I called him, but he didn't answer the phone. I'm worried about him . . . I don't know where he is. He told the nurse there was nothing more for him to do and that he would be back later."

She told me this as though she was telling someone else's story, with an odd flatness in her voice. It occurred to me that there was a broad distance between herself and the event of her child's birth.

"I just don't know what's going to happen next. I knew something was wrong, but I never expected this. Who could even *imagine* something like this." We were interrupted by the morning nurse, who was new to Natalie but not at all unaccustomed to first-time mothers for whom things have gone wrong. She didn't hesitate to come to Natalie's bedside to introduce herself.

"Have you thought of a name for the baby yet?" she asked Natalie directly. "It's important to give the baby a name as soon as you can. It's good for him and it's good for you and your husband." Natalie nodded slowly and said nothing. The nurse glanced at me as though I were about to work some magic, which I was certain I could not. She gazed back at Natalie, hopeful she might ask questions. But she was strangely silent.

"Would you like to see the baby now? We can take you to the NICU, and you can spend some time with him." The nurse was lively and upbeat, as though everything would be all right, as though everything would somehow be much better soon.

"No thank you, not right now," Natalie replied in a hushed tone. She looked at me with what I perceived to be embarrassment or shame. The nurse left us there alone. Natalie wiped away her tears and looked out the window, to the darkened day just beyond.

"Does this sort of thing happen very often? I mean babies with . . . with deformed faces? I never even heard of such a thing! And why did it have to happen to us?" Natalie looked over to me and began to cry again. Mercifully, she went on before I had time to stammer answers to her questions.

"What are we going to do now? How are we going to take care of this baby? I never expected this to happen. If I had known this was going to happen I never would have had it. Bob had to have a son, though—that's what he kept telling me over and over, even before we got married. It was going to be Bobby, Jr.—and now this. Bob's not even here, and they want me to give it a name. I don't even want to see it."

It was then and there that she asked me her desperate question, the question that sprang from her anger and grief and her unrealized expectations. It was then that Natalie asked me why it was we have children, when such terrible things can happen. It was then she shared with me her fervent wish for death for herself and for the child she brought forth that day.

Natalie Carson's question stayed with me. What was it that Natalie and Bob Carson had expected of the birth of their child? What did any parents look for as they brought new life into this world? And how might their expectations change—parents' hopes and fears, for example—as the relationship with their infant child progressed?

At the very beginning of the process, physical health will be a major concern for the parents of newborn children. And, initially, expectant parents hope above all else that their child will be whole and intact like everyone else's baby. When this basic hope is realized, parental expectation is likely to shift to a different level, one that is more specific and travels beyond the criteria that broadly determine human normalcy. There will be concern about the rate of growth and the things we call developmental milestones. There will be concern about the child's rate of learning—is he or she walking or talking or understanding his or her world in the ways that a child should? And if everything appears more or less normal, there can be a sudden shift from the concern that the child be ordinary and whole, to questions about why he or she isn't developing at the same rate as the kid next door. Does the child appear at all retarded? Or, conversely, doesn't the child seem even a little brighter than average? Perhaps a genius?

These parental concerns can include more complicated matters, such as the child's particular personality traits or ways of being—his or her success in social relationships, or the meaning of unexpected patterns of behavior. As these things are first encountered, a subtle process of attribution begins, as parents wonder where each of these traits, good or bad, might have originated.

Sociological investigations have thrown light on the issue of parental expectations of their children. A large survey performed by the University of Michigan, for example, found that parents in the United States tend to identify a few standard characteristics that they hope to promote in their children as they grow. These characteristics include such things as moral virtue, personability, independence, industriousness and persistence. It is interesting to note that those same parents did not identify or name certain other qualities that one would suspect are quite important to them: qualities such as physical attractiveness, above-average intelligence, school achievement, popularity with other children and athletic prowess. Parents might not wish to appear superficial to inquiring sociologists. Or to expect more from their children than the essential ingredients of "being a good person"—this is the phrase we know many American parents will commonly use when they mention their overriding goal in raising their children. But it is likely these same parents would be aware that such characteristics as athletic skill, attractiveness and social popularity have a certain survival value in life, as facilitators of success. Didn't we wish for these ourselves when we were children? And didn't our parents tell us they were somehow important?

On that morning long ago, Natalie Carson's expectations for her newborn baby had exploded around her. Even as he was taken from her body, she hadn't been allowed to progress beyond the most basic level of parental hope and expectations—beyond the silent prayer for an ordinary, healthy child. I recall Natalie telling me that soon after the final push—even as she lifted herself up slightly on the delivery bed to take her son from the nurse who had cleaned and swaddled him immediately after his birth—her body had begun to shiver and shake uncontrollably. She suddenly became nauseated. These sensations, like her pregnancy, had frightened her. She interpreted it as a loss of personal control. This reaction made it impossible for her to physically accept the child, returning him instead to the obstetrical nurse. Like many first-time mothers, she evinced a kind of basic ignorance—an uncertainty about what she must do and an ineptitude at parenting.

On the morning I saw her, Natalie was not at all certain she was ready to receive *that* child into her life. It had been as though the first motherly embrace would authorize a life that Natalie was understandably reluctant to live—the life of the parent of a seriously deformed child.

I can recall, however, their *second* embrace, for I was there to witness it. Natalie was still intensely anxious and ambivalent, as though she were embarking upon a journey from which she might not return. Perhaps she had been emboldened, or prodded, by the presence of her nurse and me. It must have seemed as though we had our own expectations that she behave as a mother to this child.

As she took the baby from his plastic-enclosed crib, she slowly sat back in the large rocking chair beside her. There was a long silence. She looked up at me sadly, fearfully, and then to her nurse, as if to say: "What do I do now?" We said nothing, for we had no words to say.

The sight of this mother-child reunion evoked feelings of joy tempered by anxiety. We could not react as we wished we could, as though everything would be fine. We were not even sure how the next few minutes would unfold. As Natalie slowly looked down at her infant, she sighed a long deep breath, one she had been holding in for a very long time. Suddenly, the baby felt the warmth of his mother's breath on his imperfect face, and then, quite unexpectedly—for we had been attuned to the mother and *not* the child—he gazed up at her. As he did this, the right side of his face pressed closely against her body, leaving his imperfection entirely out of view. Natalie began to smile at him, and then at us, as a stream of tears glistened in tracks down her reddened cheeks. She mumbled something to her baby—audible, but unintelligible. I could see that the baby had reacted. Again, he perked up and focused on the tearful, smiling face of his mother.

The nurse reached out to touch Natalie's arm, as she was moved by the sight of them there together. We remained still for another few seconds, silently fixed upon the mother and her infant. Natalie seemed to relax, and she shifted her gaze slowly upward, stopping as she stared straight up into the ceiling. She sighed again, quite loudly, then lowered her eyes to look at her child. Slowly at first, then much more quickly—more easily too. She took his arm into her hand and began to stroke it gently up and down. He snuggled deeper still into her breast and closed his eye for a second or two—only soon to open it again, to gaze once more into his mother's face.

■

I have followed the case of Kevin Carson for more than a decade, although much less closely in recent years because of geographical distance. He has undergone six operations on his face, beginning in the first year of life. Each of these has been performed by a highly qualified team of surgeons at a major medical center, and each operation has been but one link in a chain of surgeries to construct the missing portions of Kevin's imperfect face.

Kevin's primary doctor during those early years was Emile Troutante, an aging plastic surgeon whose specialty was the reconstruction and repair of children's faces, known in the medical profession as *pediatric cranioplasty*. Dr. Troutante explained that the very first operation corrected Kevin's cleft palate, a defect in the roof of his mouth, where the two sides of his palate failed to join together before birth. I realized that many of us hadn't noticed this defect at all that first morning after his birth. It had somehow been obscured by the larger deficit in his facial bone structure.

During a subsequent operation, Dr. Troutante constructed Kevin's right ear, an exact duplicate of his left ear in positioning and size. These two procedures went smoothly and presented few problems for his expert team of physicians. The third and fourth operations were longer in duration and required more technical skill and some daring on the part of the surgical team. They attempted to build up the depressed bone structure—the foundation for Kevin's face—to provide a basis for securing a prosthetic eye device.

Dr. Troutante had a rather old-fashioned and formal, almost European style of presentation. In our one-to-one discussions, he spoke as if not only to me, but also to an invisible audience of medical students, residents and colleagues who would be sitting just behind me—not in his small office, but in a large medical amphitheater. As he did so, he produced detailed sketches and radiographic pictures.

"*Symmetry and balance* are what we strive for," I recall Dr. Troutante saying, with a dramatic emphasis on the first three words. "*These* are the features that will yield the best overall result."

As he spoke, the surgeon gestured to a life-size clay model sitting on his desk. It was a model of a child's head; although its gender could not be discerned. The face was sleek and its features smooth and aquiline—unisex. It somehow seemed a perfect face.

"This boy's face has a sense of order," he said. "Now it will be much easier for him to . . . well, to fit in with others."

As I watched him gesture toward the model, I was reminded of a journal article I had read, written by a social psychologist who had studied people's perceptions of physical attractiveness. She reported—somewhat ironically and in contrast to what Dr. Troutante was proposing—that most people actually find the *average-appearing* face especially attractive, the face that is free of any noticeable defects and unexceptional. She found that the too-perfect face was viewed with a kind of suspicion, but for reasons she was unable to define.

I was reminded of that research because it resonated with my own reaction to the sculpted child's face Dr. Troutante had shown me. It seemed *too* perfect—so unlike the faces of children I knew. I didn't mention this to Dr. Troutante, choosing to focus on his lecture once more. I didn't suppose that he had a model of the average human face there in his office that day.

He showed me the *Atlas of the Human Form*, a series of elaborate illustrations like geographical maps of the body and each of its external parts. He told me about the neoclassical canons for the Caucasian face—a set of guidelines for determining the specific vertical and horizontal proportions of the human face. Originally formulated by artists and scholars during the Renaissance, these canons were founded upon classical Greek statuary and drawings and were later used by anatomical artists during the seventeenth through the nineteenth centuries.

Before he scheduled Kevin Carson for surgery, Dr. Troutante had duly consulted the neoclassical canons and had calculated the ideal spatial relationship between Kevin's various facial parts. He had determined the proper space between the child's nose and the midpoint of his ear, and he'd calculated the ideal distance between his chin and forehead. The goal was to develop an aesthetically pleasing model of the human facial form. This working model would, in turn, be used to plan the unfinished part of Kevin's face, which the surgeons would construct.

It seemed fantastic to me that the physician's measurements were expressed in millimeters, precisely calculated from the canons first used by artists such as Leonardo da Vinci and Albrecht Dürer during the fifteenth century, and that the three-dimensional, geometric model he had constructed would have served as a sort of blueprint for Kevin's reconstructive surgeries. My impression was that his particular approach might have been somewhat dated even then, but Dr. Troutante clung to it proudly as it had been emphasized in his own clinical training many years before.

"With this child, we sought symmetry here . . . and here, along the side of the face," he pointed to the model. "And down here, where the chin should have been. The success is in the object's shape and in the balance of the features." He paused a moment as though he were back in surgery, reflecting on his next procedure, identifying physical landmarks along the surface of his visual aid.

As he did this, I silently wondered why it was he had chosen to refer to Kevin's face as an "object." His remark reminded me of another surgeon I'd known who had once told me that he deliberately maintained a distance from his patients because he believed it allowed him to do a better job. To be too personally invested in a patient, or to fall prey to biases that can accompany sentimental love, could be a problem for a surgeon who might easily be confronted with a need to make split-second decisions in the operating room.

"And for the face, we must achieve a smooth texture to the skin's surface," the doctor continued. "There must be subtle contours. In this patient's situation there was nothing to work with on the right side—no photographs to show us how it might have looked, as in a case of trauma. There were no useful X rays of his underlying skeleton because of the depressed bone structure," he added. "So I was left to make it match the left side of his face. But I was careful to make sure it would be symmetrical both vertically and horizontally," he said, demonstrating this on the sculpted head.

He shifted his weight forward, reaching across his cluttered desk, and cupped the model's face between his hands, bringing it toward him and settling back into his desk chair. He began to gently stroke the perfect child's facial features.

"The result is pretty good for this kind of major reconstruction— his face is now very symmetrical. And I think his ears and nose are in balance," he said with self-assurance. "When I think of how it looked before we started all of this, he is a totally different boy now. A *totally different boy*," he repeated slowly and with emphasis.

But after a momentary pause he added, "Of course, there is the problem with his range of motion."

"Range of motion . . . ?" I repeated out loud, surprising myself.

"Yes. You see, we can make his face appear quite natural, balanced and aesthetically pleasing. But the muscles that underlie the face, the ones that support it and provide movement, these can be very tricky. There is only so much we can do about the face, about how it will appear, when it is . . . when it is set in motion. When it moves, you know, even as a person speaks or smiles, or he eats and changes expression. The natural range of motion is a difficult thing to correct for. We try to make allowances."

Dr. Troutante seemed a bit dejected at that moment, and I suspected he had taken this as a kind of failure on *his* part—to overcome this technical problem. But even as this thought occurred to me, his change in mood vanished. He was back to his lecture, describing the next procedure that had been completed.

Before leaving his office that day, I asked him a final question. Abandoning the teacher-student relationship I had adopted previously, I asked him how it was he came to specialize in plastic surgery. At first, my question appeared to puzzle him. I suspected he was unprepared for the more abstract inquiries of psychologists. He paused for a moment to reflect.

"Well, this might seem a bit corny, but I suppose it was initially because my father was a physician. And a rather prominent one, too, in Boston," he responded. "It just seemed natural that I would go to medical school and, well, and follow in his footsteps. He was a very respected physician," he added proudly.

"But why plastic surgery? And with children as your specialty?" I asked again.

"Well, I suppose because it is a very gratifying field to be in. For example, I take nothing—as in the case of this boy—or what has been made into nothing by trauma, such as in a horrible car accident, and I make it into something whole. This can be very gratifying because you see the result of your work—it is very real. And I . . . I suppose I became interested in children because they are so much more, well, more *malleable* than adults. I mean, they take the skin grafts so well. And the transplantations—the scarring can be so minimal over the long run with a child. And, in the end, you have a much better chance that the final outcome will look like, well . . . that it will look as it should."

Even the casual observer might sense that something about young Kevin Carson's face doesn't look quite right. His deformity from birth has largely been repaired, or at least disguised. But its remnants are revealed in defects which, while certainly more subtle, are perceptible to most who encounter him. Dr. Troutante had said to me that the range in movement of Kevin's face had been a problem he could never fully repair or render completely natural.

The right side of Kevin's face, clearly much smoother now and symmetrical in shape, nicely counterbalanced the left side just as his surgeon had intended. But it has an altogether unreal appearance, as though it had been carved out of alabaster. His skin appears tight against the bone, even puttied here and there, especially around the eyes and mouth. As a result, his face has a strangely wooden quality. Despite its proportional integrity, it cannot be considered perfect, unless you were to see it somehow frozen in time and space. Even then, one would be tempted to take a second look. For it does not seem as it should.

When Kevin smiles, it is an exceedingly odd smile, one that contorts his face. When he speaks, one half of his face moves to the left, then up and down quite naturally. The other half remains almost suspended, out of synchrony.

It was the befuddlement in the faces of perfect strangers that tortured Kevin and his mother most of all. As a result, he would not venture out into the world as much as he might have otherwise, notwithstanding the excessively enthusiastic greetings of well-intentioned relatives and neighbors. He would tell his mother: "The worst part is that look in other people's faces." He had told her this early on, when he was nine or ten years old. "I hate that look in other people's faces."

He would sometimes talk with his mother about his upset and about the sadness his face caused within him. As he grew older, though, he talked with her less and less. She told me Kevin would now share little of a personal nature—as is normal in many older children, anyway. He chose instead to retreat into his room for longer and longer periods of time. But unlike other children who become secretive at home about their inner worlds, Kevin had no close friends to confide in. Natalie knew that this could not be allowed to continue; it seemed to her an unnatural and unhealthy thing. This was the reason Natalie began visiting me once again, as she had frequently done during the first few years after the birth of her son.

She also visited because she was a single parent by then, her husband Bob having left their home and his marriage to Natalie about a year after Kevin's birth. He might see his son on holidays or special occasions, but never on a regular basis, and only when prodded by his parents or by Natalie. Because of the absence of his father, Natalie Carson often needed someone else's advice about what it was she should do for Kevin.

After initial greetings and formalities, we would behave much like old friends. Often she would pick up our conversation where we had left off, even from many months before. One day Natalie told me about the first time she realized Kevin knew that his face was different.

"He was about two and a half, and I was sitting with him in his room, just playing with him on the floor," she said. "He was looking in a mirror, just a little mirror on one of his baby toys. He looked at himself and then he looked up at me. And then he said '*Ugly.*' I was so startled by this, because I'd been doing so well with it at that point . . . and I just started to cry. He said 'Mommy not cry,' but I couldn't stop." Natalie became teary-eyed and reached for a tissue. She paused to dry her eyes and then continued.

"I told him he *wasn't* ugly. That he was beautiful to me. I told him he was a very special boy. I didn't know what else to say. And then I just hugged him for the longest time. I don't think he understood any of it, though. He just kept looking at himself in the mirror, looking sort of sad and confused, and a little bit scared because he realized that it was *his* face he was seeing there. I didn't have any idea how to explain it to him. He was so little. But that was when I started to really worry about what might happen next, because it was just when I had started to pretend everything was going to be OK. I forgot it might not be OK for *him*. I was so caught up in what it did to *me*, and that was slowly getting better, less painful and easier to accept. It all became so real to me again—like a shot. It was like I had built this shell around me and suddenly it was falling apart. I felt a lot like I did the morning he was born."

"I'm curious, Natalie, how has all of this been for you? I mean, if you had to sum it all up thus far, how has it changed you, your life, the way you think about things? Does that seem like a weird question?"

"No, not at all, it's something I've given a lot of thought to. It's like every now and then I have to . . . to take stock of what's been happening to me, you know what I mean? Having Kevin has made me think about my life and, like the . . . the *meaning* of all of this. I'm sure I've thought about it, I mean my life, much more than I ever did before. Probably more than I would have otherwise; I mean, if my life had gone another way. Before Kevin was born everything was pretty laid out and predictable. I went to school, I got a job, I got married to Bob. It was all pretty much according to plan, nothing out of the ordinary. Having Kevin changed all of that. Now I think about what all of this *really* means. And I think I have come to some pretty basic conclusions."

"Like . . . ?"

"Well, like . . . I am a much stronger person than I would have thought in the beginning. I mean when all of this happened and I didn't know what to do or what to think, it seemed like there was no future for me or for Kevin back then. It was all so overwhelming. But, over time, everything gradually became better. Much more manageable. But I had to do all of it myself. My husband was absolutely no help whatsoever, he was never there. He just couldn't deal with it. He still can't. My family was totally wiped out by Kevin's problems, and I guess so were my friends, 'cause they all stopped calling me like they had before."

"Tell me about your family," I asked.

"My parents? Well, I think they viewed me as a bad mother from the very start, I mean, because he wasn't whole. He wasn't the perfect little grandchild they had expected. And my friends? I guess they were just embarrassed or something, I never really found out. I just left them all alone."

"That must have been very hard for you and Kevin," I said.

"Yeah, it was. But I saw a side to people—people who had meant something to me. A side I never knew was there. And, let me tell you, I hated it. It was pretty cold—cold and lonely those first few months after Kevin was born."

"All I have to compare it with is what I thought it might be like. And that's like night and day. I mean, I think Kevin taught me to be a different kind of mother than I would have been if he hadn't been born with his problems."

"In what way are you a different kind of mother?"

"Well, I probably would have been a lot like *my* mother. Or like the mothers I knew who lived around me. I mean, the ones in my neighborhood. Or the ones I saw on TV. I mean, what kind of mother just walks away from her daughter because she has a baby with a birth defect? Because she can't take it? I don't think I ever really thought about what it meant to be a mother—except to take care of your kids and love them and all of that." She looked to me to say something in response, but I was focused on her words. She paused but soon realized I had little to say, and so she began again.

"To tell you the truth, I never really gave it much thought at all. You know, about what it meant to be a mother. It never really occurred to me that something more than that could happen—something different from the 'storybook' version of having kids. It's funny, I've never told anyone this before. But I sometimes think that the parents of a special child, a child like Kevin, you know, a kid who really tests you as a person—those parents *really* know what it means to love a child, to truly love a child. That is, if they don't give up first."

"Give up?"

"Yeah, you know, like my parents did with me and Kevin. They kind of abandoned us. They just couldn't deal with it. Now they spend all their time visiting my brother and his kids. He gave them what they wanted, what they expected."

"I'm sure your brother also loves *his* kids. Is your relationship with Kevin so very different?"

"Loving your kids has got be more than just taking care of them and being proud of them when they please you by being smart or pretty or whatever."

"Well, yes, I think a love that's tested by adversity can be . . . well, a more satisfying love in certain respects. Is that what you mean?" I asked.

"More than that. Much more than that." Natalie paused and seemed almost in pain, as she searched her mind for an example, hoping to find some anecdote that might help me to understand what she was trying to say.

"When I think back to when I was young, I remember my mother and father getting all excited when I was good at something, or when I succeeded. You could see they really enjoyed that. You could see the pride in their faces. But they didn't know what to do when things didn't go well—like when I failed algebra in ninth grade. I remember that day so clearly, the day I came home with the "F" on my report card. It was my first failing grade, my first low grade ever, really. My mom and dad, they just sort of shut down, I mean, they just shut down emotionally. They were shocked that I had failed, their perfect little daughter. They asked a lot of questions, like how could that happen and what went wrong—stuff like that. Sure, they eventually told me it was OK and they would help me out, get me a tutor. It took an hour or two before they realized it might not be the end of the world. It was like they just didn't know what to do. Do you know what I'm trying to say? It was like their love for me didn't include the times I let them down."

Natalie sighed with relief. Somehow she had put her feelings into words. But then it was as if she had to undo it all, as though she felt guilt over her criticism of her parents.

"But I suppose they *were* good parents, all things considered. They were probably a lot like most parents. I just never imagined I could disappoint them *that* much. It really threw me for a loop."

I nodded as if I understood at least some of what she was saying. She had not been the first person to share with me the sense of shock she and many others have felt at learning they didn't live up to their parents' expectations. This was a theme I encountered all the time with emotionally disturbed adolescents. She also reminded me of how very powerful a parent's love could be. A love that apparently could be given to a child or taken away in just an instant.

"And now I just try to live day to day. I take care of Kevin. Being there for him is part of what I am as a person. I suppose it will be that way until I die. When a child has a problem like Kevin's, he can't count on too many people to be there for him through the good *and* the bad times."

"But he knows that he has you there for him, doesn't he?"

"Yes, I think he does. But in the beginning it was as though he *wasn't* a part of me. There were times—I know I've told you this before—when I actually *hated* the fact that he came into my life, that he had to be *my* child. I asked the "*Why me?*" question over and over, until I thought I might be going insane. I think it was that initial shock, you know, from the very first day. And it probably had to do with all the hassles we went through. The doctor visits, and the trips to the city for his operations. I had to put my own life on hold for a very long time until, one day, I think Kevin *became* my life."

"Is that a good thing, Natalie?" I asked her this because it was rather common for the parent of a handicapped or sick child to give up many aspects of his or her own life, in the interest of the child. This could be, on occasion, a pattern that spelled trouble. Trouble for both the adult and the child.

"Well, I can tell you it doesn't *feel* like it's on hold anymore, I mean *my* life, my life as a person. He has to become more independent. I have to let go a bit. And I think I will, eventually. But when you asked me how all of this has changed me, the thing I thought of first is that I really feel proud that I am a parent, that I am Kevin's mother. And that I am able to . . . able to love him so much. In the beginning, just after he was born, it never even occurred to me that I could grow to love that kid as much as I do now. It makes me think everything before was somehow, well, somehow very superficial."

"But how do you feel about his situation now? Does it seem as though the surgeries have made a difference . . . for Kevin . . . or for you?"

"When I look at Kevin's face I see him the way he used to be, the way he looked most of that first year after he was born. Sure, I know they've given him the parts of his face he was born without; and they even look pretty real. But, it's strange, when I look at him, it's as though they've done nothing at all."

"What do you mean, 'nothing at all'?" I asked her in a bewildered way.

"It's like he's wearing a mask; I have this picture in my head, a picture of what he *really* looks like. Kevin's face as a baby, my baby, the baby I didn't want—at least not in the beginning. It's *very* clear to me, this picture of him. It's right here." She pointed to her forehead and stared at me intensely. "I don't think that picture of him, my memory of him even as a little baby will ever go away. Do you?"

"Probably not. But does it ever get in the way of moving ahead with things—like with your relationship, or your hopes for Kevin?"

"It's funny to say this, but I don't think I have all that many hopes for Kevin. I mean I don't expect too much from him other than that he find a little happiness in his life. Things are always going to be hard for him. You've seen his face, it still looks very odd. Everyone notices. The people we know try not to react, but you can still see it in their faces. I know he sees it, and it hurts him, though he won't admit it. Strangers don't hide it at all—they stare and look like he's some kind of freak or something. I think that I had to let go of a lot of things when I started to really want him in my life, when I started to really love him. It didn't begin right away, I'm still a little ashamed to say that, even to you—but it's true."

"What happened along the way to change things . . . to change the way you felt about Kevin?"

"Well, first of all, I had to get rid of all my dreams for him. Dreams I had even when I was a teenager. From when I wasn't even married or going steady. I had dreams about having kids some day and what it would be like and what they would become. And when I was pregnant—when I wasn't feeling sick—I would daydream about the future. About the baby son I would have and what he would be some day. It had to be a boy, you see. All of this, I just somehow threw out the window.

"I know that this is really going to sound crazy, but there are times I think we should have just left him alone. Let him be what he was. I'm not sure we ever should have tried to make him this . . . uh . . . this handsome face. In some ways it's worse than it was."

She paused to gauge my reaction to her remark.

"How is that?" I asked, clearly taken aback.

"Well, you see, before, you could tell that he was born with a very bad disfigurement. He was missing part of his face, it just wasn't there to begin with. It was a shocking thing at first, but you knew what it was. Somehow it was pretty clear what it was. A birth defect, a terrible one, yes, but something definite. Now, when these strangers stare at him on the street, I have this impulse to *explain* how it happened. You know, explain the way he looked before. Tell them that it wasn't my fault, what I had done to try and make it right, you know, the whole story. As it is now, they just look at him in a real weird way. I feel like I, like all of us, have tried to make him another child. He was supposed to be Bobby, Jr., remember? But that didn't happen. It couldn't happen. His father refused to go ahead and do it the way we had planned."

"What do you mean?" I asked. I hadn't heard this part of the story before.

"'Everything's different now,' he would say to me. 'It isn't the same now.' So I had to pick out a name—and it had to be a name that no one else in the family had. So that nobody would be *insulted*. I remember Bob saying that—so that no one would be insulted. And then I kept bringing him to Dr. Troutante, and he made it all sound so easy to fix. When I looked at the pictures of the other children he had operated on, they all looked so good. But it didn't turn out that way, really. I don't feel like I was prepared for what it would really be like."

Her comment reminded me of my conversation with Dr. Troutante several years before, and of my reactions to his somewhat antiquated and methodical approach to creating the perfect face. I realized Natalie was correct—we *had* all seemed so intent on making this imperfect child whole. It was as though his life and his humanity depended upon his looking like everyone else—or even *better* than everyone else. I paused a moment, reflecting on her words, and then I asked her for clarification.

"You mean, that you can still tell it is not completely natural. I mean the right side of his face?"

"Exactly. Sometimes I think it would have been better just to have left him alone . . . let him be what he was. It's funny, but my guilt over having Kevin—that I had failed everyone—that just went away one day. But now I feel guilty for trying to make him, well, to make him more . . . more presentable. Presentable to the world. I'm not angry with Dr. Troutante, or the others, it's just that we never really stopped to consider leaving him alone. It's like we automatically assumed he would be better off looking like everyone else. That otherwise he would be shunned and teased by the other kids. But he's teased anyway. Most of the other children don't want to have anything to do with him. He scares them."

"But perhaps it would have been far worse for him the other way. After all, it was a very serious defect. I think people might have been even more shocked and frightened," I said.

"I know, I know that *seems* right. But sometimes I just feel like we've taken something away from him in order to make it more comfortable for everybody else. My relatives, my husband, even strangers—people who don't mean anything to me. And it really hasn't made that big a difference in anything.

"Sometimes I think I tried to change what he was because I was really trying to change myself. I'm not sure I was really thinking of *him* when I decided to go ahead with the surgery. I was worrying about what everyone else wanted. And I was thinking about *myself*."

Natalie began to cry, something she had not done in my presence for several years. I felt she was now sharing something with me that was relatively new to her awareness. And although her reasoning that the child should have been left alone did not make sense to me, I began to have an appreciation for what she was trying to say.

"I just couldn't let go of the dream. The dream to be normal—to be like everyone else. To be the way I thought they wanted me to be. And that just poured over into the way I thought about my son," she said. "And now, for reasons I can't really be sure about, I feel shame over it. Shame, that I couldn't see past myself—past myself to him."

■

My encounters with Natalie and Kevin Carson have occurred less frequently in the past few years, and usually only around times of crisis. Perhaps a crisis in Kevin's psychological development, or when Natalie or is having a particularly difficult time as his parent. Sometimes she will call when she has the need to talk with someone who was there on that morning years ago when she delivered the baby who would become her only child. Someone who also carries a visual memory of the life she brought into the world.

With the passage of time, that imperfect child has emerged as more potent and complete than we could possibly have known only hours after his birth. We have watched him achieve developmental milestones like walking and talking at the same age as other children. Because of his birth defect, he has been examined and tested and prodded by scores of doctors and special teachers—including myself—during the subsequent ten years of his life. At the age of seven, he was found to display above-average scores on intelligence tests and to have acquired all of the skills he would need to achieve success in school.

He was considered an exceptionally curious child by his teachers—even a creative one—due to his rapid mastery of language and his extravagant stories of strange and imaginative creatures, beings he endowed with wondrous and fantastic powers. He showed amazing aptitude for things such as board games, learning the rules quickly and mastering the games soon after.

Like most children, Kevin Carson showed his own peculiar blend of strengths and weaknesses. And each of his achievements seemed even greater in light of the severity of his facial defect and in consideration of the burden he would carry through life. In time, Kevin would even come to reflect on his place in the larger world and the price he might pay for his disfiguring condition.

A shroud of mystery fell upon all of us that first morning long ago when Kevin was born, and for several years thereafter. The birth of that imperfect child, as with all children, was but the beginning of a process of evolution. We felt, and with good reason, that his life would be unpredictable and perhaps unhappy. It might have comforted his mother to have known of the many accomplishments her son would know during the subsequent years of his life. This hopeful bit of knowledge would have allowed me to provide more reassurance than I felt I could that morning. But the collective shock caused by his peculiar defect made us behave cautiously then, taking special care not to promise things that might never be.

Kevin Carson's case left its imprint on me. I find it difficult now to return to a hospital nursery—or to a neonatal intensive care unit—and not think back to that little boy, born with only half a face. I think of his mother and of our conversations. I think of a marriage ended, at least in part, by the birth of an imperfect child a mother and father conceived together. Bob Carson is now almost a stranger to his son—his visits in later years have become even more infrequent, and their lives have gradually grown further apart.

I will sometimes find myself gazing across the large hospital nursery filled with babies in their open cribs, the nurses scurrying back and forth to care for the infants there. Some will be asleep; others crying desperately for someone to come and hold them. Through the large windows in the nursery, and out in the hallway just beyond, I will see the mothers in wrinkled bathrobes. They are physically worn out and badly in need of sleep themselves. Instead, they stand watch outside the nursery, peering in to find *their* baby among the crowd in pink and blue.

I will occasionally catch a glimpse of an infant who simply stares out at his new world, alert and curious as some newborns can be, even during the first few hours after birth. There are times when I look for that little boy from long ago, there among the many faces of new life.

Strangely, it is as though I cannot behold those beautiful children now, or even my own children, on occasion, without being reminded of him.

CHAPTER 5

NO CHOICE

So, for the mother's sake the child was dear,
And dearer was the mother for the child.

—SAMUEL TAYLOR COLERIDGE

PSYCHOTHERAPISTS OFTEN FIND THEMSELVES in the province of what Freud and others called interpersonal *transference* and *countertransference*. These concepts derive formally from early writings on psychoanalysis and are still central ideas in many types of interpersonal psychotherapy. Transference is the process whereby a person projects or presumes certain qualities, motivations or feelings onto another person, but without any real basis in fact. These projections onto people we do not know or understand well are thought to originate from earlier relationships with significant others, such as our parents and other loved ones.

Countertransference further extends this concept to the relationship between a psychotherapist and his or her patient. From the therapist's perspective, it signifies a subtle psychological process in which the therapist's personal life experience, or previous relationships with significant people, inadvertently shapes his or her attitudes toward a particular patient. This alteration in the therapist's perceptions about the patient can, in turn, influence overt behavior and decision-making in providing psychotherapy, and sometimes to the detriment of an unsuspecting client.

These phenomena are thought to apply to the nonpsychotherapist—the average person who will encounter and interact with other people each and every day. Transference and countertransference, for example, are thought to partially explain how it is we might feel we already know someone quite well, even if we've never actually met them before. It might also account for intense and inexplicable feelings we have for certain people, though there is little or no basis for them in the reality of our actual experience. Anger or resentment directed at a relatively innocent bystander, for example. Or the passionate love that is offered willingly to a perfect stranger.

Transference can sometimes help to explain aspects of the relationships we have with the children in our lives, also, as they are revealed to us as a reenactment of some earlier time and place.

My most dramatic introduction to this particular phenomenon—a case that sensitized me to the ways children can be affected by the transference of adults in their lives—is the story of Kirsten Chase.

Kirsten was a lovely girl—not a girl, really, when I met her, but not entirely a woman. She was eighteen years old and in her first year at college. She and her father had been sent to me for guidance, for this young lady had a difficult decision looming over her.

Her father, as we spoke in a preliminary way on the telephone, told me she was pregnant. His daughter's problem was a very serious matter for him, as it should be for the father of any unmarried teenage girl, but I'd encountered this kind of situation so many times in my professional work that it seemed almost routine. By then, I'd developed a way to approach this difficulty in family life.

Mr. Chase had gotten my name from Dr. Schaefer, a medical geneticist and an expert in chromosomal analysis and the prevention of high-risk pregnancies. Dr. Schaefer was often involved with pregnancies where there was some suspicion that genetic defects might be present in the fetus, or where a parent's genetic makeup raised the possibility of a defect in the child.

Eve Schaefer had sent me several referrals in the past, but they all involved babies or young children—infants and toddlers born with diseases or abnormalities associated with their genetic legacy. At the very beginning, there was a hint that *this* might be an unusual referral, but somehow I'd failed to notice.

Mr. Chase told me Dr. Schaefer thought I might be able to help Kirsten consider her decision. As it would turn out, she had already arrived at a decision several weeks before. What her father *hadn't* told me was that everyone involved secretly hoped I might work toward changing her mind.

I met with Kirsten's father first, in accordance with his wishes.

Usually, I would meet with a teenager in the presence of the parents, at least in the beginning, as a way to discourage the family from keeping secrets. I'd discovered long before that such secrets were often at the root of my patients' problems. But Mr. Chase began our time together by explaining his need to meet with me privately.

"I don't know if you've talked with Dr. Schaefer yet?" he asked, as though she might have relieved him of his task.

"We spoke briefly yesterday," I answered. "But I usually don't discuss a case at length with other people. Primarily because of confidentiality, but I also like to hear a person's story from them directly, so there's less room for distortion," I explained. I knew all of us could distort reality, but my initial interest was always in the patient's subjective view of his or her problems.

"Well then, you may not know the whole story here. You see, Kirsten is at risk for having *Huntington's chorea*. You *do* know what that is?" he asked me, just to be certain.

"Yes . . . I do."

Now this case became much clearer. I knew that Huntington's chorea was a disorder likely to first appear in the affected person's middle-adult years. It was known to be a dominantly inherited degeneration of the basal ganglia, a part of the brain involved with both motor and intellectual functions. Patients affected by Huntington's would gradually and inevitably become demented and physically incapacitated, unless they died of other causes before the full manifestation of the disease. Some affected patients might even commit suicide rather than live on to endure the ravages of Huntington's disease.

I knew it was an invariably fatal illness, with death coming only after a course of slow physical deterioration across a span of ten to fifteen years. No cure is yet available, so doctors emphasized prevention of the disease through genetic screening and through intensive counseling with the grown children of affected parents.

"And you know my Kirsten is pregnant? We discussed it on the phone."

"Yes, yes," I said, as I began to have a private stream of thought, initiated by my new realization of the larger problem in Kirsten's case.

"And so it isn't just another teenage pregnancy, Doctor," Mr. Chase said calmly. "We're talking about two lives in jeopardy here."

I usually go with my first instinct. Phil Chase was a decent man, I thought, and a sensitive and caring father to his daughter Kirsten. He wasn't behaving like the other fathers of pregnant teenage daughters I'd known. He wasn't angry at Kirsten, for example. And he didn't seem to be out for the blood of the man who had done this thing to his daughter. Instead, he was deliberate in his approach to Kirsten's problem. He was also careful not to intrude too much. He had an extraordinary sense of respect for her, and for the difficult decision she needed to make.

"I just want her to make this decision with all the help and guidance she can get," he said. "I lost my wife to this disease, Doctor," he added. "I know what it can do."

His wife, Nancy, had died almost eight years before, after a prolonged battle. Kirsten would have been about ten years old when her mother died, although the downward spiral that is typical of the disease had probably begun some years before her death. This child very probably watched her mother's life deteriorate slowly. Perhaps, she had seen her die in agony—a much different person from the mother she had known in early childhood. Kirsten Chase might have formed unusual bonds to the memory of her mother and to the father who remained with her.

"I *do* have an opinion here," Mr. Chase continued, disrupting my random thoughts about the situation. "I would like her to decide to abort the pregnancy. To begin with, she's too young to be having children. She has her whole life ahead of her. However many years that might be," he added. "I just want her to be happy, that's all. I just want my little girl to be happy." His eyes began to mist over, and his chin trembled slightly as he spoke. But this would be as close to crying as he would allow himself to come.

"But that's all secondary to the bigger problem here—the chance she may have the gene, the gene for Huntington's." I knew she would have approximately a one-in-two likelihood for carrying the gene.

"What is it exactly that you think *I* might be able to do, Mr. Chase?" I asked him. This was my standard question in first sessions with concerned parents, to see what they have in mind and to determine quickly if there is any chance I can offer them what they seek.

"I want you to convince her to have the testing done," he said with certainty. "I've tried to tell her it *should* be done. Even Dr. Schaefer tried to sway her, but she just refuses. I want her to know what she's getting herself into here. I mean, with having the baby. She needs to know her alternatives. I don't want her to go through what I went through, Doctor."

"The testing? You mean the DNA analysis," I said. A recently developed screening test could tell the blood relatives of people affected by Huntington's chorea if they were also carriers of the gene. This test would tell Kirsten the probability she might develop the disease in her lifetime and whether her children would have a chance of inheriting it as well.

"They didn't have the test when Nancy and I first thought about having children, so it was like tossing the dice for us. It was very hard, especially for my wife, making up her mind about bringing a child into that situation. Nancy's father died of Huntington's when she was a teenager. She knew there was a chance she might have it, too, and that she could give it to our children. She worried a lot about it until one day she just up and said to me she wanted to have a baby. I didn't know what to say. I knew in my heart it was *her* decision to make."

Mr. Chase paused, looked down at the floor, then up again. "And to be quite honest with you, Doctor, I didn't know anything about the disease, really. I didn't know a damn thing about being a parent either. I was just trying to make it in the business, you know—I was all wrapped up in my career just then. To be blunt, I really hadn't given it all that much thought until she'd made up her mind," he added candidly. "I didn't think about it one way or another. It seemed, well, it all seemed kind of *abstract*," he said, as though he wasn't sure that was the right word for what he meant to say. "And so, by that point, I mean when Nancy told me she wanted a child, I just sort of went along."

"So you hadn't formed a real opinion about having children?" I asked.

"No, not at all. I don't think most people just starting out in a marriage think all that much about what it means to have a kid, do you? But I *did* love my wife, Doctor, that's for sure. And so I figured if *she* was willing to have a child, then so was I. I thought she knew more about the whole thing than I could ever hope to know." He abruptly sat up in his chair, as though trying to come back to the present and away from the past. "But that's all behind me. I just want what's best for Kirsten," he said. "She's all I've got now."

"It's clear you care a great deal for Kirsten, Mr. Chase," I said.

"I still don't know if it was the right decision, though, you know what I mean?" he added. "At this point, I can't imagine my life without Kirsten, so from *that* point of view, I'm glad we had her. But my life's not over yet. How do I know what's waiting for Kirsten and me just around the corner, in ten years or so? Now, with what I know about the disease and what it can do to people, I just can't be certain what's right or wrong here. I mean, I can't see me going through all of that again with . . . with Kirsten."

Phil Chase sighed briefly, but quickly became more focused and businesslike in manner.

"Kirsten should know the odds, and the test can tell her that. It will tell us both. She *should* know, Doctor, don't you think I'm right?"

His eyes pleaded with me to tell him what he wanted to hear. But I offered no real opinion—as I'd been trained to do. And so he just went on, as if he'd known all along it was a question I wouldn't answer.

"All of this has brought it back, you know? I mean, Nancy's death and those last few years with the disease when it was really at its worst. But Kirsten says she *won't* do it, Doctor! She *won't* submit to the test!" he repeated desperately. "And I can't *make* her do it. I promised my wife I wouldn't do anything like that. Or tell her she couldn't have children. Besides, I don't think I could make her even if I wanted to. But someone has to make her realize what the consequences could be—what this might mean in her life. I'm not just talking about *now*, I'm talking about the rest of her life. And the baby's life, too."

He looked over to the empty chair beside him, as though his late wife were sitting there quietly in the room with us.

"She's still with me, you know?" he said, as he turned his gaze back toward me. "I mean, my wife, Nancy. She's still with Kirsten, too. We loved her very much. But I don't want Kirsten's love for her mother to bias her decision. She needs to make her *own* life. She has to make her *own* decisions now."

"I understand," I said, although I didn't really comprehend the full meaning of what he implied.

We both stood up, as our time together came to a close. As he walked to the door, he turned back to me and said something altogether unexpected.

"You'll notice her *eyes* when she comes to see you, Doctor. Everyone does," he added. "She has her mother's eyes. In fact, she's the image of her mother."

By the end of my session with Kirsten's father it was clear he wanted me to discuss the matter with his daughter and to serve as an objective adult in the process. By *objective*, though, I think he wanted me to be logical and to see the wisdom of having the testing done—and to advise Kirsten to end her pregnancy. But I couldn't promise to convince his daughter of anything. I'd explained to him that I sought to help my patients arrive at their own conclusions, if I could. I would listen to their reasons. I would try to understand their feelings. But I wasn't about to press a decision on Kirsten any more than her father would or could.

■

My session with Mr. Chase about his daughter had, in turn, made me recall a conversation I'd had with the referring physician, Dr. Eve Schaefer. A few months before, she'd given me a brief lesson on how genetic screening tests were performed. Coincidentally, she had used the method for detecting the marker for Huntington's disease as her example.

She explained to me that the screening involved taking blood samples from many family members—both affected and unaffected relatives—and not simply from the person who sought an estimate of his or her own risk. In addition, attempts would be made to obtain available tissue samples from relatives known to have died from the disease—perhaps in the form of frozen brain tissue samples "willed" to succeeding generations by relatives who had suffered from the disease and died of it, and who had been told of the potential value to their family members in providing their diseased tissue for study. Findings from these samples would also be collected and included in the complex DNA analysis, along with information from the patients' extensive medical histories.

Although the screening was not considered absolutely accurate and there was a margin for error, it was more accurate than the traditional estimate of a fifty-fifty probability that the disease would appear. If sufficient information was available, the outcome of the DNA analysis of the family's genetic patterns and medical histories could allow doctors to raise or lower the statistical likelihood that the disease would manifest itself in a person's lifetime. Using a complex statistical formula, geneticists would calculate that risk ratio for a given person by taking many factors into consideration at once. The number of relatives with the marker associated with the Huntington's gene, the age of the person in question, the gender of the affected parent and similarities in the time of onset among family members were all variables that would contribute to the mathematical model scientists used to derive a final estimate of risk.

In this way, a computer-generated mosaic would be constructed, unseen by human beings, situated deep within the complex mathematical model constructed to analyze so many variables simultaneously. The geneticists could only hope to understand the meaning of this fourth-dimensional image through the numerical output of a risk-calculation computer software package they called LINKAGE. The output from this large computer program would allow them to increase or decrease the probability for an individual carrying the marker for Huntington's disease, using information specific to that person's family pattern. And this knowledge could only be gained by considering the whole family as a single, complex unit.

"This is how science can change people's lives for the better!" Eve Schaefer had pointed out to me enthusiastically, as she ended her description of genetic screening. "By preventing these horrible diseases from the very beginning! *This* is also why I get so frustrated when I hear someone say that science isn't relevant to everyday life. I see it working all the time. And we've only begun to realize the power of molecular genetics to change the world."

Although I wasn't about to dispute her claim, I was also familiar with some of the thornier issues this subject raised. I asked her about the tendency for roughly a third of all people suspected to be at risk for Huntington's *not* to seek genetic testing. These were the ones who chose not to know their actual risk—or the likelihood that they carried the gene.

"Have you ever run into a patient who *doesn't* want to know he or she has the gene for a disease?" I asked. "Like Tay-Sachs? Or maybe Huntington's disease?"

She'd nodded excitedly, even before I'd finished my question. She stammered as she attempted to reply.

"Oh, oh, yes, yes . . . several patients have told me that!" she said emphatically. "But I can't for the life of me understand why someone *wouldn't* want to know," she said, puzzled. "And especially if they're thinking about having children of their own. I can understand they might be anxious about their own lives—not wanting to know whether they will die of the disease or not. But why would anyone want to take the chance of bringing a child into such . . . . such misery?" she said, looking to me for an answer. But I simply nodded and let her finish what she was saying.

"I see so many parents with children who have chromosomal abnormalities, and they always ask me: '*Why wasn't there a test for this? A test we could have taken before we had the baby!*' And I have nothing to say to help them. There *aren't* tests for most of these disorders!"

She moved closer, forewarning me she was about to make some important, final point.

"And when we *do* have the science to tell them—to tell people what the probability for a defective or diseased baby will be—these people don't want to know! It's utterly ridiculous!" she exclaimed, as she threw up her hands in disgust.

She assumed I agreed with her, but I hadn't formed a definite opinion about the issue. I remained silent, suggesting I understood her point of view.

But something inside me was uncertain about the matter, because my next words were intended to provoke Dr. Schaefer even further, to urge her to see the issue from yet another perspective.

"You know, this reminds me of a story I heard recently," I said. "The story of a woman who helped isolate the gene for a genetic disease. She was one of the key people in tracking down the gene by collecting detailed family histories in a geographical region where the disease was rampant. She had interviewed all the members of certain families in that rural area—the family members of the people known to be affected by the disease. It happened to be a place where there was a lot of intermarriage, and there was a high prevalence of the disease there. Her work in the field helped geneticists identify the carriers, and later they isolated a marker for the gene defect."

"Well," I continued, "the researcher's *own* mother had been diagnosed with the disease and died of it at a young age. In the end, the researcher wasn't sure *she* wanted to have the screening test done for herself!" I said. "I don't know whether she actually went ahead with it later on. But at the time, she was quoted as saying the test could have many repercussions in her life and that she needed time to think it over—although she could see the value of it for many people."

Dr. Schaefer nodded, as though she'd appreciated the unexpected twist. But her next words left me uncertain.

"All I know is that I've dedicated my life to this, you see," she said emphatically, "to eliminating unnecessary disease and misery in children. And its just *very* frustrating when these people throw it all away because of some . . . well, because of some *psychological* reason."

■

As I greeted Kirsten Chase in the waiting area outside my office, I was quite taken by her physical beauty. Beauty, I thought at the time, that resonated from within. She was tall and slender, an auburn-haired young woman with hazel eyes. Bright and piercing eyes that just looked right through me.

"Hey, you've got red hair and freckles, too!" Kirsten said to me, after sitting in one of my most comfortable chairs. Then she laughed a silly laugh. That type of remark was common in my conversations with some of the teenage girls I met in my work. Her use of humor to break the ice, for example. And her subtle attempt at what I perceived as harmless flirtation.

"We people with red hair and freckles just *have* to stick together, you know," she added with a smile. "Did the other kids make fun of you, too? I mean, did they call you 'freckle- face' when you were a little boy?" She giggled, hoping I might become flustered. "I'll bet they called you 'red,' didn't they?" she finally asked.

"Once in a while," I said with a grin, although it had actually been much more frequent than that. Her comment, rather than putting me off, had taken me delightfully off guard.

She must have felt comfortable with me as well, for she curled her long legs under her body and shifted her weight to the back of the chair, as though getting situated for a long chat with an old friend. I noticed she had a small book with her. It was very similar to a book my mother had kept on her nightstand, although she never used it. I guessed it might be a diary of sorts, the kind one might buy in a five-and-dime store. It had a tiny latch that locked across the pages.

The diary Kirsten held in her hand, though, was worn, and the plastic binding had begun to rip off along the spine. It was obvious it had been used frequently, for many of its pages were torn, and they stuck out of the book here and there.

I looked up from the book she held against her body and gazed at her face more directly. *Her eyes . . .* I thought. Those strange and beautiful eyes her father had mentioned. He hadn't exaggerated in the least; they were stunning. *Such beautiful eyes . . .* This response was quite unusual for me, for I began to sense a basic attraction to this young woman, despite my having only just encountered her.

"Well, Doc, I've really got myself in a jam here," Kirsten said, in a way that suggested she wanted to get right to the point. This comment broke the spell her magical eyes had created in me—I watched as she proceeded to caress her belly gently back and forth with her hand. Softly back and forth, in a loving motion.

"I'm pregnant, you know," she said almost proudly and with only a slight hint of nervousness.

"So I've heard, Kirsten," I said solemnly. I said it more as a parent might, as a father might who had the good sense to see the seriousness of her situation.

"It was *real* dumb, I know. And please don't lecture me about birth control and all of that!" She pleaded with me like a child. "I *know* it was a dumb thing, but now it's done," she said with a sigh. "And I know my father wants you to talk me into getting the test, but I've made up my mind already. Believe me, I've given it a lot of thought." She was almost as determined as her father. An inherited trait? I wondered.

"Why don't we just start at the beginning, Kirsten," I said. "Can you tell me how all of this happened?"

This was a standard question for eliciting the personal stories of my patients' lives. So standard, in fact, that I'd just said it without thinking about how it might sound. With a verbal and cooperative eighteen-year-old, I assumed I could talk much as I might talk to an older, adult woman. Or at least I was willing to try. But the way I had posed the question set me up for her quick sarcastic reply.

"You *do* know about the birds and the bees, Doctor, don't you?" she asked me cheerfully, again in that flirtatious tone.

"Yes, I do, Kirsten, but I'm more interested at the moment in hearing *your* version of things. I've talked this over with your father, and now I'd like to hear your side," I said. "This is *your* time, to use as you wish. We can make jokes, or we can discuss the situation seriously," I said, much in the way my own father might have said such a thing to me.

"OK, OK, I'm sorry," she said. "It's just that if I don't keep a sense of humor about this then I'm going to be in *real* trouble." She lifted the book she carried.

"This is my mother's diary," she announced solemnly, as she raised it high in front of her. It was light blue and shiny, with smudges of fingerprints across the cover. Kirsten unlatched it. It wasn't locked, the tiny brass mechanism having broken after years of regular use.

"She left it for me when she died. Well, actually, she gave it to me about a year before she died," Kirsten informed me. Then she looked up at me with a somber gaze.

"She could barely talk—at least, she couldn't say anything that made any sense. But one day she just handed it to me." Kirsten paused briefly and looked at me again. "You know my mother had Huntington's, of course?" she added quickly, trying to gauge my reaction with a direct stare.

Her eyes didn't blink as she focused on me intently. Her face was without emotion. She was uncertain what I might be feeling or thinking at that moment. And, for some reason, she wanted to know.

"Yes, your father told me about it," I said.

She nodded slowly, although her eyes remained fixed and steady on me. But then she suddenly looked down, breaking her powerful gaze, and began to drum her fingers nervously across her mother's diary.

"Well, that can be pretty rough. You know how it can go?" she asked again. She wasn't sure I was familiar with the more intimate details of the disease.

"It was pretty bad for Mom . . . and not so much at the end, either. By then she was pretty much out of it, you know, not really herself." She abruptly straightened in her chair as a cold shiver went through her body, much as her father had done at the memory of Kirsten's mother.

"The worst was when her mind started to go. Just a little at first, then it kind of went all at once. That's when she gave me her diary." She fondled the precious book, rubbing it softly against her arm. Then she raised it up again for me to see more closely.

"*This* is what helped me know what to do, Doc," she said. "It's all right here. Can I read some of it to you?" she asked.

"Yes, if you like," I said. It was then that I noticed she'd already placed her finger between the pages of the book as a marker for some special passage. She suddenly became more excited and opened the diary, ready to state her case to me, a complete stranger, as if I were judge and jury in this delicate matter.

"Here . . . here it is," she said, "*this* is the part I want to read to you."

She began to recite a specially selected passage, but in a softer voice, and one more adult in tone than only moments before. This was what she read to me.

> "My sweet Kirsten turned three today . . . we had the party Phil and I planned all month. It was a big success. There was a bunch of neighborhood kids there, we had plenty of cake and ice cream. But Kirsten sat on Phil's knee most of the time, as if she didn't understand why we were making such a big fuss over her. She was confused about it all. Someday when she's older I'll tell her. I'll tell her what she means to me."

Kirsten reflected for an instant, as the power of her mother's words took hold of her once again.

> "But how will I say it? How will I tell my baby how she's changed my life? Before I had her, I was just a big mess. Always worrying about the H.C. and what it was doing to Daddy. And to me."

Kirsten paused again.

"H.C. is Huntington's chorea," she explained. I nodded that I understood. She motioned with her head as if to say good, then found her place in the diary again.

"And what it did to me. All that time I wasted, the times I worried it would happen to me. I never realized there was really nothing I could do. What if I did get H.C., like Daddy? Even if I did, there would be nothing I could do. Except maybe kill myself. But I was already killing myself worrying about it night and day. My baby changed all that . . . she really did. The day Phil and I decided to have our baby, I started to live again. I had a reason to live, I had to stop the worrying. My baby was more important. More important than me. No matter if I got H.C., or if I died young. The only thing that mattered was my baby, and Phil, and the time we'd have together. You kept me from giving up, sweet Kirsten . . . my baby. I needed *you* in my life to find my way in this crazy world."

"You see?" Kirsten exclaimed proudly. "Having *me* was fighting back! It was her way of fighting back at the disease. At her father's death and what it did to her! It was my mom's way of getting rid of all the fear she had inside her."

Kirsten Chase's lovely eyes were filled with confidence now, with a certainty that what she was feeling for *her* unborn child had shown the way to what she must do. And that somehow everything would work out for the best. Just as her mother had written many years ago.

"If she didn't have *me*, it would have been like, well . . . like giving up," She said, as she closed the diary with a snap.

This woman-child was smiling at me now. She apparently felt no sense of overwhelming fear or anxiety over the situation. She had worked this out for herself, it seemed. She would have this baby because *she* wanted it, and because she wanted the life it represented. She had moved well beyond the dilemmas that teenage pregnancy might bring to more ordinary girls. Far past those to a decision about the affirmation of her own life and her mother's life as well.

"Don't get me wrong here, Doctor, I can see why some people would want to know. I mean, they'd want to know whether or not they carried the gene—the H.C. gene. I can see why some people would want to know if they're going to get it," she said. "But I don't want to! I'll never want to know." Kirsten paused just then and rubbed the diary along its weathered edge. "At least, I don't think I ever will."

Her last remark suggested that she had left room for other possibilities—a sign of her burgeoning maturity. But I didn't think this was about to make her swerve from the course she'd already set. I remembered the seriousness of Kirsten's circumstances, though, and I felt compelled to question whether or not she might be making an error in judgment. And was the projection of her mother's life onto her own and her baby's a "healthy" thing? Did this powerful transference lend a distinctive meaning to her baby that prevented her from understanding and appreciating the dangers still to come? Had she really given careful consideration to the life-threatening risks that she and her child might face?

"Have you thought about how you will take care of the baby?" I asked her—to begin to understand more about the possible loopholes in her decision. "I know how important it is to you—that's very clear. But are you certain you will be able to take care of the baby?"

"I gave it a lot of thought," she replied, as she brushed her long hair behind her. Her face was filled with youth and energy. Her words seemed wise and well conceived.

"I have to get my father to go along with it, of course. I've already figured that part out. But it won't work if I can't get him to help me. If I can't get him to see the baby will be important to him, too."

"How do you plan to do that?" I asked her. "He seems to think it's a very risky thing to do—because of the possibility of H.C."

"I know he does, and he thinks I'm way too young besides." She stretched out her long fingers and looked them over. "And guess what? He's probably right! But I figure I'm not like everybody else. I have this thing hanging over me that none of my friends can even understand. The H.C. thing, you know?"

"I know," I said. I realized that the rules for everyone else might not easily apply to Kirsten Chase's special situation.

"So my life will be different from now on. I mean, I don't plan to go out and try to have more children with, well . . . with the risk they might get H.C." She looked up at me with a serious gaze. "But I'm not going to run away from this, either. I'm not going to run away from life!" Kirsten rubbed her belly once again, to show me she meant the child she'd conceived. "And getting the test right now isn't going to change that at all."

Kirsten looked away and didn't seem the strong and self-assured woman I'd experienced only moments before. She sniffled slightly and rubbed her eye with the side of her forearm.

"If there's one thing I've learned from my mother—and from all the pain Daddy and I went through before she died—it's that a fifty-fifty chance is still better than no chance at all."

She looked down once again, to her mother's diary. She touched the surface of it gently.

"And I don't judge other people, either," she explained. "I mean, the girls I know who decided to have . . . to have an abortion. I just know that this is for me to decide. And I'm sure about it, here inside," she motioned to her breast. "It's the *right* thing to have my baby."

Kirsten had obviously given her situation considerable thought. I remained touched by the way she'd found help and guidance in the record of her dead mother's words. And she didn't seem at all like the other adolescent girls I'd interviewed before. She was certain *this* was the right thing for her and that it might be helpful for her father, too.

I wondered if the experience of losing her mother at such an early age, and the trauma that terrible time had exerted on Kirsten and her father, also served to place her on a developmental track apart from other children. And did Kirsten's risk for Huntington's set her on a life course that would compel her to mature more rapidly than an unaffected child? Did she now realize she would, almost of necessity, be different from those who could have no inkling of the pain and uncertainty she'd know in her life? And had all these things combined to allow her to have such certainty about life and living and the meaning of her child?

"Daddy has got to get on with things," Kirsten finally announced, interrupting my thoughts about her situation. "I mean, he's been so down and unhappy all these years since Mommy died." She unfurled her legs from beneath her—sat up and stretched in a lively manner, to animate herself after sitting in one position for so very long.

"Daddy's just *got* to learn to live again," she told me with no uncertainty whatsoever, and in a way that suggested her baby might be the solution to that as well. Unwilling and unable to remain somber for very long, she giggled slightly and smiled at me again. She flashed her stunning eyes in my direction. For one last time, she gently patted the new life she sustained within her.

"This baby might be just what the doctor ordered!"

She smiled at her little joke, then stretched her arms out and upward toward the ceiling. She paused to look around my office, stopping for a moment to gaze at the pictures of my children. Then she looked back to me with a more serious expression.

"The way I see it, Doc, is this: If the baby means so much to me—which it does—if it means so much to me because it's *this* special before it's even born yet, then I can't see messing around with that. You know what I mean?" she said, in a manner that left me without the need to question her at that moment.

"So it's like *I have no choice.* Do you know what I mean? There's really nothing else for me to do but have my baby."

Then a strange thing began to happen to me.

With her last few words, I sensed within me a rising feeling of disapproval. And it was very much a *feeling*—for my mind understood what Kirsten was saying. But suddenly, it was as though I'd suspended my professional, objective and uncommitted stance. I was rapidly becoming more and more irritated with this woman-child before me. And I couldn't understand why.

Here she was, I silently said—only eighteen years old and she thinks she has it all figured out, those impossibly difficult ethical dilemmas. Didn't she know that greater minds than hers or mine had debated these matters and been left with less-than-satisfying conclusions? Didn't she know that only the zealots or overintellectualized academics among us appeared to have definite opinions about such things—opinions they were always ready to foist upon everyone else?

Who *was* this child, anyway? Telling *me* the ways of the world, and with such a smug sense of self-assurance. And, on top of that, to make it all seem so simple, when it wasn't. I began to suspect that Kirsten was just another know-it-all teenager. Those things I'd studied about these children at the threshold of the adult world suddenly appeared quite true. Their egocentrism. The irrational idealism they could espouse. The arrogant belief that somehow *only they* knew what was right.

The theories about the psychological nature of teenage children, framed by perplexed adults pressed to make some sense of adolescence, suddenly seemed helpful in defining my rising suspicion about this woman-child and in understanding that Kirsten just wasn't old enough to know what she was talking about. This view of her, in turn, made me feel somehow wiser than she—and more powerful as well.

If she were *my* child, I'd talk some sense into her. I'd show her the error in her thinking. She needed to be told about the realities of life, about the more practical concerns all of us had to face. Why, if *I* were her father, I'd . . .

Those eyes suddenly came back to me, back into my awareness—bright green, flashing with a luminescence that shone from within. And the auburn hair, her freckled nose, the quick sense of humor and infectious laugh. I'd felt a strangely powerful bond with this girl only moments after we met. But why was I behaving this way? What was wrong? Why was I losing control of the situation? Where were these thoughts and feelings coming from?

Just then, I remembered *Kathy's* eyes—they were hazel green, too, weren't they? Kirsten did seem so much like *her*, so much like Kathy, the woman I thought I would love forever. The girl I'd fervently planned to marry one day. Kathy—the woman who might have been the mother of my child.

But *my* Kathy's eyes had been filled with tears the night she told me—that night she told me of her difficult decision.

"*We have no choice,*" she'd said. "There's nothing else we can do."

It was the night she finally decided what she would do about her unwanted pregnancy, about the unplanned child we'd conceived together. She explained to me her reasoning and told me of the long discussions with her concerned and caring parents.

"It just doesn't make any sense right now," she said to me sensibly. "We're too young to have a child. We have to make a start—make something of ourselves. We have our whole lives ahead of us. There will be time for children later," she added. A peculiar phrase I felt certain had originated with her parents.

I'd listened to her words but had little to say that night. For I had no experience with such decisions, let alone a *definite* opinion about having children. I was barely an adult then myself, and the meaning of children in my life was a matter left to a far and distant place. Reserved for a time when I would be older and able to give the matter more careful thought. Saved for a time when a child might be more convenient, too.

The child who might have been!

Off and on over the years, I'd thought of Kathy and that child who would never be. I fantasized that our child together would have been a girl. She'd be about seventeen years old now—I'd calculated her age from time to time, but not so frequently that it became an obsession. I would imagine what I might be doing with her, and I wondered what would she be like? And how might *I* be made different by her presence?

My unfinished business about that child was not that uncommon—I had heard or read about very similar reactions in many other people. Typically, a certain amount of grief could be experienced by a woman who opted for abortion. And, in recent years, it had become more evident that men could also share in these feelings of loss and self-doubt over the child who had not been brought to term. In some adults, though, this reaction might not reveal itself until many years later—when they were in a different position or frame of mind. When they had developed a sense about life that allowed them to reflect anew on the broader meaning of their decision. And, I would suppose, as they evolved toward a clearer view of the role of children in their adult life.

This change in view or mood brought on by a decision made years before—and before its ultimate meaning could possibly be known—might be called a "sleeper" effect. A psychological term for emotional repercussions that could only be felt with the passage of time, or with a maturity that brought with it new perspectives on the meaning of one's life.

As I contemplated *that* child—Kathy's and mine—I abruptly realized it was *Kirsten Chase* who sat before me now. This was Kirsten, who was the image of *her* mother. But she had also become an apparition of *my* child who never was.

In an instant I understood the sudden and unexpected rush of feelings toward Kirsten Chase and why I shared Mr. Chase's deep concern, and intense fears, for the child he loved so dearly—the child he stood to lose in his own lifetime.

Kirsten looked at me with alarm, for she'd noticed the change in my expression and a hesitation to continue. I think she also saw a hint of my rising sense of irritation with her—a difficult thing for a "parent" to hide from a child. She wondered out loud if it had been something *she'd* said.

By then I was in better control, although not entirely calm or collected, as the full nature of that strange and unexpected countertransference had come into my awareness. I assured Kirsten that everything was all right, although I wasn't referring to *her* situation. I told her she must have misunderstood what she'd seen—misperceived what she'd recognized so clearly in my face.

I remembered the phrase Kirsten had used moments before—when she was talking about *her* baby.

If the child is this special to me before it's even born, then I can't see messing around with that.

Her words captured my own visceral instincts in this case. Who was *I* to attempt to alter or influence her heartfelt decision? Right or wrong—and I could never know which—the decision was *hers* to make.

And *unlike* my indecision those many years before when confronted with the question about the meaning of a child, Kirsten's peculiar circumstances had prepared her to make a clear and resounding answer. She would have her baby despite the risk for Huntington's chorea.

I tried to smile at Kirsten in a gentle and reassuring manner—in the way a parent might to comfort a child who seeks approval—to confirm it might be all right to take personal control over her own future and over the destiny of her child. I smiled to let her know I thought she might indeed be a woman now. A woman capable of making her own life choices.

She seemed extraordinary at that moment—a child really, but one with a mature sense of certainty about herself and the baby she carried. I silently wondered how many parents could have such presence of mind before the birth of a first child. How many young adults who would become parents were able to articulate and ascribe such intensely personal meaning to the arrival of a child into their world—and to trace the child's connection to them in compelling intergenerational terms?

■

To the best of my knowledge, Kirsten continues to choose this uncertain future—to live her life without the special and intimate knowledge medical screening could offer her. She still hasn't submitted to the genetic testing that would tell her the probability that she might inherit her mother's deadly disease.

She has made other choices instead, beginning with her new life as a young mother. I know this because she visited me one day, quite unexpectedly, about ten months after we'd first met. She looked older then, on the day she came to show me her new baby daughter. But her vibrancy and youthful enthusiasm were still intact.

Her father, Phil, was with them—I spied him first as they were coming down the hallway. Returning from a visit to her pediatrician, Kirsten had wanted to walk by my office on the chance we might say hello. It worked out just as she'd planned it. We had our brief reunion in the waiting area.

Kirsten wore a broad and happy grin, as if to tell me everything was just fine. Her baby was healthy, and everyone was delighted with her, a new life that had come into their world. Even Phil Chase beamed with pleasure as he gently took his granddaughter from Kirsten and wrapped his large arms around her.

"Here she is!" Kirsten exclaimed with joy, and before we'd even exchanged greetings. "I told you she'd be something special."

Her tiny baby, a girl, looked at me with eyes so brightly blue, her face framed by wisps of strawberry-blond hair just beginning to blossom into curls.

As I moved closer, I sensed enormous energy in Kirsten and her father. The somber anxiety they'd known before was somehow gone for now. We stood there in silence for a moment or two, as if there was no need for small talk, just looking at the baby, then back and forth to one another. Mr. Chase finally interrupted this joyful silence with a cliché I'd heard many times before.

"I guess where there's life, there's hope," he said simply, as he looked back down into the face of the lovely baby girl he held in his arms. "We just take one day at a time now," he added. "We're having a lot of fun with little Nancy around the house."

When they left that afternoon, having said goodbye, I watched them briefly as they traveled down the long hallway dappled by beams of sunlight coming from the bright day just beyond. I could see Mr. Chase talking to his granddaughter pointing to the colorful and interesting sights in the garden space outside the hospital. Kirsten gently patted her father on the back, and they laughed over the baby's reactions to the world around her.

The three of them together left a strong image—they formed a mosaic in my mind. A picture of three generations, and a family still. I recalled they were scarred by immense tragedy and loss, terrible events they might know again. But for now, they chose to live as others did. They would wait and see what the next day might bring, enjoying moments in life even as they cherished their memories of the dead.

And in making that choice, they were linked to one another in ways science might never truly understand.

CHAPTER 6

A BAKER'S DOZEN

Setting out in this world, a child feels so indelible. He only comes to find out later that it's all the others along the way who are making themselves indelible to him.

— EUDORA WELTY

THE IMPOSING DARKNESS in the room at the end of the children's medical ward foretold of the lack of hope there. Not only was that particular room out of the mainstream of the place, being situated physically distant from the nurses' station that is the hub of activity on any medical unit, but I also knew it was a place sometimes reserved for those children with the poorest medical prognosis, the ones expected to die, and perhaps quite soon, for whom there was little left to do, except to keep them as comfortable as possible.

I knew that the two occupants of that darkened room at the end of the hall were in the hospital for what would likely be their final visit. In fact, they might die at any moment, though there seemed to be little drama surrounding that fact. It saddened me that a hospital room might be their last refuge on earth—and that the vision of this place would be their final memory.

As I entered, I saw a child who was familiar to me: Rene Cicciarelli, a seventeen-year-old girl diagnosed many years before with *cystic fibrosis*. It may seem odd that I would refer to her as a child, but I had watched her grow from a much younger age and then was forced to see her wither physically, when she should have blossomed into a young woman. And perhaps because of that, I chose to remember her as the child I'd known only a few years before.

Rene's gaze was fixed toward the ceiling above her bed; her eyes shifted toward me as my shadow was cast into the room by the light just beyond the threshold. My own attention briefly focused on the mechanical ventilator situated next to her bed. It hissed rhythmically as it automatically breathed for her, forcing optimum amounts of oxygen through a tube inserted in her trachea, into her irreparably damaged lungs. The machine had been put in place only a few days before, under emergency conditions, when Rene's breathing had become so difficult that her doctors felt she would die. Caught up in the press of the moment, her parents pleaded with the doctors to do anything and everything to save their child's life. And so all measures were taken.

Rene's flashing eyes hinted that her mind was as active as it had ever been. I knew she would be very frightened, for she had told me many times *this* would be the worst time of her young life—the day when she might become dependent upon life-support equipment, with all that that could mean for a person at the end stage of cystic fibrosis. Like others diagnosed with the disease, she had long dreaded the time when she would be given the choice to be placed on an artificial respirator. Although it might prolong her existence, it also meant the loss of much of the autonomy she'd managed to retain in her day-to-day life. And it could signify the beginning of the downward spiral toward death that is characteristic of her disease.

I'd known Rene for several years by then, and I came that day for what might be our final encounter, since she was not expected to survive the week. Her physical condition had worsened significantly in the past few months, and her body was now literally "shutting down"—the term her doctor had used during a medical conference about her case only a few days before. Because of Rene's rapid organ failure, her parents were approached by the physicians with questions about the need for continuation of her life-support systems, specifically about leaving the ventilator in place, which might keep her alive a while longer as the rest of her body became increasingly unable to function.

After agonizing over the doctors' questions, Rene's parents had finally agreed to leave the decision to their daughter.

Rene chose to allow her death to occur that much sooner, by discontinuing the life support provided by the ventilator. I knew when this would happen, and so I had come to see her at least once more.

She was more agitated than usual, and I knew she was fully aware of what was about to happen. She was anxious and frightened, and not really accepting or understanding of her fate. Perhaps as a result of this, she was angry and resentful.

"This really stinks, Doc," Rene said hoarsely, after the respirator tube had been removed. "Why does this crap have to happen to me? What did I ever do to deserve this?" she asked, expecting no answer from me. "I'd fight this to the end if it wasn't for my family," she added.

Her thoughts were not clouded or distorted by the imminence of death. In fact, her final words to me that day were spoken quite clearly and with a steely confidence that was characteristic of her. And with no sign of ambivalence or regret.

"You know I don't want to die," she whispered to me, her breathing labored and painful. "But I love my family so much." As she spoke, she gestured with her long, thin hand toward a bunch of fresh flowers placed on a small table nearby and to the cluster of colorful, half-deflated balloons that floated tenuously, only inches above the head of her bed. She paused to gather her strength to speak again, and as she did, she glanced toward the collage of photographs and greeting cards affixed along the wall beside her bed. She looked tearfully and angrily toward me once again.

"I don't want them to suffer any more."

In the opposite corner, another gaunt young woman lay fitfully on her bed, weakly gasping for each breath. Her name was Susan Shea, and she also was well known to me. But Susan's half of the room, in contrast to Rene's, had a strangely different quality. She was not attached to a respirator or a monitor of any kind, for example. And so the sound and sight as she lay there dying were not as medical or modern as on Rene's side of the room.

Although she seemed in pain—each labored breath brought on barely perceptible spasms in her body—she would only sigh in muted groans, randomly reaching up into the air space above her as if to grab hold of some unseen person or object. Someone or something she envisioned there above her, or just behind her tightly closed eyes. It was as though she were grasping for death to take her.

Susan also had become familiar to me over the years, having returned to the hospital for many preventive medical treatments, or "tune-ups," as the medical staff were apt to call them. And for emergency visits related to the assorted medical crises typical of her disease.

Susan was another "cystic" in the shorthand language of a busy medical staff. But Susan the cystic was still an unusual *child*, in light of the fact that she was actually a young adult of twenty-six years of age. It is common practice in some hospitals to treat young adults with chronic diseases in pediatric or adolescent units for as long as is feasible. This is especially true for patients with cystic fibrosis, who might have come to the same pediatric unit scores of times during their relatively brief lives. The doctors and nurses would be understandably reluctant to let their longtime relationships and rapport with these patients end simply because of chronological age. And I suppose they might also view these patients in much the same way I saw Rene Cicciarelli, as children still—having known them long before their disease became rampant and so destructive to their being.

And like so many other times before this final visit, Rene and Susan were placed in the same room for good reasons. They were both female, for example, and closer in age than most of the other child patients they might room with. And they both had cystic fibrosis, first diagnosed when they were newborn infants.

Susan and Rene had come to know each other well over a number of years, having been admitted to the hospital many times for intensive medical treatments that might prolong their lives or to recoup from the life-threatening bouts of respiratory illness and common colds that the more typical child could easily weather at home.

But this time I knew Susan and Rene were together in that particular room for another reason, one that would not be discussed openly. Both were dying rapidly, the course of their disease having now mercilessly reached its endpoint.

On those frequent occasions when both of these young women were in the hospital at the same time, opportunities arose to compare and contrast their lives. They and their families were different in how they coped with the gradual and insidious horrors of their common disease. Even Susan and Rene would make such comparisons, talking freely with one another about the changes or the milestones in their lives. Susan once confided in me that she felt a failure next to Rene, because Rene seemed so brave and unaffected in the face of her increasingly debilitating disease.

I was struck by what had seemed to me a large disparity in the lives of the two girls who were victims of an identical genetic defect. Medical research has shown that cystic fibrosis is a result of a problem with chromosome number seven—a defect in DNA that is known to alter the integrity of life at its most basic, cellular level. For the person affected by cystic fibrosis, these changes would eventually mean a very gradual deterioration over time—beginning in childhood—and then death in early adulthood for the majority of patients with the disease.

Before death came, however, the developing children would be forced to endure many assaults upon their bodies from within. Multiple organs could be affected and compromised by the disease. And with time, the ability to breathe efficiently and effortlessly would be greatly reduced. This would lead to lowered resistance to respiratory infections and to pulmonary obstruction.

Visible physical changes would inevitably appear in affected children as well, often during early- to mid-adolescence. A pronounced and dramatic *clubbing* deformation of the fingers and the toes, and a gradual emaciation and weakening of their bodies. From time to time, I would be called to see such patients, as the full extent of nature's cruelty was revealed. And especially at that most delicate time when they began to struggle with already difficult questions about identity and the meaning of life. Sensitive adolescents could be crushed by the power of this disease.

More than ninety percent of our DNA is devoted to making us similar to one another, while only about three percent is dedicated to making us different. All of the things we tend to think of as the ingredients for individuality, those qualities that provide the basis for how we're defined as persons, come from so little genetic material.

But these comparatively small differences between Rene and Susan were detectable even on the day I visited their deathbeds. And some of these distinctions, at least in my mind, appeared to have their origins in the families from which each child had come.

I considered the Cicciarellis first, a large family that professed traditional working-class values and beliefs. Rene's father worked long hours outside the home, while her mother remained at home, caring for their many children—thirteen, to be exact. And their extended family lived in close proximity to one another, all residing in one of the older and run-down sections of the city.

The Sheas, on the other hand, were solidly middle class, well educated and financially comfortable. Both of Susan's parents worked at white-collar jobs and managed to juggle the demands of taking care of three children between them, demands made that much greater with the arrival of Susan, their baby with cystic fibrosis.

In Susan's case, unlike Rene's, the decision was made early on not to use artificial life support, as evidenced now by the absence of monitors and elaborate medical devices around her bed. The decision had been made several years before by her parents, who had considered these matters well in advance of any pressing need to do so. It was thought to be in Susan's best interest to plan ahead.

"Why prolong her life only to have her feel more pain?" they had asked their family doctor, who was somewhat surprised that the Sheas had worked through this difficult issue so thoroughly in advance. "By then she will have suffered long enough," they concluded.

Susan's side of the hospital room was different from Rene's in other ways, as well. There were no greeting cards posted along the wall beside her and no balloons suspended from the metal braces behind her bed. This absence of another world reaching out to her from beyond that darkened room might give the impression that Susan had no place to go from there—even if she were to survive this latest round with death.

At first glance, her world appeared to be that hospital room, peopled only by the staff who saw to her medical needs. And yet I knew that was not accurate, for I'd met her family many times during their regular visits to the hospital. But as I approached her that final day, and as I sought to say goodbye and offer whatever comfort I might have to give, I could sense a strange fear within myself. A fear clearly borne within my response to the spare and sterile space in which I found her, as I became more aware of an unrealized and unanticipated loneliness in death.

"This is probably it," Susan said to me solemnly, and with resignation, as she slowly opened her eyes at the sound of my coming closer to her side. "I'm finally going to die."

I sat silently beside her, for I had no immediate words to say.

"It's just as well, I guess," she added with a subdued moan that masked the great physical pain I was convinced she was experiencing.

"We've been waiting for this for a long time," she added quietly, and with no emotion.

As I left their room that day and passed by the nurses' station to leave, I encountered Rene and Susan's primary nurse, a young woman who'd known them both for several years.

"It's really surprising, isn't it?" she asked me. "How badly Rene is taking this, I mean."

I stopped and looked at her somewhat perplexed, for I truly didn't understand what she meant.

"I mean, Rene was always the stronger one . . . the braver one. And Susan was so meek and afraid all the time," she explained. "And now when it's time to die, they're so different. I mean, they're the opposite of the way they used to be."

Not all of my visits with Rene and Susan had been so dark and daunting. Many times I had stopped to say hello during their hospitalizations, and we would talk about their lives. This was primarily true of Rene, the more social and friendly of the two, who could engage in lengthy conversations with anyone who happened by, despite the depleting effects these talks might have on her already strained breathing.

And the two of them when they were in the hospital together were a sight to behold. It was as though long-lost friends had found each other once again, a reunion that came to serve some important purpose in their lives. These became times to compare and to learn from one another, perhaps to share things that really couldn't be divulged with any other person.

I think those times they would meet and interact were as therapeutic as anything else the hospital might have offered those young patients. Just as the medications and the rehabilitative therapies would strengthen their bodies to cope with the world outside of the hospital, their time together somehow boosted their morale. It helped each of them know she was not the only one.

I recall one particular exchange with Rene and Susan, and the thoughts I had that day.

"You ever heard of a baker's dozen?" Rene asked me with a smile, as she sat upright in her bed, busily writing a letter to her boyfriend. As we talked, Susan lay back resting, her head propped up by pillows and her bed covers pulled up to her chin. She listened intently to Rene's stories about her life beyond their hospital room.

"Yes, I think I have," I said, "But why don't you tell me exactly what it means."

"Well, it's when you get one extra!" she replied. "You know, like when I make an extra cookie or muffin—just in case. And if they all come out OK, then I get something unexpected—you know, more than I thought I'd get!"

"You must have learned that when you worked for your father," I said, remembering he was a baker.

"Yep, he taught me that," she said with pride. "But he told me about it in a funny way. You know how funny he can be."

"Yes, he does have a sense of humor," Susan interrupted quietly. "He's a lot of fun when he comes to visit us." Rene looked over to Susan and giggled. Then Rene began again.

"See, there's thirteen of us kids in my family, and whenever somebody asks him how many children he has, he always says the same thing: 'I got a baker's dozen!'"

She laughed gently and with the prolonged and difficult wheezing that afflicts adolescents and young adults with cystic fibrosis when they try to carry on even the briefest of conversations.

"You know I'm still working in my father's place," she announced.

"Really? I didn't know that," I replied. "I thought you stopped doing that last year." I remembered there had been a big fuss over Rene's job in the bakery—her doctor had greatly disapproved.

"No, I'm still going there a couple of days a week," she said. She paused for a moment, and her mood seemed to darken. "It's getting a little harder, though. You know, the breathing part." She motioned to a small oxygen tank she carried around with her when she was having a bad day, and to the long transparent tube she inserted into her nostrils. "But I'm hanging in there," she added fiercely.

Rene's father, Lou Cicciarelli, was a master baker. He'd followed his trade for over forty years. This fact was relevant to his family in many ways, more so than most parents' employment might be for their children. For example, when each of his children turned thirteen years of age, Mr. Cicciarelli arranged to get him or her a part-time job in the large commercial bakery where he worked. Thus the children would be given the opportunity to make a little pocket money and to learn about their father's work. That brief time each child would spend in the world of their father had become a tradition in the Cicciarelli family. And strangely, it was not at all a thing his children sought to avoid—as some offspring might be apt to do. Instead, the hours his children would spend in the bakery appeared to have some special meaning for everyone in the family.

" 'This way you got something to fall back on . . .' my father always says," Rene said, mimicking her father's gruff and gravelly voice. " 'At least you'll know how to make a good loaf of bread,' " she added, as her attempt to copy his manner of speech made her begin to cough uncontrollably.

A bakery was probably one of the worst places for an adolescent with cystic fibrosis to work. The excessive amount of airborne, powdery dust would irritate and exacerbate Rene's already compromised ability to breathe. Her doctor had warned her many times to stay away from such places. He pointed out in no uncertain terms that it wasn't good for her health, that it could seriously compromise her longer term respiratory capacity. But Rene had insisted on experiencing the rite of passage her older brothers and sisters had known and was determined to work that job in her father's bakery.

Rene's family was there for her when she needed them, but they generally stood back when she asked for the chance to prove herself, or to be like everyone else. It didn't always work out so well, because it was clear that sometimes she just didn't accept her physical limitations, and she would often fail to take the care she should.

Her father once alluded to his philosophy about such matters, as we talked informally about children and parents in the pediatric ward.

"You got to treat 'em all the same, Doctor," Mr. Cicciarelli explained to me. "I got thirteen of 'em. Kids, I mean. And I love each one in a different way."

He took out his overstuffed wallet and opened it wide, and as he did, the plastic sleeves burst forth and unfolded toward the floor. I could see they contained no dollar bills or credit cards, just photographs of his large family.

"See all these kids, Doctor," he said with a hearty laugh, as he dangled his precious pictures in the air. "They're all mine!"

He gazed at the portrait gallery for a second and then looked to me more seriously.

"Most of 'em are off on their own now, 'cept for Rene, of course. But I tried to be the same guy for each and every one of 'em. No favorites, you know! You have to love each one the same, or you get into trouble," he added, as he looked up at me intently and with a clear sense of pride. "None of my kids are in trouble!"

His enthusiastic attitude went against the grain of my own professional training, which led to the biased thought that just about everyone in this complicated world had some sort of psychological or situational problem to deal with. But as he went on, the sheer force of his charm and unassuming manner began to sway me from my more reasoned, clinical view.

"I tell 'em this: 'Look, each one of you has a little special place here,'" he said, as he pointed to his chest and his heart within. "'You're all the same,' I tell them. 'But each one of you is special!'" he quickly added with a grin. "That leaves 'em speechless, Doc. That's the mystery I leave 'em to think about."

"The mystery?" I asked.

"Yeah, see, I let 'em try and figure out how they can all be the same to me—and still be so special in my heart!"

Rene's resistance to her doctor's advice—her will to normalize her daily life—reminded me of something a psychologist had written in a book about chronic disease in children. The author, a specialist in psychological issues of children and adolescents with cystic fibrosis, was one of the first to point out an interesting fact about some of these children. It has long been thought in mental health circles that *denial* as a psychological defense mechanism is a rather primitive response to life stress, and as a consequence, that it is not effective in promoting eventual adjustment. Those people who use denial to avoid their problems are thought to be candidates for more serious psychological crises, since you can refuse to acknowledge your problems for only so long.

This belief was based largely upon repeated clinical observations that mentally ill patients who deny their problems would almost invariably have a poorer outcome when compared with persons who used defense mechanisms theorized to be of a higher order. Some minimal level of acceptance of one's problems was the first step toward insight and better adjustment in life.

But in the case of the child with cystic fibrosis—and perhaps for other persons forced to endure major incapacitating conditions or events with no cure or relief—psychological denial appeared to function somewhat better. By refusing to let their disease change their day-to-day life all that much, seriously ill or incapacitated people might attempt to remain as normal as possible for as long as they were able. And while there might be a price to pay eventually—perhaps in a poorer medical outcome—the people who chose to deny the effects of problems could appear to fare much better psychologically than their peers who allowed themselves to experience the full brunt of a disease or chronic condition.

I knew that denial was one of Rene's major coping strategies as she went about living with her debilitating and terminal disease. In the beginning it would get her into difficulty only with her doctors and nurses, with the people who'd been trained that denial of disease was not good and that it was important to face up to one's problems and accept the limitations they might include.

When asked about her *noncompliance*—the term that doctors use for the situation where the patient doesn't follow their sound medical advice—Rene was quite direct.

"I *like* working in the bakery," Rene would announce firmly. "It's the only place I feel like I can really *do* something. I mean, *make* something. And besides, I want to be like all the other kids in my family. You know, to spend the time with my dad."

Susan Shea and her family took another approach. They accepted the reality of their child's diagnosis quickly, many years before they could have truly felt the full impact of it. They listened carefully to all that they were told and read about the disease on their own. The

Sheas were soon lay experts on the unhappy subject and prepared to deal with the worst. They mastered the skills the physicians and nurses taught them, learned how to treat common symptoms and what to do to prevent problems on the horizon. They emerged from the initial adjustment period with a sense of acceptance and under-standing about Susan's future life, and with the realization she would be very different from their other two children, that she would need special care and attention from that point on. There would be things she could and couldn't do, for example. And they knew that she would die at a relatively young age.

The Sheas were considered "good patients" by their doctors, who knew that they would comply with advice. With time, they adjusted more comfortably to the fact that Susan would never be normal, that many precautions needed to be taken.

"She's very weak," Mrs. Shea had said, that first day she called to set up an appointment for me to see Susan. Her physician, suspecting depression, wanted me to interview the young girl, for she seemed listless and unhappy to him.

"She has to conserve her energy to get through the day," Mrs. Shea warned me. "Is it possible for you to come to the house and see her?" she asked, with mild irritation over the inconvenience. "It's such a long way to walk, from the parking lot to the hospital. I just know Susan will be out of breath by the time we get to your office."

"I don't usually make home visits in a case such as this, Mrs. Shea," I said. "Is Susan feeling poorly this week?"

"Well, Doctor, I know I don't have to tell *you* that she has cystic fi-brosis, now do I?" Susan's mother admonished me, as though this might change my mind. "I'm sure you know these children are very fragile."

Susan's life had been different from Rene's in other ways, as well. She stopped going to school soon after the more serious physical signs of the disease had appeared—at about twelve years of age. Since then, she'd received tutoring intermittently from a special teacher in her local school district and was allowed to pass ahead to the next grade without formal evaluation. It hadn't seemed all that important to push her on academics or to grade her, either. Homebound much of the time, Susan withdrew into a world of watching television and eating food, though she gained little weight because of the deranging effects the disease wreaked on her metabolism.

As a result, she seemed tired much of the time, and more sickly. And quietly unhappy to those people she met when she was compelled to briefly travel from her home.

"We're just so afraid she'll catch a cold," Mrs. Shea once told me, when I saw them during a hospital stay. She told me that visits to the hospital were particularly stressful, because of the likelihood Susan would contract yet another viral infection there.

"She has to be very careful all the time. We feel it's best she stays at home and goes out only when it's absolutely necessary. To preserve her lungs, you know," she said. "To give her more time."

"Do you think she should get more involved with some children her own age?" I had asked Mr. and Mrs. Shea during one hospital visit, concerned that the child had become so reclusive.

"She has us!" Susan's mother had replied quickly and with confidence in the fact that somehow this would be enough. "And besides, I think she's accepted her fate," she added, although I wasn't certain what Mrs. Shea meant.

From what I could tell, Susan's more immediate fate was to take most of her meals in her room and to travel outside the house only when she needed to go to a doctor's appointment, or for those times when her parents couldn't arrange for a sitter. Perhaps as a result of this daily regimen of isolation and inactivity, Susan seemed pale and strangely silent whenever I saw her—no matter the season of the year. Her immediate family members were also subdued and somewhat aloof. And they seemed sad, too.

Susan and her family were obviously more serious and sad than the Cicciarellis—a distinction made clear when the two families happened to converge on the hospital at the same time. Susan and Rene's room could fill up with various friends and relatives of the Cicciarelli family very quickly. On some occasions, they would have to take turns going in to see her, as the many brothers and sisters or uncles and aunts filled the hall outside her door. Parents of many of the other children in the hospital would ask the nurses what was going on, only to be told it was just the Cicciarellis visiting their Rene.

But these differences could sometimes lead to problems between the two families.

"Can we get Susan into another room?" Mr. Shea had whispered to me one day, as we passed each other in the lobby of the hospital. "We like Rene and all," he said, "but they can be awfully boisterous sometimes."

"I'll talk with the charge nurse about it," I offered, although I knew no such change would be made. "But I thought Susan and Rene liked to see one another?"

"Well, they do. Of course they do," he said. "But we're not sure it's good for her to get so . . . well, for her to get so excited. It affects her breathing, you know," he added, as if to rationalize his discomfort with the situation. "And there's always someone visiting Rene—it never stops. Even though she's so ill," he finally said, in a puzzled manner.

■

"Did you go to the M-and-M yesterday?" a young resident physician asked me casually, as we stood in line together in the hospital cafeteria. "It was on those two cystics that died a few months ago."

The M-and-M was shorthand for the weekly morbidity and mortality conference—a formal presentation and discussion of patients who, while in the hospital, had deteriorated medically or who had died there. These conferences were a way of examining those particular patients whose downhill course or abrupt demise might somehow be instructive to the medical staff to improve their understanding of the very worst possibilities in disease and trauma and to enhance their ability to deal with similar situations as they arose again.

"I generally don't go to those," I replied. But the M-and-M for the two young women I had known over several years would have been of some interest to me. And so the resident's question had piqued my curiosity about that particular conference.

"So what did they conclude?" I asked the resident, as we moved slowly down the cafeteria line.

"Well, Dr. Marcus compared the two patients' lung status. He showed how they were both in about the same crummy shape when they died.

"He had pictures, of course," he added, referring to the elaborate and sometimes grisly color slides the pathologists would often show

at an M-and-M. "He tried to make the point that the younger patient—I think she was seventeen or eighteen . . ."

"Seventeen," I replied impulsively. "Rene was seventeen-years-old."

"Yes, well," he went on, "Dr. Marcus said she could have lived a few
years longer, if only she'd been a bit more compliant. And if her parents had made her listen to her pulmonologist's recommendations. I
guess she was heavily into denial," he added finally, to impress me
with his facility with psychological jargon.

Then the young doctor innocently shook his head in disbelief at
the prospect of a patient who wouldn't have the good sense to follow
physician's orders. And perhaps at the possibility that the patient's
parents must somehow share the blame for her early death.

"You would have found that part of it interesting," he said, as he
prepared to move on into the lunchroom. "Someone brought up that
the noncompliant cystics seem to deny the real seriousness of their
disease. We couldn't really understand how she could go for so long
like that," he said. "And why her parents just seemed to let her get
away with it."

I remained silent, my memories of the two women returning once
again.

"Dr. Marcus also mentioned briefly that one of the girls had been
quite agitated before she died—even though she was the one who
wanted to end it all."

He looked to me for some reaction, but by then I was immersed in
my own thoughts.

"Somebody who was there said she had a bad death," he finally remarked.

He reminded me that doctors these days will sometimes talk about
what they call a "good" death. This term is applied to the demise of
persons who appear to have accepted their own mortality, terminal
patients who have had the opportunity to make a final peace with
the world they are leaving behind them. The "good" death—as dis-
tinguished from a "bad" one—is facilitated by a relative absence of
pain or upset, physical and psychological. And so many physicians
who preside over the terminally ill will do whatever they can—within
the bounds of acceptable medical practice—to help ease the physical
burden of the dying patient.

Even in cases where physical pain or distress is not a problem, how-

ever, there can be human deaths framed by intense bitterness and regret. Thus, more and more in recent times, counselors, clerics, nurses
and various mental health professionals have begun to focus on the
psychological and spiritual aspects of treating terminally ill patients.
Some dying persons' final hours or days can be filled with feelings of
guilt, sadness and self-doubt. These are the deaths marred by a different sort of anguish, deriving from the belief or revelation that one's
life has somehow been grossly misspent, or due to the experience of
intense anxiety or apprehension that arises from the realization of
one's own mortality and the imminence of death.

When a child dies, though, the psychological effects can be even
more complicated to understand and difficult to endure. The drama
that can unfold in the child and parent can be more far reaching, for
the death of a child seems to us unnatural and incomprehensible.
Unlike an elderly person, the child has only begun to realize life's potential, and the ordeal involved in a child's dying can alienate parents
from a predictable world they've come to know, as they learn that
their child can perish long before they do.

"It just isn't supposed to be this way," several parents have told me,
with anger and sadness, after the loss of a child to disease or trauma.
"My child is supposed to bury *me*."

When a child is dying—and nothing can be done—it is as though
each and every person close to that young person is somehow temporarily denied hope themselves. I, too, have known this feeling,
when I could begin to sense that the death of a child I worked with
infringed upon and threatened my own belief in life. The premature
death of a child presents so many difficult things at once that it can
suggest a kind of randomness and a cruelty to existence. This is a realization that few of us are adequately prepared to acknowledge, let
alone accept or deal with.

It is an unsettling feeling that might typically last for a moment or
so, before something within us acts to dispel it. It is an acute awareness that life and death can, at times, be so utterly unpredictable and
unfair. And that, at any given moment, we can lose the people or
things that are most important of all—our own health or sense of
personal security, for example, or the people we love and cherish
above all others. Even a child, one who may embody our hopes and
dreams within his or her very being.

For most of us, though, such a feeling or experience *must* be merci-fully brief, for there appears to be a mandate within the living to go on. For others, though—and especially those whose lives are inti-mately bound to the life of the child who dies, as in the case of a par-ent or a grandparent—the loss of hope and the experience of despair can endure much longer. But I have also observed that the impact of the death of a child can take many forms, determined in some mea-sure by the manner of life that precedes it. Similarly, in the case of the parent who has lost a son or daughter, the significance of their child's death can be powerfully influenced by the psychological meaning of that child when alive.

Because of the intensely emotional aftermath to the death of a child, many parents will report years later that they never really re-turned to normal—to the person they were before they lost their son or daughter. Most will, in fact, go on as best they can with life, perhaps comforted by a belief in God, or determined to will themselves onward to nurture their other children or the loved ones who still remain.

A few parents I have known have been affected in ways that seem both cruel and extraordinary. Some will become clinically de-pressed—and not for only a brief while following the loss of their beloved child. Instead, it will seem to me as though they are now de-pressed forever, as they go on to mourn what they lost when unantic-ipated life events blindly took their child away. Other parents will become angry with a primal rage that sometimes seems to seethe within them long after their child has died. They are unforgiving of whatever is responsible for the fate of their child, and often they can-not forgive themselves for being powerless to help. They will see the world as unfair and random and having little that can be relied on. They can even become quietly asocial, excluding other people from their lives as their pain and discontentment enlarges over time.

Still others will effectively drop out of life and take up an alternate persona. A new job, perhaps, or a different place to live. Sometimes they will find a new spouse or family—all to transform what they were *before* their esteemed child was lost and to distance themselves from the memories and life they knew before.

As I think about these parents—the ones whose lives are so dra-matically transformed through the loss of a child—there is no single theme that serves to link them. I have encountered parents for whom there appear to be many great regrets, remorse based upon the things they did or didn't do when their child was alive and with them. The words or joyful experience they had foolishly put off to another day, for example, when it would be more convenient or less burdensome. Some have intense guilt over these feelings of regret, though I cannot be sure if their guilt is based in reality, or is a magnification due to their immense emotional trauma. But it is a feeling I've encountered in the parents whose adult life seems entirely recast by the death of a child.

On the other hand, I've known parents who had appeared to approach each day when their child was alive as a celebration of life— in the way Rene Cicciarelli's father had—parents who knew how to enjoy their time with their children and to savor and nurture each child they felt so blessed to have. Yet even these parents could show the very worst psychological effects from a child's loss.

There is a threshold of inner psychological life that reminds bereaved parents, each time they unhappily cross it, of an essential hollow within their lives, an incompleteness that may arise from regrets over an unlived or inadequate life, or from feeling they were not the parents they should have been when their child was still alive.

I have come to believe that how the death of a child is eventually dealt with by a loving adult—and it can never be an easy thing, for certain—has something to do with his or her memories and the emotions these personal remembrances will bring. The grieving parent who copes with a child's death is the one who finds it possible again to *celebrate* that child—and the time the parent had with that child—by relishing recollections of the deceased son or daughter. And in this act of celebration and commemoration, a process that will continue for the remainder of their lives, these parents are somehow able to avoid crossing the boundary to the thoughts and feelings that will leave them desolate and empty.

"It's for the best," Susan Shea's father sadly remarked to me, as we spoke briefly several days after his daughter's death. "This has been a burden for the family for so long," he added. "And she was in such pain there at the end."

Although his words might seem harsh and unfeeling, he loved his child very much—of that fact I am quite certain. His love for Susan was as intense as the devotion her entire family had shown to her over so many years. But her father's comment hinted that Susan's life and death had been framed largely by the harsh realities and limitations of her illness and not by the possibilities that might have allowed for another sort of life for her. As such, her death seemed a rebirth for her family or, in her father's words, like a burden coming to an end.

In my mind's eye, that closure on a life contrasts sharply with my clear recollection of a brief encounter with Rene's father, as we sat down over coffee more than a year following his daughter's death. Partly as a response to the loss of Rene, he had begun to volunteer his services at the hospital, doing whatever he could. He told me of the nagging depression he now knew, a profound and troubling sadness that began within days after Rene died. As we spoke, he seemed to me wholly different from the man I once knew.

"I still carry her pictures here," he said, as he pulled out a weathered wallet from the back pocket of his baker's dusty-white pants. "Although sometimes I think it's not so good."

He flipped through the wallet, which was bursting at its seams, filled as it was well beyond its intended capacity with pictures of his thirteen children—pictures now of the living *and* the dead. He showed me a picture of Rene—all smiles—from a happier time, in her early adolescence. I suspected he thought I might need to see this visual reminder to recall her once again, but that was not the case.

"You know, this is the first time she ever hurt me," he said oddly, as he returned the photograph to his wallet.

"All her life, she was nothing but a pleasure, even with all the problems she had to put up with." Mr. Cicciarelli became teary-eyed; the depth of his sadness now seemed as great as had been his immense enthusiasm for life in earlier days.

"And now that she's finally gone, I'm just not the same anymore, you know," he said. "People try to tell me I still got all my other kids left—as if they can take her place. I know they mean well, but that hurts me even more."

Mr. Cicciarelli began to sob, his tears trickling down and dangling from his grizzled, unshaven chin. He made no attempt to wipe the large tears from his face—they would just hang there for a moment and then spill down onto his shirt.

"I don't have my baby anymore," he said softly to himself, as he gazed off to some distant place.

Then he looked back to me again, desperately clutching his hand to his moistened chest. A man tormented by his memories, and by a father's love for a dead child.

"Rene's left this big hole in me that nobody's ever gonna fill."

CHAPTER 7

THE WIZARD

Blind fortune still bestows her gifts
On such as cannot use them.

—BEN JONSON

"YOU HAVE A CHESS SET!" the handsome little boy exclaimed that first day I met him in my office. He ran to the opposite corner of the room and began to examine the chess pieces on my table. He looked more closely to study the detail in the wooden figures, sculpted to resemble horses and kings and castles. I knew this boy was only six years old, but he seemed familiar with the game of chess and showed a keen interest in learning more.

"It's a wonderfully complex game," he said, startling me with his relatively advanced use of language. "*Wonderfully complex,*" he repeated somewhat flatly.

"Wonderfully complex . . . wonderfully complex . . . wonderfully complex," he whispered over and over, in a regimented and monotonous manner.

This kind of repetition in children—called *perseveration* by psychologists, and unusual in a child his age—was the first clinical sign that something might not be right with this young boy. It was likely he'd heard this particular abstract phrase from someone else, but the melody it created when spoken pleased him, and so he chose to repeat it over and over.

He paused and picked up a bishop—one of the more abstractly formed pieces—from the wooden board. From this act alone I could tell the boy might be somewhat out of the ordinary. A more typical six-year-old would be apt to pick up the knight or rook pieces first, because they resemble something real, to refer to them as "horses" and "castles" and then use them in some concrete way.

The boy examined the bishop carefully for several more seconds, turning it slowly around, as though appreciating its smooth contours and the elegance of its sleek design.

And then—just when I thought he could say it no more—he said it yet again.

"Wonderfully complex . . ."

This young boy, whose name was Randy Easton, finally looked over and ran toward me, stopping abruptly, only an inch or so from my body. He tugged at my shirt to pull me down to his height. His eyes, as they peered up toward me, were strangely nonexpressive—almost empty. But his body jerked here and there, as though it was somehow electrified and partly out of his conscious control. He jumped up and down with excitement, as he uttered sounds that told me he was becoming even more delighted over his discovery of a chess set in my office.

Randy's obvious physical clumsiness and his very poor judgment about social etiquette were yet two more signs that he might have a diagnosable problem.

I stooped down in front of him, and he responded in an odd manner by moving even closer to my face. Much too close to the face of an adult stranger, and it made me rather uncomfortable.

"Do you play chess?" he asked seriously, as he continued to stare at me with that vacant look. I was forced to pause a second to refocus my gaze upon the little boy's face, which by now had completely filled my visual field.

His eyes, though, were moving to and fro, focusing quickly and almost randomly on many of my features—and not at all looking into my eyes.

"Yes, Randy, I play a little," I answered with apprehension, and then I moved over to sit on a nearby chair. He followed me as I moved—like a shadow figure—and stood beside me, unaware I might have changed position to put a more comfortable distance between us.

"It's wonderfully complex, isn't it?"

"Yes, I suppose it is. It *is* a very complicated game," I offered.

"Yes, a complicated game . . . a complicated game," he mimicked and rehearsed. "I just wish they'd make a video game that was as complicated as chess."

"Oh, you play video games?" I said, thinking that discussing them with him would be a way to quickly develop rapport.

"Yeah, but I master every game I try," he said sadly, and not with any sense of pride or accomplishment. "They're all too easy," he added quickly. "I wish they'd make a game as complicated as chess." He paused, and then his face brightened, as if some great insight had been revealed to him in that split second.

"Do you know how to program computers?" he asked me excitedly. "That's what video games are, you know . . . they're computer programs they put on a tiny thing that has a memory. It's just a tiny teeny little thing—a little thing they call a *chip*," he said, with joyful emphasis on this final word.

"I know a little about it, but I'm not an expert," I offered, though I could tell he was still attuned to the word he'd said only a moment earlier.

"They call it a chip . . . a chip . . . a chip. Chip . . . chip . . . chip." He laughed over this repetition, and his playfulness with the sound of language. And then he stiffened suddenly, as another tangential thought dawned on him.

"Let's write a program *now*!" he demanded abruptly. "Let's write a program for a video game of chess!"

"I think that would take a long time to do," I informed him. "People take months and years to write the programs for computer games."

Randy moved in front of me again, although by now most six-year-old boys would have sat on my couch, or on the floor where I keep a supply of toys. He tried to sit on my lap—an unusual gesture for a child his age to extend to an adult stranger. I shifted his attention back to the chessboard and stood up to prevent him from carrying out this touching but socially inappropriate gesture. He reacted by reaching out and finding my hand, and he held onto it firmly, as we walked over to the table. He was still completely unaware of any effect his physical proximity might create in me.

"You know chess only has so many moves," he instructed me, giggling loudly. "You can understand it if you remember every move there is," he added seriously, going through the motions of opening a game. "I don't know all the rules, though. I'll learn them when I get better at reading." He seemed sad that he couldn't take up the game immediately and become a grandmaster overnight.

I began to reach out to pick up a piece from the board. Randy stiffened and yelled: "No, no, no!" I stopped and looked at him as if to say: "What's wrong?"

"No, no, no!" he exclaimed again. I could see he was not about to tell me why.

"Why don't you want me to pick up the chess piece?" I asked him gently, my hand still suspended over the board.

"You might not put it back just right," he warned me. "And then we'll *really* be in a mess."

I recognized his rigid preference for sameness as a telltale symptom for at least four clinical disorders, and so I inquired further.

"You think we'll be in a mess if we don't put it back just right," I said. "Why?"

"It just isn't good to move these things around. Not when they're put where they oughta be," he warned me matter-of-factly.

"Mommy always does that, and I tell her cut it out . . . cut it out. Put it back now, Mommy . . . put it back."

"What does your mommy say when you tell her that?" I asked.

Randy began to hum and shake and dance a rhythmic dance. He looked along the barren wall adjacent to where he stood. I repeated my question once more.

"What does your mommy say?"

He quickly homed in on me with a hostile stare, realizing I was going to persist toward an answer. He seemed irritated with my simple question, and his face conveyed an overreaction of major proportions.

"*I don't know what she does!*" he said forcefully, and with a very clear nonverbal message that I stop asking him such difficult questions.

"Let's talk some more about *chess*," he implored me, as he began to dance clumsily and once more hum his bizarre tune.

Randy Easton and his parents were sent to me by a psychologist at a local public school. He was described as a first grader with very high intelligence, and an uncanny knack for acquiring and retaining new information quickly. Although he was judged to be rather odd, he had already completed some of the academic requirements for the fifth grade in science and math. His performance in language skills was also superior, but he showed significant weakness in reading comprehension. The findings of the formal evaluations he'd received already suggested he was a talented child, but one who might require special handling. For this reason, he might not advance to the second grade.

I still recall the final phrase in an informal note I received from Randy's school psychologist.

"*This child is an absolute whiz,*" she wrote. "But Randy shows certain unusual quirks in his behavior." There were more than a few quirks to Randy Easton's story.

Randy's mother and father, as some parents are apt to do, insisted upon meeting with me *before* they brought their son to my office. This was a tendency I'd noted in a few middle-class and upper-middle-class parents—people who were cautious about subjecting their child to the mysterious methods of mental health professionals. It was also typically related to their ambivalence in seeking professional help for their children or themselves.

Randy's mother, a successful consultant in financial matters, seemed haggard and worn. She was anxious about our meeting, and I thought she seemed very eager to begin. Mr. Easton arrived separately a few minutes later, dressed in suit and tie, having come directly from his position as an actuary with a large insurance firm. He appeared fatigued as well, but not nearly as world weary as his wife. He managed a slight but superficial smile as we greeted one another, but he looked past me as we shook hands. His wife remained vigilant and dour throughout our session together.

"They tell us our son is *gifted*," Mrs. Easton began, with a sardonic tone. "But I personally don't think *gifted* is the best term to describe Randy."

Her husband sighed audibly, as he looked out the window next to his chair.

"Why do you say that, Mrs. Easton?" I asked her directly. Her cynical attitude was unusual in a middle-class mother who'd been told her child was intellectually or creatively gifted. I'd met many parents by then who seemed so very *disappointed* to learn their child's IQ was *only* in the average to above-average range.

"It isn't a simple matter of being gifted," she replied almost bitterly. "It just isn't as simple as that. You're supposed to be the expert here," she added. "Maybe you can help us sort this whole thing out."

Mrs. Easton began to recite a litany of complaints about her young son—problems that seemed to begin when he was about three years of age. By the time he was four, she told me, she felt frustrated and at her wits' end. It seemed to her that Randy's problems were just worsening every day now, and she saw no signs of improvement. She told me his behavior was widely erratic, ranging from times of frenetic hyperactivity and emotionality, to prolonged periods of silent and brooding introspection.

Randy could stay with an activity for hours on end—always some new area of interest, such as learning how a clock was put together, or understanding the workings of the gas engine on the lawnmower. He would follow his mother around the house and ask a thousand questions—and this at the age of three or four!—only to then become silent for hours thereafter as he became utterly engrossed in the current object of his interest.

"He was a *beautiful* child in the beginning," she said. "But as soon as he could walk he began to shut me out. He would talk to me alright . . . and he even seemed to need me—to need someone. But I gradually realized he only needed me when he was trying to understand some object, or . . . or some *thing*. We never really connected . . . you know what I mean? We never really connected emotionally. And I don't think he ever really looked at me or acted like I was his mother . . . or, as though I was *anyone* who might be special to him."

She was firm and appeared to be objective as she described those early years with her son, Randy. The only emotion I could sense in her was muted anger, seething just beneath her tired but controlled exterior.

"You should have seen him do puzzles, Doctor," she continued, but with no perceptible trace of pride in her son's amazing skill. "It was fascinating at first. But then it began to frighten me . . . I mean, the way he behaved when he'd sit down to do a puzzle. I'm not talking about the puzzles a toddler tries to do. I mean the kinds of puzzles a grown person would have trouble with—you know, jigsaw puzzles."

"Some children can show those kinds of unusual abilities early on, Mrs. Easton," I said. "But what was it about Randy and those puzzles that *frightened* you?"

"He would solve a puzzle—say a puzzle for a seven- or eight-year-old—maybe a hundred pieces. But he didn't seem to enjoy it at all. He was so . . . so, concentrated on it. And then, when he was done, he wouldn't want to touch it anymore. He'd throw it on the ground and tell me get rid of it. 'Too easy,' he'd say to me over and over. 'Too easy . . . too easy . . . too easy,'" she repeated monotonously, emulating Randy's irritating tendency to perseverate.

"Until I felt like just *smacking* him across the face."

She shook her head in disbelief, as though she was reliving a particular time he told her this.

"And so I'd go out and get another one—a *harder* one. After a while, it became like a game between the two of us—almost like a challenge. Could Mommy find a puzzle that Randy couldn't do? " Mrs. Easton said these final words in the way a child might.

"Doctor, we're talking about a three-year-old child who could take one look at a puzzle piece and know exactly where it should go! He didn't even have to look at the picture on the box," she added dramatically.

"*That* was the frightening part?" I asked.

"Not really . . . it was the way he would shut everything out . . . me, the dog . . . my husband . . . he would just shut us all out, while he concentrated on that one puzzle." She looked over to Mr. Easton, but he continued to gaze out the window to the sky just beyond.

"The scary part was the way he'd act . . . as though we didn't exist. And he still does that whenever he gets interested in some weird thing or another. It's as though nobody in the whole world matters at all. Just that damn puzzle, or whatever it is he's trying to figure out." She looked down at her hands, as she rubbed her palms together nervously.

"And if anyone tried to help him—or even if you moved the pieces around—he would get angry and shout and put it back exactly the way he thought it should go." She paused. "He absolutely hates for anyone to change things around from the way he has them. His room

... his things ... even his toothbrush, for Christ's sake."

I paused—waiting for a moment when Mr. Easton might direct his gaze back into the room—in the hope of drawing him into the conversation. After a few seconds of silence, he seemed to come out of his self-induced trance and quickly looked in my direction. We made eye contact only briefly, before he adjusted his gaze ever so slightly above my own. Then he began to speak.

"Randy is a very special child," he started slowly, and with an odd flatness to his voice. I suspected that he'd said this same thing many times before, perhaps to other people who were concerned about his son.

"He talked in sentences at two ... and not *short* sentences, either. We knew he was highly intelligent from that point on ... at least *I* did. He excelled in just about everything that meant learning something new. His only weakness was that he was a little clumsy. Now, he's more than a little clumsy—even I'll admit that. So he'll never be a Larry Bird," he added with a quirky little laugh. "But I was no athlete, either."

"Did you have a similar experience with Randy?" I asked him. "I'm referring to your wife's feeling frightened by his being in his own world so much of the time."

"Well, she's right about that ... he can be very aloof, and especially at times when he's caught up in some project. You know, when he's interested in something new and challenging. But it didn't bother me as much, I guess. I'm a little like that too."

"There *are* a lot of similarities," Mrs. Easton interrupted, seeming almost happy this fact had now been publicly revealed. "I mean between my husband and Randy. Sometimes I think it makes him blind to the things that Randy does. And he minimizes the seriousness of Randy's problems," she added, looking in her husband's direction.

Mr. Easton turned away from his wife and peered aimlessly through the window again, effectively tuning her out of his immediate perception.

"I don't think he would even be here at all if *I* hadn't insisted on it," she added, indicating her husband with a sideways gesture. "He thinks everything will be alright."

Mr. Easton turned to us again, but I couldn't really discern whether he'd heard what his wife said: he seemed preoccupied with the view just outside my window.

"I *was* a lot like Randy when I was younger," he continued. "I wasn't as intelligent as he is, but I was quiet and in my own world most of the time. But I sort of grew out it, I guess." He looked at me as though I could somehow validate this summary evaluation of himself.

"Now I have a job I'm pretty good at, and we have a nice house and nice things. I still don't mix with lots of people too much, but I don't really *have* to do that anymore. I do what's expected, and everyone pretty much leaves me alone. Which is the way I like it," he added.

I wondered silently where this aversion to others first began.

"Sometimes I think Randy's biggest problem is all the other people he has to please. I'm talking about his teachers . . . and the other kids. All these people who expect him to act a certain way." He looked over to his wife. "Even his mother. I think even his own mother wants him to be different from what he is."

Mrs. Easton wouldn't meet his gaze, and I sensed they'd had this conversation many times before. So we sat there in uncomfortable silence for a few more seconds.

"It's not that simple," Mrs. Easton said, looking directly at me as she began to continue her description of her son. "He has no friends! *No friends at all!* That's not normal, Doctor! I don't have to have a Ph.D. to know that. And when I make an effort to get him to mingle with other kids, he acts . . . well, he acts crazy!"

"I wouldn't call it *crazy*," Mr. Easton interjected with irritation. "He doesn't know *how* to act," he pleaded. "He's at a total loss when it comes to playing with other kids. So he gets silly and goofy around them, and they don't know what's going on with him."

"He *scares* them, George!" Mrs. Easton retorted. "You can see it in their faces. He scares the hell out them when he starts getting hyper and weird . . . and for no reason at all." She looked to me again.

"He gets *real* strange with other kids, Doctor," she said. "He starts to make noises and says all these crazy things, like words that don't mean anything. And he mixes up his sentences."

Mrs. Easton looked back to her husband briefly, to gauge whether he was even listening. He was staring at his shoes intently.

"And he's always patting himself all over," she added. "Like this . . . just pats himself all over." She demonstrated this odd behavior for me. "You can imagine what the other children think when he starts in with that!"

Mr. Easton's subdued anger toward his wife now became more apparent. Up until that point he had successfully repressed it in my presence. But that wall seemed to weaken now, as he began to defend his son more forcefully.

"Why don't we start talking about all the things Randy does that are pretty remarkable?" he asked her point blank. Then he looked over to me again.

"You've read the reports, haven't you? So you know he has an IQ that's off the chart. They can't find a test to give him that he can't perform at the top." He shook his head back and forth, puzzled by why this very important fact might be ignored by his wife.

Mr. Easton was technically correct—Randy's performance on IQ tests qualified him to be designated as superior in intellect. His son's scores on at least two major intelligence tests had been within the top one percent of the population of six-year-olds who provided the basis for the testing norms. And, I recalled, almost seventy percent of children would be expected to fall within the average range. So from that point of view alone, Randy Easton was already an extraordinary child.

"Sure, he has some problems knowing how to act in public . . . and especially in knowing about people. At least, that's what the school psychologist told us—and I think she's probably right. That's his big blind spot—understanding people. But, other than that, he's a great kid," he added. "You'll meet him, Doctor. It takes a while to get used to him, but once you do . . . you'll see, he's a great kid."

"Try *living* with him," Randy's mother interrupted angrily, as if she were determined to dispel her husband's bright illusions.

"Try putting up with his weird behavior in a group of children and their mothers. Try taking him to a store and having to endure the stares of people—perfect strangers—who think he's afflicted with some goddamn disease. Go try sitting with him in church and having the old people look at you like your child is nuts, or . . . or . . . possessed by an evil spirit."

She paused to catch her breath—and to see if her words had swayed me or her highly distractible husband.

"It hasn't been a picnic, let me tell you, Doctor. There's something very wrong with this kid. I just hope you can tell us what it is."

"And what if he *can't?*" Mr. Easton blurted out angrily, confronting his wife. "What if *no one* can find anything really wrong with Randy? Or if there's no name for it . . . and no treatment? What will you do then?" Mr. Easton was clearly frustrated by his wife's attitude and by her extremely negative attitude toward the boy. He also appeared to know in advance that his son's problems were going to be difficult to resolve.

"I guess I'll just have to keep on putting up with it," she said angrily.

"Sometimes I think you just *put up* with me as well," he responded. "Sometimes I think you'd just like to get away from the both of us."

Mrs. Easton looked at me with an embarrassed smile, as though she'd never intended for this visit to the child psychologist to turn into such a heated discussion of her marriage. I suspected that she was much more comfortable with the spotlight on Randy—and not at all on herself.

"Look, George," she said firmly. "It's one thing for me to marry you and live with you . . . I mean, sure, I knew you were a little odd." Mrs. Easton glanced over to me. "We even talked about it before we were married. But with a child . . . no, not *a* child, *my* child. With *my* child it's all different. He's my flesh and blood . . . *I'm* the one who brought him into this world, you know?"

She reached into the small purse she held in her lap and took out a fresh handkerchief. She brought it up to her eyes as if to dab tears from her cheeks, though they didn't seem that moist.

"I can put up with you being the way you are, George," she added weakly. "It's just not my fault. But when I look at Randy and I see how . . . how *strange* he's become, I just die inside. And you're right, there *are* times when the only thing I want is to get away from him, but I can't. I know he's my son and I have to stay. I have to take care of him until he's old enough to go out on his own."

She folded the dry handkerchief into a square, then clutched it tightly in her palm.

"But I *don't* have to pretend to *like* him," she said bitterly. "I *don't* have to act *thrilled* to have him in my life."

■

In 1944, a Viennese child psychiatrist named Hans Asperger wrote a clinical research article published in a rather obscure German publication. It was a document that went largely unnoticed for many years thereafter—perhaps due to world events at that time and to the fact that his clinical work pertained to a relatively rare clinical syndrome of childhood. Although he originally referred to this unusual pattern of child behavior as *autistic personality disorder*, researchers who studied the same phenomenon in later years would subsequently call it *Asperger's syndrome*.

Odd as it may seem, Dr. Asperger was primarily interested in describing and rehabilitating a collection of children who had not been successfully absorbed into the Nazi-inspired sociopolitical organization known as the German Youth Movement.

Dr. Asperger originally set out to better understand those children who seemed to shun involvement in the Aryan youth groups. Of course, some of these children and teenagers might have avoided affiliation with the movement simply because of a family or personal attitude against the efforts of the state. But as his work progressed, Asperger eventually focused more narrowly on those children who could *never* fit in, the ones who couldn't possibly connect with the large social network that the German authorities had sought to create.

Asperger hypothesized that their failure to associate and affiliate in groups seemed to be the result of an inherent psychological inability to relate to other people.

At about the same time in the United States, another child psychiatrist, Leo Kanner, published an influential article that described the clinical phenomenon of *early infantile autism*. Apparently unaware of the similarities in each other's work, these two clinicians attempted to expand our knowledge of a small subgroup of patients who were not well defined within medicine or psychology. Children who, beginning at a very young age, appeared to inexplicably withdraw from the social world around them. However, there were major qualitative differences between autism—the more extreme form of withdrawal that Dr. Kanner described—and the pattern that would come to be known in professional circles as Asperger's syndrome.

If Randy Easton had been evaluated by a European psychiatrist, for example, there was a good chance he would have been seen as an Asperger's patient. It was clear he didn't fall into the category of autism because of the fact that he could relate to the people around him much better than children who were classically autistic. However, his behavioral characteristics *were* suggestive of a milder form of autism, or at least, of some important delay or defect in his social and emotional development.

As I reviewed the list of key characteristics and symptoms that Hans Asperger had originally described in his 1944 paper, I could not help but be impressed by how accurate a description he provided for my new patient Randy Easton. "Highly intelligent children with interesting peculiarities," Asperger had written. He emphasized that the syndrome was characterized primarily by "the innate inability to form affective contact." Other researchers would later refer to this as basic deficits in understanding and expressing emotionality and in the ability to decipher the emotional and nonverbal cues that are embedded in the social behavior of other people. These children could even have problems in sorting out relatively basic emotions within themselves.

For example, what might be instantly apparent to you or me in a social interaction—perhaps the affection or anger that can be communicated clearly in the facial expression of someone we might encounter—would be difficult for a child with Asperger's syndrome to discern. And even more complex nonverbal signals, such as the curious look or fleeting glance intended to cue us that another person expects we will respond in a certain manner—might be lost on the child with Asperger's syndrome, who, for whatever reason, cannot possibly decipher them.

In addition, the young German children Asperger originally described were linguistically precocious, although they were also apt to show many peculiarities in their use of words and sentences. They might invent new words—*neologisms*—that were original and idiosyncratic to them. They were likely to produce illogical or incomprehensible sentences, especially when they were emotionally excited. But they wouldn't seem as psychologically disturbed as the classically autistic child, and their overt behavior would not be as dramatically asocial or withdrawn.

Some very young children with Asperger's syndrome were endowed with unique and special skills or abilities, and they could display intense and obsessive interest in the everyday objects around them. They might become fascinated by the physical features of their toys, for example, or by discovering common implements in their home. They seemed compelled to understand the inner workings of various household appliances and other mechanical devices—perhaps even to the point of taking them apart and then putting them back together again.

As they grew older, these eccentric children would become intellectually absorbed in the study of other complex or obscure phenomena. The structure and patterns inherent to music, for example. Or the ancient origins of names and words. They might become engrossed in understanding computers, astronomy, or the weather. A few of these children were reported to become obsessed with the elaborate game of chess.

Though children or adolescents like these might dazzle their parents and teachers with displays of unusual and odd intellectual powers, they could also be extremely clumsy and inept in tasks that required simple gross motor ability, such as in sports. They even had difficulty in the simple maneuvering that is required to allow them to move smoothly through the physical world. More significant, perhaps, was that they seemed no more skilled than infants when attempting to master the rudimentary tasks of social interaction. They struggled to grasp the universal precepts of human emotion.

Children with Asperger's syndrome were more likely to be boys, and some studies had suggested a similar pattern of behavior might be found in the childhood history of a parent or some other blood relative. A few reports hinted that medical problems during pregnancy or the birth process might contribute to the origin of this disorder. But no one knew for certain, since the condition, like autism, was relatively rare and difficult to study.

If I were to use the term Asperger's syndrome to describe little Randy Easton's behavior, what would be the value?

It was somewhat reassuring to know that a number of researchers felt this pattern had a reasonably good outcome as the child grew older. That is, many of these children might eventually find a place for themselves in the adult world, perhaps in jobs that happened to match their unusual pattern of intellectual or creative abilities. They could carve out a space for themselves in the lives of other people, as well, and even marry or be befriended by people who were much like themselves. And they might even be loved—by someone who could see past the oddities and the quirks in their behavior, a person who took the time and effort to see the person *beyond* his or her peculiar disability.

Unlike autism—in which the longer term outlook is bleak—Asperger's children could pass as ordinary people more easily. With a bit of luck and practice—and despite their peculiar quirks—they could seem within the normal range of adult behavior. But *only* after years of practice—and only when they were given the adult's greater freedom to shape their lives at will. I also knew that a few of the professionals who worked with such children had found that psychological support could be helpful to these children and their parents during the more trying times, especially during adolescence when they might be held up to ridicule by others and thus be forced to isolate themselves all the more. Such children might benefit from special coaching in how to cope with social situations, or what to do when meeting someone new. Simple tasks such as learning to initiate and maintain eye contact with a stranger or a potential friend. Even if the child could not discern what the other person might be feeling or thinking, he or she could be taught to behave in certain routine ways, to minimize the risk of alienating or frightening other children.

In the case of Randy Easton, such a practical approach might be best initially. The research on these children suggested that insight psychotherapy or methods that attempted to allow the child to learn about himself were probably ill-fated. My time with his parents, though—and especially my approach to his distraught mother— might have to take an entirely different tack.

"Oh, no!" Randy said with alarm, as he fixed his gaze precisely on my right shoulder. I was mystified about what he might be staring at, but then he reached up slowly and plucked a tiny bit of lint from my woolen suit coat. He drew it toward himself and examined it— turning it from side to side to attend to all its features. Then he simply dropped it and watched it float through the air toward the ground. He giggled and hopped about nervously as it sailed slowly downward.

"Randy, is there anything special you'd like to do while you're here today?" I asked him, having exhausted my limited knowledge about the game of chess, video games and computer programming during our previous sessions.

He looked at me seriously, and I thought he was carefully pondering my question. His brow knitted, and he began to look around the room. He would stop and focus on every object he might spy and appear somehow to record it in his memory. As he did this, he would pat himself at random—and at different locations on his body. He hummed a tune that seemed chaotic and completely foreign to any form of music that I knew.

"I want to talk with you about video games again," he finally responded, after seeming to give my question such careful and prolonged deliberation.

"Did you know that Nintendo games are very predictable?" he asked me.

"Predictable?" I responded quizzically. Silently, I wondered if *this* was the way he talked about such things with the six-year-olds in his world. If so, it was easy to understand why he might have such difficulty making friends with other children.

"Each screen in a Nintendo game is in a special order," he explained. "And all I do is memorize the screens." He began to pat himself on the leg and mumble. "That way I know what's coming next. And I know when to jump or shoot or kick."

"I'm not sure I really understand what you mean," I said.

"I know," he said sympathetically. "Most grown-ups don't get it like us kids," he answered. "We just do it in our heads." He skipped forward, covering a yard or so across my office floor and almost tripping on the carpet as he did.

"Do you play Nintendo?" he asked me pointedly, though he was gazing down intently in front of his feet at the rug, which had suddenly attracted his immediate attention.

"I've played Mario Brothers once or twice," I replied.

"Easy . . . easy . . . easy . . . easy game . . . easy game," he sang out loud.

"I've got it all right here," he said, as he pointed to his head. "I got all the screens right here. I mastered that in a day," he announced proudly. "Only took a day . . . only took a day."

"*Wow*," I responded with genuine enthusiasm, having tried to play that game myself. "*That's really great!*" I effused. "To be that good at Mario Brothers—and in only one day!"

My change in expression, and the way I'd suddenly become emotionally excited over his amazing feat, seemed to throw him off balance. He stopped his skipping back and forth, his smile erased. And his hands and fingers, previously moving about like tiny birds in flight, suddenly stiffened at his sides. The abrupt enthusiasm embedded in my words had served to confuse and disorient him.

"What do you mean?" he asked me nervously, and with an almost tortured expression on his face. I tried to undo the damage my remark had apparently caused, repeating what I'd said, but *this* time without the overt emotional display.

"I *meant* to say that, well, not too many people could do so well in a video game like that, and in such a short time," I whispered calmly. "I thought it was really great that you could do that."

"Oh . . ." he stammered, clearly reassured. "Why didn't you say that to begin with?" he chided me—and then moved on to his next seemingly random thought.

His overreaction to my behavior reminded me that one therapeutic technique that can be useful with a child like Randy is to rehearse his reactions to hypothetical social situations. In this way, a child can be quizzed about his understanding of what might actually be happening in a social interaction, but, even if he does not completely comprehend the nuances of interpersonal communication, he can be taught how and when to respond to the more predictable cues that other people give.

I had tried this approach more than several times on Randy, and once or twice he seemed to profit from the exercise. We went over what to do and say when meeting another child for the first time, for example. And we rehearsed a way to react when someone seemed excited or angry or happy.

These things were not simple for Randy, because he had great trouble distinguishing the difference between feelings like sadness and fear, or upset and excitement. But we went over such things again and again, until he had learned there were important differences in the meanings of expressed emotion.

This time, though, I shifted to a situation at home. I wanted to explore his ability to perceive feelings within himself and to examine his relations with his mother and father.

"Pretend you're in your house, Randy," I started. "You know—the way we used to pretend you were with the other kids at school."

Randy whistled and patted and skipped quietly up and down. But he shook his head to show he'd understood my request.

"You've done something you shouldn't have . . . and you're about to get in trouble," I continued. "Your mother and father are there, and they've just caught you in the act."

Randy smiled and laughed and jumped some more, as if I'd described an exact scene that was repeated often in his household.

"What happens next?" I asked.

"Ha, Ha . . . that's a good one," he began. "It happens all the time. I did something wrong, you see. I dropped the box too loudly and now I'm gonna get it!"

Rather than demonstrating fear or anxiety, Randy flashed a broad grin, inappropriate in response to the likelihood of trouble.

"What happens next, Randy?" I prompted him.

"Ooooooh . . . my motherrrrr . . ." he whispered, as if he were telling a ghost story around a nighttime campfire. "She's coming to tell me: No . . . No . . . No!" He straightened up with electricity. His body went erect. "Mommy says, 'You little monster!' "

And with that, Randy mimicked a loud monster, growling "Aaaarghhh . . ." as he stomped about the room.

"And then?" I asked him. "What happens next?"

"Daddy, Daddy, save me!" he screeched in falsetto.

If Randy was experiencing any emotion at all as he portrayed this scene, it was much too scattered and diffuse to be discerned. He stood up straight, and his body locked tightly, as if he'd snapped to attention. He wrapped his long, skinny arms around himself and then tucked his head down snug against his chest.

"Daddy, save me from the monster!" he sang out. "Daddy, save me from the monster!" His long thin arms unfolded from around his frame and reached out to grasp some unseen object he imagined.

"What's the monster thinking, Randy?" I prompted him. He paused with his dramatic scene and looked to me as though I'd ruined his fun. Frozen in his tracks—his mouth agape—he began to respond in his ordinary tone of voice.

"Now how in the world do I know what my mother's thinking?" He shook his head back and forth, disappointed in his child psychologist's ineptitude. "What do you think I am, some kind of *genus* or somethin'?" He'd heard this word before, but he'd failed to get it exactly right.

"Well, how about you," I tried again. "What are *you* thinking when your mother catches you doing something you shouldn't?"

This question would fail as well, for Randy hadn't any clues. He paused for only a brief moment, then began to skip about again. I could tell our "game" had gotten much too boring or difficult for him, and so I'd lost his attention altogether.

I decided to make one more attempt, since our various interactions had never before led us into the province of his life at home with his parents. I asked him, in very broad terms, about his relations with his parents and about how he felt toward them. He couldn't articulate his feelings at all, and his verbally constructed ideas were almost gibberish. But I could tell he knew something wasn't right—and that he accurately perceived his mother's disgust over his behavior. He had shown me this before, when we'd talked about the reactions of the other children to his odd ways.

Of course, his quirky behavior did not seem odd to him at all, which was the "curse" intrinsic to his condition. He was hopelessly in the dark about what might really be the cause of what even he vaguely perceived to be a problem.

It suddenly occurred to me, though, as we struggled through that strange conversation about thoughts and feelings and his parents, that Randy expressed himself largely in his physical movements and in the peculiar manner in which he spoke. For example, the harsh loud tones and swaddled position he used to convey his many run-ins with his mother. Or the higher-pitched but softer intonations, and his greater physical ease, as he evoked memories of his father.

It was clear he could distinguish qualitatively different sorts of feelings for each of his parents, though he had not grasped the universal linguistic code that would help him to communicate such intimate knowledge. To capture and express the very essence of his own emotions, he had only those strange inflections and clumsy motions his mind would allow him to produce.

■

"I've brought this book to show you, Doctor," Mrs. Easton said as we sat down to begin yet another session about her son. Mr. Easton seemed aloof from us again, although I knew from past experience he would join in when he felt it was necessary.

His wife held a tattered copy of a former bestseller that I knew had been published many years before. In fact, I'd read it myself as a student in college. It told the fascinating story of a severely autistic child—the sort of child that Dr. Leo Kanner had first described in his classic paper on early infantile autism in 1943.

"I wonder if you can tell me if Randy is autistic?" she inquired coolly, but with quiet determination. "No one has ever used *that* word yet," she added. "But it's been on my mind ever since I read this book."

Her words didn't get Mr. Easton's attention, or so it seemed by all outward appearances. He fixed his gaze on the walls or the floor, then out the window, toward the dark storm clouds forming in the distance.

Unlike others who might casually look here and there during a counseling session, though, he didn't appear at all bored. Instead, he seemed quite caught up in an examination of the objects and physical world around him.

"I think everyone is trying to *protect* him, or something," Mrs. Easton continued angrily. "They keep saying he's gifted . . . but when I press them, they'll admit he's strange as hell." She flicked the pages of the paperback book. "I'm not saying Randy is entirely like this boy, but there sure seem to be a lot of similarities."

"About all I can say at this point, Mrs. Easton, is that Randy does display autistic *features*. Other than that, I *can* tell you that he doesn't have what are considered to be the primary symptoms of autism. He is much better functioning, for example, than the boy that book describes," I said. "Today I hope to talk with you about how we might approach the problems your son is having," I added. "I'd like to spend some time talking about how we might work together to make things better for him . . . and maybe a bit easier for the two of you."

"Doctor," Mrs. Easton said, "if you really want to know the truth, I'm not here for a whole lot of advice about how to change myself. I want answers about this kid!" She flipped nervously through the worn pages of the book in her hand.

"I mean, I really don't think I've got that much energy left . . . energy enough to change the way I feel about my son. The way I see it now," she added, "I'm convinced this child is a lost cause. I've tried everything I can think of, and nothing makes it better! My attitude right now is that I'm going to start giving all I can to our daughter, Amy. *She's* the one who's gotten the raw deal in all of this. Everything's gone to this weird kid . . . I mean Randy. And she gets *nothing*, because he just takes it all!"

The force of Mrs. Easton's emotion, and the cold manner in which she spoke about her son reminded me briefly of a phenomenon that had been described in the 1960s by a child psychologist named Bruno Bettelheim. He had talked about the "refrigerator mother"—the term he used to describe the mothers of many autistic children he had seen. Based on this clinical impression, he and others hypothesized that the cold and withholding manner in which these mothers treated their children had actually *caused* the autism in the child. But, alas, as can often be true of theories based solely on subjective observations, the direction of causality was probably the reverse of what he'd envisioned.

That is, the cool almost uncaring manner these mothers could show had actually been the result of bearing and living with a child who rarely, if ever, gave them emotional cues. Autistic children rigidly avoid such direct contact with any person, including their mothers and fathers. It is not so difficult to understand that over many years of this sort of difficult interaction, a mother might easily tune out and put a distance between herself and the child she'd tried to love.

And so the concept of the "refigerator mother" became obsolete, as evidence mounted that the origins of autism were likely to be biologically based in the children's brains.

I hadn't paid much attention to Mr. Easton, as I listened to his wife express her anger and frustration. When she paused, though, I looked over toward him to monitor his reaction and was surprised to find him staring at me directly—with that same vacant look I'd seen in Randy's eyes.

For a second or two, he seemed to examine *me* as closely as he'd previously analyzed the various objects in the room and the intricate array of clouds in the sky outside my window. Finally, he ended his close scrutiny, and began to speak.

"You . . . and my wife . . . and all the experts in the world . . . you can use whatever words you want to describe my son," he said firmly, "but, you know, you'll never *really* understand him. I don't think anyone can. Randy is just too complicated," he added more softly and with a sense of resignation about this one, overriding fact.

Mrs. Easton snorted loudly one more time—her disgust with her husband resounded through the room. But Mr. Easton was not the least dissuaded from his opinion about the boy.

"What it all boils down to is this: he's just a wonderfully complex child," Mr. Easton finally said, with the fierce and hopeful sense of determination a parent will show when talking about a beloved child's unknown future.

"He's just wonderfully complex . . ."

■

Randy is now in junior high school, but his behavior is much the same. Like all atypical children, he continues to have considerable problems being accepted by his peer group—and even by several of his teachers. These educators, well-meaning individuals who are sometimes at a loss about how to deal with Randy's unusual pattern of abilities, will sometimes become frustrated with their failed attempts to get his attention.

It is difficult, for example, to keep his interest for very long on a subject he already knows quite well—or if it seems too boring for him even to bother. This is a trait that characterizes many students, of course, but with Randy the response to boredom can be much more dramatic. If he fails to become engrossed in a particular subject or activity, it is likely he will go off on wildly creative or seemingly random tangents, and that will usually land him in trouble.

Some researchers who have studied Asperger's syndrome argue that giving Randy a medical diagnosis—a label that identifies him as afflicted by a disorder thought to have its basis in the brain—might serve to help him in the long run by making clear that his problems are not under his direct control and that he is, after all, likely to be the product of an unusual biological abnormality.

Others suggest he should be treated like every other child, since there is a good likelihood he will improve with time. But certain clinical studies of this particular syndrome suggest the core deficit in understanding critical aspects of social interaction and emotions will remain significant throughout the life of the child with Asperger's.

Randy Easton's life will move on. With or without solutions.

Mrs. Easton, clearly disenchanted and even embittered by her lot in life as Randy's mother, now channels most of her love and attention to Randy's younger sister, Amy. This little girl has no signs or symptoms of any disorder, certainly no features of anything so rare or exotic as Asperger's syndrome. The bulk of Mrs. Easton's anger and frustration, though, appears to be reserved for Randy, whom she cannot allow herself to accept. And who, perhaps, she will not allow herself to love.

Because of this, she will not be able to appreciate or see the wondrous feats that Randy could conceivably accomplish one day. As a result, she has little investment in what he is right now, or in what he might become in the future. On the other hand, Mr. Easton, whose childhood course and personality were quite similar to his son's, takes a very different view of young Randy. He assumes a perspective that frees him to cherish this extraordinary child and to view his son through a hopeful, though rose-colored, lens.

I would guess that the psychological identification I observed between Randy and his father might now typify Mrs. Easton's evolving relationship with her daughter. Some parents clearly have a tendency to gravitate emotionally to the child who is much like themselves, and especially when that child's traits are perceived in positive or self-fulfilling terms.

Children can be like the projective tests psychologists use—those techniques that employ ambiguous or uncertain images. As we gaze upon a child, and if we resonate to what we see, it is likely we will discern pleasant things that are in some manner connected to ourselves. If we find we do not like the child we see, however, we may experience him or her as foreign or unfamiliar, and not at all as part of what we are.

The danger that resides in such a complex process of parental identification or alienation is that we adults may fail to recognize the simple gift that *is* the child, as we search to find something of ourselves.

CHAPTER 8

HITTING THE NOTE

Alas, one must die . . .

— A MOTTO ENGRAVED IN STONE AT A
MEDIEVAL HOSPICE IN TOURS, FRANCE

"CODE BLUE . . . PICU! *Code blue* . . . *PICU!*"

To the uninitiated, this pronouncement over the public address system in a large hospital would be without meaning or any real effect. It might not even be noticed, let alone understood, by visitors unaccustomed to medical places.

"*Code blue* . . . PICU! *Code blue* . . . *PICU!*" It repeats again.

This time, there is a greater sense of urgency in the woman's voice, as if no one had heard or responded to the first announcement. As though no one had understood *exactly* what she'd meant.

I might hear this particular phrase now and then, sandwiched amid the background drone of frequent hospital announcements. Some of these involve illegally parked cars or the daily "special" in the hospital cafeteria. Others are informational in nature, having to do with the many meetings and case conferences that take place each day in a large medical center.

People who are familiar with the special vernacular of hospitals, however, will know that the phrase *code blue* carries a very specific and dramatic meaning. In common parlance, a code blue means that a human being is dying.

Typically it will be an elderly patient, or perhaps the victim of a major motor vehicle accident. Sometimes it will be a heart patient who already lives on borrowed time. No matter who it may be, however, the death of one patient will not significantly alter the schedule or the tenor of the hospital. Life and work must go on—especially in a hospital, a place where death can be an hourly event.

"*Code blue . . . PICU! Code blue . . . PICU!*" It repeats once more.

"PICU"—pronounced *PICK YOU*—is an acronym for the *pediatric intensive care unit*, a small, high-tech unit in the hospital, set aside for children in need of specialized, twenty-four-hour medical care. In some cases, these are children who linger near death following a long illness or accidental trauma. Or they might be children who are at risk for sudden cardiopulmonary crises that can seriously threaten their lives.

It is also a place where the normal and expected in family life collide quite suddenly with the unknown and the uncertain.

Although the code blue message has repeated several times, it takes a moment for me to become aware of its actual meaning. As I come to understand its special significance, I am sipping the final residue of my routine morning cup of coffee. It finally occurs to me that a child I know may be dying, even as I sit in my usual place so early in the day.

I had been in the PICU the night before, and I reviewed each of the cases briefly. There had been four children in the PICU then, but it can be a busy place and by now, the next morning, there could be others.

There was a tiny baby boy—perhaps only three or four weeks old—afflicted with spinal meningitis, a virulent life-threatening infectious disease. How or why he contracted it, no one seemed to know. But the *why* of it had seemed less important than what might happen to him next, as he lay deathly ill only a short while following his birth.

There was a young girl—an infant under a year in age—diagnosed with what sounds like an exotic disorder when first encountered. The diagnosis listed in her medical chart was *shaken-baby syndrome*—a peculiar name under which are grouped the signs and symptoms seen in a physically abused child. Not surprisingly, I'd encountered this very bad situation before, for this young child's condition had been called a *syndrome* because doctors all over the country had seen so many children with an almost identical pattern of physical findings.

The other two children in the PICU yesterday—a girl and a boy—were older. The boy I hadn't reviewed formally, but I'd glanced briefly at his chart. He'd fallen out of a third-story window in his apartment building and broken his neck. The girl I knew very well. Her name was Maggie Chessler. She was a twelve-year-old with a rare form of cancer—in the hospital yet again, for a final and desperate series of treatments.

As I went over each case briefly in my mind, it occurred to me that each of those four children had fallen prey to one of the natural enemies of children—at least the enemies I knew to be most common. First, and seen more frequently than anything else, was accidental trauma—the motor vehicle and household mishaps and the sudden unexpected destruction they could cause.

Next was the diseases, chronic and acute—the ones that had no cure—and the physically handicapping defects that the child might be born with or develop sometime thereafter. In short, the many things that can go wrong with the health of children.

And then there was the little girl with *shaken-baby syndrome,* so third on my list of the natural enemies of children would have to be their parents and other adult caretakers, and the considerable damage they were known to do.

After I reviewed each of these four children briefly, my thoughts turned again to Maggie Chessler. Her young life had now begun to wind down, after a long, fierce battle with cancerous tumors scattered throughout her body and her brain. Because of their repeated visits to the hospital, I had many opportunities to talk with both Maggie and her mother. As a result, I became very fond of the girl— which can be a risky thing to do with a terminally ill child.

It was now two years since her initial diagnosis. The course of aggressive medical treatment had gone on and on as more tumors were discovered growing in her brain. Some of these tiny malignant growths were resistant to the various treatments, while others had almost immediately disappeared after her initial chemotherapy. This had offered Maggie and her parents a shred of hope. It allowed them to anticipate some chance for victory over a disease known to kill nine out of ten of its victims.

Maggie was fated to be in and out of the hospital many times over the course of two years—on a frantic "roller-coaster ride," as Maggie's tearful mother had once remarked to me.

"But we're in this thing together, Maggie and I," she'd added bravely. "We're going to beat this disease, you know?"

Strangely, though, during all that time, I'd met Maggie's father only *once*, and at the very beginning of Maggie's ordeal.

Maggie and I would talk frequently as I made my daily rounds through the pediatric ward. I would stop to say hello, and she would always have a smile for me and some bit of interesting news about herself. She kept me up to date about her friends and exploits outside the hospital, as well as the progress of her treatments.

In my field—since I am so often caught up in the troubled lives of psychologically disturbed children and their families—Maggie was, in many ways, like a breath of fresh air. Although her life had been ravaged by a disease that can strike anyone, no matter their social class, intelligence or personality, she had remained cheerful and strong as before. She was a normal, happy child, whose body had now miserably failed her.

I recall one particular conversation I had with Maggie Chessler, early on, just after her diagnosis. It lingers in my memory because it taught me something I hadn't known firsthand before encountering her. She taught me about the child's capacity for inner strength and forgiveness—even in the face of enormous personal adversity.

"Do you like poems, Dr. Garrison?" Maggie asked me one day, as I casually walked into her hospital room to say a quick hello.

"Well, yes . . . I guess I do," I replied.

I could see she was writing furiously in a black-and-white composition notebook, the kind children use in grade school. As I entered her room, Maggie stopped momentarily to gaze across the room in search of inspiration.

"I'm writing a poem about myself," she announced with pride. "It's about my life and being in the hospital."

"Really?" I said with genuine interest. It was heartening to see she was able to keep busy despite the difficult treatments she had to endure. "I didn't know you were a writer."

"This one's about death, though. My mother thinks it's not good to think about death too much. She keeps telling me everything's gonna be alright."

"And what do *you* think?" I asked her.

"I don't know . . . I just don't think about it all that much . . . and when I do, it really doesn't get me down or anything." She went back to her poem, as though this was much more interesting than her own predicament.

"What got you interested in writing poems?" I inquired. "I don't remember your doing that before." Maggie's face brightened. Her brown eyes flashed in her beautiful face, which was framed by a bright, multicolored scarf around her forehead that hid her hairless scalp. She had lost all of her lovely blond hair following the most recent round of chemotherapy.

"My teacher told me I should write about my life. It's a journal for English class," she said. "I decided to write some poems. They're easier than long, long stories. And it's fun to try and make them rhyme."

I moved closer to her side and sat down in a chair by her bed. She shifted her body to look at me more directly. Clearly, she welcomed a visitor while her mother was busy talking to the doctors.

"Do you want to hear one?" she asked me happily. I nodded to say I did.

"OK. Let's see," she mumbled, and began to look through her bound notebook for the poem that might be best. Then she went to the last page she'd been working on—to the poem she had been composing just before.

"Here's one I haven't finished yet . . . but it's kind of sad." She looked at me to gauge whether or not I might be too sensitive to hear her melancholy verse.

"That's OK," I said to reassure her.

"Good," she said with a smile, glad that she would be able to share her unfinished elegy.

"There is no reason to fear the end," she read. "For everyone has got to die." She looked up to me, not with fear or anxiety, but with apparent pride—and perhaps to see whether I approved of her writing. Then she looked down again to her notebook and read the next line she'd composed.

"It's *life* that we are given . . ." she said with a flourish, then looked up at me with a quizzical expression.

"I can't figure out how to finish it . . . there are so many words that rhyme with 'die.'"

184

"You'll come up with something," I said. "Besides, it sounds really good to me . . . I mean, the part you've written. But you're right—it does seem a little sad at the beginning."

"Yeah, that's what my mother says," she sighed. "But my teacher told me to write about my life. So I'm writing about what might happen—my doctor told me it doesn't look real good." She said this with wide-eyed innocence, not sorrowfully, or with any trace of self-pity.

"My mother says this isn't fair . . . you know, that *I* should get this sick and all." She looked back down at her unfinished poem.

"What do you think?" I asked her. "About it being unfair?"

"Well, I think I just got bad, bad luck," she offered with an ironic laugh. "Sometimes people die young, and sometimes they die real old . . . like my grandfather." She fiddled with her yellow pencil, tapping it lightly on the bed. "Don't get me wrong," she added, looking me in the eye. "I don't *want* to die or anything. I just want to have some fun before I do."

We sat in silence momentarily. I was contemplating the very real potential for Maggie's death, but she was more concerned with finding the next line for her poem. She seemed to comprehend the weight of her own words, and so her mood darkened temporarily.

"But I have to stay the way I was before," she finally said. "I mean, before all this stuff started. I know I got a bad disease, but we're in it together. My parents and me, I mean. We're in this thing together."

"You and your family are very close," I said. "So you don't feel alone in all of this?"

"I don't really like what this is doing to them, though," she added. "My dad's quiet all the time—and once I caught him crying."

Maggie closed her notebook as she said this, and it was clear she would try to finish her journal later.

"Daddy's afraid I'm gonna die," she whispered to me. "And he's really different now . . . from the way he was before." She seemed much sadder as she thought about her father, and then she just seemed to snap out of the mood that had been created.

"Oh well, it helps to believe in God, you know," Maggie said, making a conscious effort to put a cheery tone into her voice. "Mom and I pray sometimes . . . and that helps us both."

I nodded my head, remembering that religion and a personal belief in God *did* serve as a coping mechanism in the face of death. Several studies of terminally ill patients had shown that people with a faith in a higher being seemed to accept their fate much better. They told the researchers that their belief in God helped them to avoid interpreting their own misfortune as random or unfair. And such people are more likely to report a sense that a kind of peacefulness awaits them after death.

"My mother prays I get better," Maggie said. "But I just pray for my family. I ask God to take care of them if I die . . . and especially my father."

■

The PICU is a relatively recent development in hospital units, having first come into being during the polio epidemic that struck mercilessly before World War II. Children affected by that deadly crippling disease were kept alive with mechanical ventilation, in huge machines called iron-lungs. In the 1950s and 1960s, these crude and cumbersome devices were replaced by modern and more efficient artificial respirators—machines that could be used to save or maintain the lives of children with all kinds of physical disorders.

Soon thereafter, medicine began to refine the techniques for cardiopulmonary resuscitation—a specialized approach for responding to cardiac arrest and heart death. Use of these procedures had reduced the mortality rates in hospitals dramatically. In children, cardiac arrest was usually brought on by congenital cardiac defects, or by anomalies in the rhythmic beating of the heart. Children with such conditions often needed constant and expert medical monitoring, or they could die quickly and unexpectedly.

The PICU is a hospital unit where the parents or friends of children have little to do, except wait. On other units, parents can easily play and talk with their children, or perhaps take them for a walk or a ride in a wheelchair to other parts of the hospital. In the PICU, though, they can only sit or stand around, or try to catch some sleep in typically claustrophobic rooms provided to the parents of children in such a medical unit.

It is common for me to encounter these parents as they pace back and forth down the long, sterile hallway that is adjacent to the PICU. Their faces appear understandably drawn and grave, as they cope with one of life's very worst disasters, the critical illness of their child. It is my impression that in that same hallway, many parents seem likely to reflect upon their own lives—and on the meaning of the child they might lose.

There is, of course, usually very little of a practical nature that parents can do or say that will alter the course of the dramatic events in the PICU. These mothers and fathers are forced to stand along the sidelines—perhaps for the first time in their lives as parents—as their child's fate unfolds before them.

Parents in the PICU also wait to discover whether it will be *their* child who lives. And, as each child's situation reaches its own *denouement*, these mothers and fathers will sometimes brood over whether or not the child they see before them—the one lying seriously ill in the PICU—will be at all the same as the one they knew only yesterday, the child they might have taken for granted, before this terrible thing happened that puts his or her life at stake.

And some of the parents who accompany their child to the PICU will dream a dark and frightening dream. Though they will be told of their child's excellent chances for survival, it is as though these words go unheard and are without effect. "It will be *my* child who will be the one to die," they will say to me. "I just know it. I have this feeling deep inside that *this* will be the end."

It will seem as though they are in a kind of fateful lottery—a contest in which they are certain it will be *their* child who will be chosen to die.

Perhaps it is this essential pessimism I've often encountered in PICU parents—fueled by their natural anxiety—that helps to explain the subtle but gradual psychological distancing that can go on there. Sometimes, though, it will not be so subtle at all. It can seem as though a few parents are preparing to say goodbye. Preparing to bid farewell to their child—to the son or daughter they knew before all of this began. And in some extreme cases, it will appear as though a parent has said farewell very long before.

What most people don't realize is that—unlike adults—nearly eight out of every ten children who enter an intensive care unit survive to return home again, and usually within a relatively short period of time. Many of these survivors emerge from the PICU experience largely unscathed, at least in terms of major, long-term physical effects. They quickly seem to their parents, and to others who knew them well, as though nothing had really changed at all. This common outcome will seem nothing short of incredible to friends, neighbors and relatives. But most of all, it will feel like a miracle to their parents, who, unlike others, have firsthand knowledge of the electrified air of tension and dread that resides in such a place.

For the child, despite the often intense and sudden drama in the PICU, the days there can eventually be forgotten. Once the acute crisis period has receded, the ordeal will gradually become a time of terror placed comfortably in the past.

The physician I knew best in the PICU was Dr. Frederick Morris. I prefer to call him "Fred," for, in his most agreeable and humorous manner, that was what he was apt to tell anyone he met: "Just call me Fred!" Then, after a split-second pause, he would add with an impish grin: "Only my mother has to call me *Doctor* Morris . . . to keep her in her place!"

Most of us felt comfortable in his presence. The children in his care—after they came to know him—would smile when they saw him coming their way. This was somewhat unusual, since many children who are patients in a hospital actually become *more* anxious and afraid when they see doctors or nurses heading in their direction. They are afraid of the pain that such people must often bring.

Fred Morris was a highly trained critical-care doctor, specializing in the treatment of children in life-or-death situations. He was also an avid fan of jazz music. It may seem odd I recall *that* specific detail about him first, but it captured something essential about the man and about the nature of his work. He was a dabbler in jazz himself, having struggled over many years to master the saxophone. But it was the music itself that fascinated him—its spontaneity and the uncertain course jazz improvisation could so easily take.

And there was the fact that Dr. Fred Morris could draw interesting parallels for me, between the work he chose to do and his appreciation for jazz.

"You never really know what will come along next," he said to me one day, as we talked in the hallway outside the PICU.

"It might be a car accident victim with multiple contusions and lacerations—you know, a kid in the emergency room, bleeding all over like a stuck pig. Or it could be a little baby's head swelling up like a balloon." He opened up his two hands, creating an invisible sphere the size of a basketball.

"It might be one of the cancer kids coming out of remission and suddenly taking a nosedive." He motioned, his hand slicing downward through the air like a swimmer diving off a platform. "Or maybe a drowning . . . or a newborn with pneumonia."

He shook his head as he seemed to recall a few of the more dramatic cases and rescues he'd been involved in.

"Anything and everything can come in here, so I'm constantly improvising. 'Cause it's never the same—and yet, it's really *always* the same. You know what I mean?"

I didn't completely understand his analogy, for I had no intimate knowledge either of jazz or intensive-care medicine. But his interesting comparison between his job and playing jazz has stayed with me all the same.

"The principles are always there, you know. To be used over and over again. The basics of pathophysiology. Look, I'll show you." With that, he took a pen from my shirt pocket and scribbled a formula on a piece of scrap paper he held in his hand.

"Resistance equals pressure over flow," he said, as he wrote it out, holding the paper against the wall beside us. $R=P/F$, he'd scribbled down—a basic formula for measuring the rate of blood flow in a patient. This somehow made it all seem very simple and elegant.

"But with each one of these kids you can get a funny *riff*—a weird and funky variation on the theme. Something just doesn't go the way it should, ya' know?" he said, jabbing the pen back in my shirt pocket with a surgeon's perfect aim.

"And then the kid starts crashing down, and I'm left to improvise. You know, I have to make it up as I go along. That's the hardest part—knowing when to go a different way from the one I took before. To do it seat-of-the-pants and not just go by the book."

"So then you try something else, something different? Because it has a chance of working?" I asked.

"Yeah, right," he answered quickly. "'Cause when you've used all the tricks you know and they don't work, you're on your own, man. *Watch out!*" He said this last thing to startle me—and perhaps, to impress me with the sense of danger in his daily tasks.

"And *that's* when I hope I hit that note just right," he twiddled his fingers, as though he were playing his jazz saxophone. "*That's* when I hope to God I do it *exactly* right."

"But how do you know?" I asked. "I mean, how do you know if you've hit the note just right?"

"The kid starts perking up," he said happily, his hand rising up slowly like a bird caught in the currents of the sky.

"Now, I don't always know *why*, or even *how*, I did it exactly right. But I'll know I did it right. It'll just *feel* so right."

Fred smiled at me and seemed to savor just such a moment from his recent past. But then he looked me in the eye, and his expression changed completely.

"But sometimes I don't," he added, his hand moving down slowly to his side.

"In this place, I miss the note, the kid gets sicker just like that!" He snapped his fingers loudly. "The kid'll just die," he added sadly. "I *hate* it when one of 'em has to die."

■

"*Code blue canceled! Code blue canceled!*"

The woman's voice on the public address system was noticeably without emotion now, even lifeless. But her words transported me back to the here and now. The drama in the PICU had somehow ended, so I slowed my gait by half. Maybe it had been a mistake— Maggie Chessler *didn't* die just then! Or was it that she *did* die—before emergency resuscitation could be delivered? Then again, perhaps she had just bounced back from death. Such things did happen in that frenetic and uncertain place.

As I turned into the long hallway to the PICU, I found myself in keen anticipation. Since I was worried the code had been about Maggie, I recalled my visit with her mother the evening before in the PICU, as I prepared to leave the hospital.

"What's wrong with all these parents?" Mrs. Chessler had whispered to me—though there were actually no other parents in the PICU at the time.

I reacted with a quizzical look, since I really didn't know exactly what she'd meant.

"You know, why don't these kids get any visitors?" She motioned with her head in the direction of the little boy who'd fallen out his bedroom window.

I shrugged my shoulders as if it were a complete mystery—why no one had come to see him after the first few days following his unfortunate accident. I'd read the boy's name was Jason Marks. He was unconscious and considered brain dead. He'd been jumping on his bed for fun, but it was foolishly positioned directly in front of a large window. Young Jason had broken his neck and sustained massive internal injuries in the three-story fall to the concrete walk below his bedroom window.

It was mid-July, and it had been exceedingly hot that week, so even windows without screens had been opened wide in those houses in the city that went without air conditioning. Everyone in the PICU knew that summer was the season for children falling out of windows—just as the winter months predictably brought on the viruses and serious cases of secondary pneumonia. And so the arrival of that young boy of nine or ten had been seen as only one case in what was likely to become a seasonal epidemic.

But Mrs. Chessler was right. It did seem strange that young Jason lay there alone all night and day, with no loved ones to monitor his condition. The doctors and the nurses, of course, would check his vital signs every fifteen minutes.

"And what about *that* poor thing," Mrs. Chessler added—pointing furtively to the infant with the odd diagnosis of shaken-baby syndrome. She had no one with her, either, as she lay unconscious in the PICU. Since her case involved social services, I knew quite a lot about what had led up to that child's hospitalization. The results of extensive X rays had been typed up neatly and placed at the very front of her medical chart. I'd read them carefully the first day she arrived on the unit.

The findings of her CAT scan had been described in almost incomprehensible technical detail. The radiologist who interpreted the penetrating, high-tech photographs chronicled the aftermath of what he called "angular acceleration-deceleration effects" on the baby's brain. He went on to note the "diffuse subdural hematoma,"— many minuscule sites of bleeding that were peppered throughout the young child's gray matter. He remarked there had even been evidence of "white brain matter shearing"—a splitting off of sections of her neural flesh, the part of her body intended by nature to be hidden away and protected within her tiny skull.

Child abuse can take many forms, but this particular variation was primarily reserved for babies and small toddlers who could be easily picked up by their parents or caretakers and then shaken back and forth with little difficulty or real effort. The mother who had inflicted this upon her baby, we would come to find out later, had been frustrated by her child's endless crying. And, in the end, the baby had been violently shaken in a desperate attempt to end her shrill wail.

The infant's tiny shoulders had been gripped between her parent's adult arms, and the child was shaken so hard and long that her brain began to slide about, from side to side and back and forth within her skull, until the damage was done. After such a prolonged shaking, a baby's brain might bleed, though usually quite slowly. Or it might swell to twice its normal size—the result of a liquid substance produced by the body and intended to salve the injured tissues inside the head. Each of these subsequent conditions could lead to death or permanent brain damage.

Strangely, the first sign might be bleeding retinas—for the eyes are a kind of window to the brain. Using a technique called MRI, magnetic resonance imaging, to take pictures of the head, hospital personnel could detect a predictable and systematic pattern of tiny rips and bruises at the back of the eye and in the front of the brain. There was reason to suspect that there were many more shaken babies in the world than ever came to the attention of the medical profession. But the ones who ended up in intensive care and needed to be treated by a critical-care doctor were more likely to be the ones who were shaken first and then struck or thrown against a hard surface or object. The floor, perhaps, a wall, or the wooden side of their crib—whatever happened to be nearby, as their parent vented a rage upon them.

Mrs. Chessler interrupted my train of thought with yet another question about this child with shaken-baby syndrome.

"What kind of parent would do *that* to a baby?" She looked at me intently, as though I might actually have the answer.

I shook my head, to show I understood what she was asking, but didn't have a ready explanation. And, in the long run, speculation about the exact motivations and circumstances underlying child abuse were always somehow incomplete and failed to adequately account for this all too common situation.

Her question, though, reminded me of a father I had once evaluated who had done this same thing to his young child. He admitted to me that he found the whole thing unimaginable. He couldn't believe he had such power within him—power enough to cause such damage to his child.

"All I did was shake him—to get him to stop it! To get him to stop his damn crying," he pleaded. "I didn't know I was that strong. Strong enough to do *that* to the baby."

I'd felt some sympathy for him at that moment, thinking he knew regret and shame over the incredible harm he'd inflicted on his child. But that feeling vaporized in the next instant, as he nervously asked me: "This isn't going to get me into trouble, is it?"

"A lot of parents *do* visit," I finally said to Mrs. Chessler, and I motioned to the empty chair where that new mother had stood watch over her baby with meningitis. I knew she had left only briefly to get some dinner.

Meningitis was a relatively common problem in the PICU, since over thirty or forty children a year might contract the more serious form of bacterial meningitis and end up being treated in the hospital soon after delivery. That tiny newborn was almost always asleep, despite the noisy monitors situated around his enclosed metallic crib.

His mother would typically be sitting there beside him, staring off into space. Except when the nurses could coax her to take a short break.

"I just don't understand it," Mrs. Chessler said. "I never would have believed it if I hadn't seen it for myself. Every time Maggie and I are here in the PICU, it's the same—these poor kids don't seem to have anyone at all! It just makes me want to cry."

She shook her head again in confusion and disapproval. She was sincerely empathetic to the sick and lonely children situated around her. But then she showed insight into the matter, by drawing an analogy between this incomprehensible pattern and her own husband's failure to visit Maggie more than once or twice during the entire time she'd been in the hospital.

"Well, maybe it's too hard for them to come here," she offered. "It *can* be a pretty scary place. With all the alarms and buzzers and the bloody kids that come in through those doors."

She looked toward the large, automatic entryway to the PICU and seemed to remember one or two of the more dramatic cases brought into the unit during her long vigil at Maggie's bedside.

"And *my* husband, for example," she added. "Now he's got this thing about hospitals, you know."

"What *thing?*" I asked her, since I had long been curious about the mysterious Mr. Chessler.

"Well, he says he's afraid if he sets foot in the place it'll bring Maggie a dose of bad luck." She chuckled at the flimsiness of his rationale. "But it's really just that he can't take it, don't you see. He can't take seeing her there so sick—and the effects of the radiation and chemo just . . . well, it just knocks him down, so to speak."

I nodded my head as if I understood, though I thought she was being a bit too kind. I think she suspected I might feel that way, because she went on to state a stronger case on his behalf.

"He loves Maggie *very* much," she said calmly, for she believed that with all her heart. "But he gets real upset when he thinks she might . . . well, when he thinks she might leave us. It makes him kind of . . . well, kind of crazy." She looked toward Maggie, who was sleeping soundly, and above her, to the monitor that registered the beating of her young heart. "He calls her every single day, you know!" she added as an afterthought.

194

"Sometimes I worry about *him* the most," she whispered gravely. "Maggie and I—well, we've kind of come to grips with this thing. But my husband, I think he would just rather pretend everything's going to be fine and the family will get back to normal. But when Maggie has a turn for the worse—or she has to come back into the hospital for another treatment—he's like a man possessed."

"Possessed?" I echoed back.

"Well, he just starts doing all these chores and projects around the house—anything to get his mind off her illness. It's sad sometimes, I mean, it's sad the crazy things he comes up with that need doing, because he can't really talk about what he's feeling, or what he's really afraid of. He keeps busy just so he can be doing something besides thinking about his Maggie dying."

"I guess everyone has their own way of dealing with the bad things in their life," I responded weakly.

"Oh, you men are *all* big babies," Mrs. Chessler said with a chuckle. "Things like death and dishes—and especially sick children—are more than you can take."

I laughed, too—though her words rang sadly true.

"How's your husband taking all of this now?" I asked, "I mean, Maggie's latest relapse?" Mrs. Chessler had offered me the opportunity to learn about an important part of Maggie's life that I'd previously not been allowed to explore.

"Oh, he's a little better this week," Mrs. Chessler responded. "I talked with him earlier today on the phone." She looked down to the floor meekly. "He said he'd try to get to the hospital this Saturday—if she ends up having to stay over the weekend. Of course, we all know he won't." As she said this, I think she observed a connection between her husband, on the one hand, and our brief discussion of parents who never visited their children in the hospital on the other.

"But he really doesn't *have* to visit," she finally said. "Maggie and I understand it's hard for him to see her like this." She looked over to the abused, unconscious baby girl lying in the next bed.

"He loves her very much."

I must admit that there does appear to be a discernible pattern—one that can be unsettling and difficult to understand when first encountered. There's a tendency I've noted, though I have no statistics to prove it, for more than a few fathers to *not* regularly visit their sick children in the hospital.

I don't think this is because they do not love them, or that they love them any less than a more obviously devoted parent might. Nor do I think the reverse—that they somehow care for their children *too* much and the prospect of losing them is so incapacitating that they are too depressed or frightened to visit.

Instead—for some men, anyway—I think it is because of a kind of panic that overwhelms them when they are in hospitals. And for a few, this intense anxiety can strike them even as they *think* about their children becoming ill.

When the fathers do not visit, I am left only to imagine the fear of death and their children's mortality in their faces and to try to understand it if I am able. Usually I will hear they are at work, keeping even longer hours than they did before their child's crisis first occurred. I suppose work can be a kind of coping mechanism for men— a way of doing something, anything, while they wait to know the worst.

One insightful young father had told me that, when his little boy underwent surgery for a serious heart condition, he *deliberately* buried himself in his work, to keep hold of the sense that he was somehow effectual. He said he needed to sustain the feeling that he mattered in all of this, even if it only meant making a little extra money for his family. He said he felt without power and useless, sitting day after day at his sick child's bedside.

This pattern of fathers' not visiting their children can be especially evident in the pediatric intensive care unit, where the life-and-death struggle is all the more striking. And, since the PICU is a place for the very sickest children, who may be unconscious or the focus of the most aggressive medical interventions, there can be a tendency for others as well as fathers not to visit.

For example, even though I cared about Maggie Chessler, there would be times I might walk right past her bed in the PICU. As I reflect on my reactions to her case, I can recall almost trying to *avoid* spending too much time with her, as she lay there deathly ill. I'd read about this phenomenon in a medical textbook once, about the known pattern in families, as well as among medical staff members, to unconsciously avoid too much contact with a dying child or other patient. When I read about it, though, I never imagined *I* might also fall victim to this unfortunate quirk in human behavior.

But where did this originate? A fear of death? And was it *Maggie's* death, or my own? Or was it related to the fleeting nightmares all parents have, about what might happen if one of their children became gravely ill or died? All I knew for certain was the palpable anxiety *I* felt each time I encountered Maggie in the PICU, as she moved closer to her death.

Is it possible my anxiety, aroused by that terminally ill child, was, in turn, related to the behavior I've observed in some parents of hospitalized children? And could it have something to do with all the parents I've *never* met—the ones who just don't come at all? If *my* child were seriously ill, would I be like the men whose visits are so brief, who seem like shadows moving through the place?

That was what Maggie's father had been like, beginning soon after her disease was first diagnosed. But I was in no position to judge him, for I was strangely uncertain just how *I* might react in Mr. Chessler's miserable situation.

■

As I moved closer to the PICU doors, I suspected Fred Morris would be on call that day. He was always at his post. And so I expected to see him first as I entered the place.

Oddly, I recalled now that Fred had majored in English literature in college. His particular interest was poetry. I suppose my initial surprise on learning this was partly based on the fact that he was so immersed, day to day, in the *physical* problems of human beings. His work, after all, involved the acute medical crises of the very sick children under his care.

I knew that his particular subspecialty used a fixed number of very pragmatic medical procedures to sustain children's lives. And Fred would appear to perform them routinely, with honed skills that derived from years of advanced medical training and clinical practice.

He'd learned what are called *invasive medical procedures*—emergency techniques that could easily make a layperson wince or faint.

These procedures could cause even other medical staff to be quite uneasy, for they might be unaccustomed to seeing such heroic and desperate procedures performed on the smallest of children.

For example, some observers would be forced to look away as Fred inserted a *Swann-Ganz catheter* into a young child. This common procedure entails placing a needle, called an *introducer*, into the child's subclavian vein—a blood vessel located in the chest just below the right shoulder. This would become an entry point for a journey into the child's beating heart. A long piece of flexible, clear tubing would then be threaded into the vein and slowly worked along until it reached through the child's right ventricle, ending at the pulmonary artery. The catheter tube, when in place, would be used to monitor the blood flow and measure the heart's efficiency. The knowledge this type of monitoring device provided could be crucial in caring for critically ill children.

I recall that Fred had a way of performing that particular procedure in a kind of rough-and-ready but graceful manner. He would lift the younger child up ever so slightly, if he could, and then lay him or her down flat again. He'd gently slap the entry site with his sterilized gloved hand—as if to warn the body he was coming in. Or perhaps to distract a conscious child from the shock or pain of the needle's entry. I really never knew which.

The needle would be inserted quickly, often with some amount of blood produced as it entered. Fred would insert the catheter with one strong and confident push, then slowly wiggle it in and slide it toward the heart.

The sight of intensive-care procedures could be upsetting, for doctors and nurses might handle a child in what could easily seem to the observer to be a harsh and almost insensitive manner, not at all the way that children *should* be handled.

"Doesn't that hurt him?" a young medical student had once asked Fred nervously, as she watched him perform this procedure on a tiny baby boy. "I mean, it seems unnecessarily rough."

"*Dying* might hurt him more," Fred had answered quickly, undistracted from his delicate task.

"Besides, if you think *this* is bad, you should see a circumcision," he added with a hearty laugh—loud enough to wake the dead.

"Now with *that* little piece of business they just strap those poor bastards down. And they don't give 'em any anesthesia, either. They just slice it off—snip, snip, snip . . . 1, 2, 3"—he motioned with his fingers—"and with *no damn ceremony whatsoever!*"

Fred had looked up at the medical student just then, to gauge whether his words had any effect. Her delicate sensibilities—at least as they pertained to the handling of little children—had been disturbed by what she'd seen, and so she persisted. I could tell she might also be trying to figure out if critical-care medicine was a specialty she could ever hope to master.

"But *when* do you get used to it? I mean, when do you get used to handling a child like *that?*" she asked him. "Do you have to *forget* they're children?"

Fred paused, then slowly looked up at her again.

"When I forget they're kids, I quit this fuckin' job," he said somberly. "'Cause then, *I* might as well be dead."

This interesting man had also been trained to master an array of elaborate and complex electromechanical devices. They would be situated around and within the small bodies of his patients, continually spewing out numerical and graphic data. Such machines and monitors produced a cacophony of odd sounds, a bizarre symphony only the trained medical ear could hope to disentangle.

Those monitors were especially daunting in the case of a newborn baby, perhaps an infant such as the one I had seen only the day before in the PICU, for the large and noisy machines dwarfed the tiny patient. Fred Morris had the strangest ability to detect extremely subtle changes in the complex, auditory world of the PICU.

Once, as I watched him lecture to a small group of physicians-in-training, he suddenly pricked up his ears to a sound that no one else had heard. His mind seemed to be translating a single noise—almost like a nuance in a foreign dialect—and then analyzing its particular meaning within an instant. This reminded me of a quirky and obsessive ethologist I once met. She had lived among an exotic species of animal for many years and, for anyone who cared to listen, she could mimic the peculiar animal sounds she'd learned and then explain what each one meant.

But, of all things, Fred's first love had been *Poetry?* Most of his competitors for acceptance to medical school would have majored in the "hard" sciences, like biology or chemistry. And perhaps a few in mathematics. The admissions committee members must have been curious about his motivation to get into medical school. Would he attempt to bring humanism into the largely pragmatic world of the life sciences? Did he think his abstract knowledge of the language would help him save human lives?

Then again, they might simply have viewed him as a scattered sort of genius—which was what he was, of course.

One day I was moved to ask him, "Do you ever get to use poetry in your work?" He smiled as though he knew what I was after.

"No, no, no!" he said emphatically. "That stuff'll get me in *real* trouble here. I stopped thinking of myself as a poet the first day I spent in emergency medicine."

"Why do you say that?" It hadn't been the answer I was expecting. I couldn't believe he'd abandoned this passion so abruptly.

"If I spend too much time thinking about things like why *I'm* alive when some of these kids have to die, I wouldn't last a week in this job."

"I know what you mean; other doctors have told me the same thing. Like the ones who deal with cancer. They say they try to put it out of their minds—the unfairness, the lack of reason. And especially when it comes to children."

"Most of my kids do OK now. It's the ones that lie there day and night, just staring at the ceiling, with no one to talk to but me and the nurses—they're the ones that get to me. They never prepared me for *that* lesson in life. You know, the one about the parents who never visit." He seemed genuinely sad as he said these final words.

"Yeah, that was a surprise for me, too," I said. "And I'm supposed to *understand* human behavior."

"Well, maybe *you* better not think about it too much, either," he said, laughing.

But then he moved closer to me. "You know what *really* gets to me, though? Sometimes I look at a kid coming into the unit, and they'll resemble one of my own kids. And just for a second or two I think: *Hey! That's my kid they're wheeling in here!* And then I start shaking. I'm a friggin' basket case! I can totally lose my edge! It's like I get this wave of panic, you know? It just hits me like a truck!"

He shuddered visibly, and it seemed as though he was reliving one such moment. I thought this to be a rather remarkable admission of vulnerability for such a seasoned rescuer of little children. But I also knew him to be a sensitive and loving father to several children of his own.

"This probably sounds crazy to you, but sometimes I'll even go out and call my wife. You know, just to make sure they're all right. It's really weird, man," he added, "this *power* kids have over their parents."

"It's like you sort of, well, you just *panic?*" I asked.

"You bet it's panic! Whew!" he sighed. "That's when I think about hanging it all up. You know, just spending time in bars for the rest of my life."

"I don't understand," I said. "What would make you quit?"

"Well, somehow I can take this stuff when it happens to other people's kids—you know, *strangers'* kids. But I don't know what I'd do if it ever happened to my own. I think that would do me in."

Uncomfortable with the moment, he sought a way to end our conversation. "Sometimes I think these parents are the scum of the earth," he said. "You know—the ones who never visit."

Then he paused a second to reconsider.

"But how do I know *I* might not do the same—I mean, if it was *my* kid lying in the PICU?"

■

"So what's the story, Fred?" I asked nervously, as I finally arrived at the unit. I quickly scanned the entire space, but as I did, I somehow failed to pick up any specific details. It all became a blur.

"Hi-ya, Billy-boy!" he greeted me, as though there was no reason for alarm. He patted me on the back, in his strong and reassuring manner.

"I heard the code. What happened? Who was it?" I asked again. I thought I said it calmly.

"Relax, my friend, relaaaxxx," he glibly said, putting an arm around me and moving his face closer to my ear.

"*I hit the note on that one,*" he whispered proudly. A broad grin broke across his face. An odd sort of poet, I thought silently.

And then off he ran through the PICU doors, en route to the emergency room to deal with some life-or-death disaster.

As I looked around the unit to determine just who had "coded" only a few minutes before, I noticed the young boy who'd fallen through his bedroom window. He was situated off in one corner of the largest unit room, still unconscious. His monitors seemed lifeless, too. The dull inactivity of the machines encircling him hinted his brain was gone, at least the parts of it that had made him who he was. Maybe *this* was what his parents had sensed, as well, for again there was no one with him in that dark and lonely corner.

I turned to Maggie's bed, and she was there, trying to read a book. She managed to offer me a wave and a slight smile, and so did her mother, who sat beside her with quiet determination.

I felt reassured. Maggie *was* still alive, though I knew her time was running out. But it wouldn't be today. At least, I hoped it wouldn't be today.

I would find out later that it *was* Maggie who had been pulled away from death and into life again. It had been an unexpected cardiac arrhythmia, instantly detected by the heart monitor situated at her side. Her heart had dangerously skipped several beats, but Fred had managed to set it right by administering immediate resuscitation and several powerful medications.

Now she simply sat there, as though nothing at all had happened. Which may seem odd, but Maggie had been that close several times before.

The newborn infant with meningitis? There he was, asleep again, his young mother at her station. She waited anxiously for him to awaken from his limbo state. I wondered how long she was willing to wait before she might somehow begin to distance herself from this child, a child she never truly had the opportunity to know as a person.

But where was the *other* girl? The baby shaken so violently by her mother? Where was *she* today?

Her space was taken over by a much larger child, an older girl I didn't know.

"She died last night," the nurse called out to me, as though she had been watching my every move and had easily read my thoughts.

"Sometimes one of them has to die," she added calmly, but with compassion and a sense of resignation in her voice.

"Sometimes one of them has to die," she repeated quietly to herself.

"Who was with her?" I asked, though I already knew the answer. This was a question I would often ask, when a child I knew had died in the PICU.

The nurse just shook her head as if to say "no one" and then looked back down to the medical chart in front of her.

The poet Edna St. Vincent Millay wrote that "Childhood is the kingdom where nobody dies." But her next line of verse was more telling: "Nobody that matters, that is . . ." I knew this was just a poet's license, and she'd written these words with a different meaning in mind. It is her *second* phrase that haunts me now.

"Nobody who matters . . ." she said.

Were they the ones I have encountered? The children who are left to die alone, or in the company of strangers. Are they the children whose parents and friends have somehow already said goodbye—and so very long before?

But then again, there are so many more parents who faithfully remain beside their children, as Maggie's mother did. I would hazard to say that there are even certain cases in which the child whose life is threatened by disease or trauma will, in fact, be valued *more* than when they were healthy or intact. We adults *do* have this unfortunate tendency sometimes to take the most important things in our lives for granted.

I'm reminded of a cliché I've heard again and again, used by the parents I know whose children have come very close to death. They'll say, "You don't really appreciate them until you might lose them."

And I recall one father in particular, whose young child had survived a battle with leukemia. He said something similar to what Dr. Fred Morris had told me one day in the PICU.

"I never realized the *power* children have over their parents," he said in awe. I already knew that the intense experience with his child's disease had brought him to a time of sobering self-reflection. "That power is really scary."

■

Maggie Chessler died at the age of thirteen years. She peacefully succumbed to her disease at home, with her family by her side. In death, she was the same extraordinary person I had come to know several years before. I was told she even joked and told stories with her parents and relatives only hours before she passed away.

From among the collection of her poems—the verses she composed while in the hospital—I've saved a few to remind me of Maggie. The nurses who had been impressed by her writing had typed them up, mimeographed copies and stapled them together in booklet form. They remain, for me, keepsakes of a very special child.

In her poem about death she wrote:

> There is no reason to fear the end,
> For everyone has got to die.
> It's life that we are given,
> Like birds, we have to fly.

T H E   C L A S S   O F   ' 6 3

What I had not foreseen
Was the gradual day
Weakening the will
Leaking the brightness away.

— S T E P H E N   S P E N D E R

IN MY WORK WITH CHILDREN and their parents, a common theme has been the loss of a dream. The loss of the dream that is a person's child.

It's quite clear to me by now, despite what they might say to the contrary, that the private imaginings and personal ambitions of many parents depend on the lives of their children. I think this may be one of the reasons why offspring appear to be the recipients of such intense and unrelenting love from their parents, for to love one's child is, in some ways, to love oneself.

From a darker perspective, this provides at least a partial explanation for how children can sometimes become the target of their parents' self-serving or aggressive impulses. Most children cannot hope to facilitate the realization of their parents' lifelong dreams and ambitions. At least, not right away. If this is to happen at all, it typically involves a gradual process, a lengthy period during which parents can nurture their own dreams through the life of their child. But some children will never be able to fulfill their parents' expectations.

Because dreams take considerable time to realize, there is a need for making plans. But when these plans are altered in some unexpected way, or when they must be abandoned altogether because of unforeseen circumstances, parents can experience powerful psychological responses, reactions that can surprise in their intensity and are revealing of the deeper psychological value of children to their adults. The loss of the idealized child or the failure of the parents' dreams can be a psychological event that will transform the very nature of adult life.

When I think about the dreams of parents—and more generally about the psychological meaning of the child in adult life—I cannot help but remember Elliot and Grace Mason and the story of their son, William. For them, the introduction of the unexpected and the loss of their idealized child was not at all a sudden event or an abrupt process. It was far more gradual than was true for most of the other children and families I've known, the ones who endured traumatic events or the onset of some psychological or physical illness.

The Masons' story, by virtue of the fact that most of the critical events were placed in their past, revealed to me much more subtle aspects of parent-child relations. In some ways, their tale is the most revealing of the many I have considered. For it taught me about the compounding power of the child across the wider span of adult life.

It was a busy time in the emergency room that first day I met Mr. and Mrs. Mason and their son, William. I'd been called down from my office and away from my scheduled appointments for the day to help a family in crisis. Or so I'd been told. This was not a usual event for me, since most emergency situations will be handled adequately by the physicians and nurses. After all, they are in the business of knowing what to do when things look their very worst. They specialize in keeping cool heads when everyone around them seems to be falling apart.

The staff in the ER hardly ever needed to call outsiders to handle a problem, so I suspected from the beginning this might be an extraordinary case. And perhaps a case where I too might be limited in my ability to help these people in crisis. The nurse who called had told me simply that it was a parent-child problem, and she'd hung up the phone before I could ask any questions. That was often the way things were done in emergency medical settings—the staff of doctors and nurses would take care of one situation, then quickly move on to the next. So I didn't know what the actual problem would be with the Mason family.

Would it be a child abuse case? Perhaps it would be yet another adolescent suicide attempt, or a verbal threat to self-destruct. Those were among the most common psychological or social problems of children seen in medical emergency rooms.

As I entered the ER, the nurse who'd called rushed over and handed me a medical chart. "They're in Room Two!" she exclaimed, as she quickly turned around and went in another direction.

"This one threw us a curve," she added as she jogged back to the other patients waiting for her down the hall. "We thought we'd call the *child* psychologist to help out," she added with a little chuckle.

I opened the medical chart and began to read the first page, since the face sheet would contain essential information about the family. It is my custom to find out how old a child is first, before I do anything else. That one piece of knowledge allows me to prepare my overall approach to any clinical problem, an approach that will be geared to the developmental levels of the child and to the potential issues of the parents I will see. I checked the date of birth at the top right section of the face sheet. I'd become facile at calculating exact ages based on the date of birth. But this one made me look twice.

William Mason was born . . . wait a minute, there must be a mistake. His chart said *1937*! That would make him over fifty years old!

A grown man? That can't be right—it must have been an error made by a hasty nurse, or a clerk's typo during admission to the ER. But when I gazed further down on the sheet, to the very brief description of the presenting problem scribbled there, I realized there'd been no mistake.

"Elder abuse by adult son," was all they'd written.

As with any case of the unexpected, I begrudgingly let go of my prescient vision of the Mason family. This had been an image based upon memories of all the families I'd seen before, and on a latent sense of definition about myself and what it was exactly I was doing there. My expectations were now replaced by a blank—I had so little experience with this sort of situation—and I suddenly found it difficult to imagine the Masons at all. But they would still be sitting there in Room Two, despite my lack of preparation, waiting for some unknown doctor to appear.

The nurse had written *elder abuse*, and I now knew this *child* named William would be almost my age. He wouldn't be actively violent, though, because then the ER staff wouldn't have left him alone in the same room with his parents. In my mind, I quickly reviewed some "facts" about the presenting problem, which is a habit I've developed over the years, especially when I encounter an unusual or extraordinary case.

I knew, for example, that the abuse of older parents by their adult children was said to be a growing problem, brought on in part by the mere fact that so many of the elderly were living longer than ever before and by the tendency for more older people to stay at home or with their adult children, rather than enter expensive or substandard nursing homes.

Although abuse of the elderly had probably been a problem for many years in our society, it was just now coming into view. Many felt it was even worsening as a result of social and economic factors. In my area of the country, for example, a survey of social service agencies that systematically investigated such cases found a one hundred percent increase in elder abuse, as compared with only three or four years before. The writers of that report estimated this would represent only about ten percent of the entire problem, since there was a strong and natural reluctance on the part of the elderly to report the abuse or neglect, or even to seek help from others outside the family.

As a group, older parents tended to live quietly with the abuse and neglect they received from their adult children. After all, the consequences of a formal investigation could lead to changes the older person might abhor, such as being placed involuntarily in a nursing home. Or, if they couldn't be placed, they might suffer from reprisals or retribution from the abusing child, as the legal and social service systems moved along at a snail's pace.

Many caseworkers who were familiar with this problem had pointed out how difficult it seemed for parents to admit their child was hurting them, a psychological barrier that inadvertently protected many abusers of elderly parents. It appeared to be an extremely powerful influence, since national statistics on elder abuse suggested more than half of all known cases were discovered and reported by people other than the victims themselves.

I entered Room Two with some trepidation, for I sensed I would be navigating through uncharted waters. Although the nurse who originally called me had probably reasoned this to be essentially another case of parent-child conflict, I suspected that very little of my prior training or experience would prepare me for this clinical encounter. I was not trained in thinking about adult children and parents in the same terms as I might use to describe their relationships during the early periods of human development. In fact, in my entire field relatively little was really known about the nature of the ongoing parent-child relationship once it had passed into the child's adult years, at least not in any scientific sense. We simply hadn't framed questions about this relationship as a direct extension of childhood or adolescence. It was as though the parent-child relationship somehow ended, or ceased to be of interest, when the child came of age.

As I opened the door, the first person who came into view was Mrs. Mason. Her first name was Grace, and it captured much about her outward appearance. She was nicely dressed, her hair arranged neatly, suggesting regular visits to the beauty parlor. She had a serene face, and my first association to the sight of her was to think how much she seemed a "grand" lady. She reminded me of Eleanor Roosevelt, of all people, in the way she sat there so noble and unbowed, despite the present circumstances and her immediate surroundings.

Once I'd fully entered the room I was able to quickly view Mr. Mason and their son, William. The elder man was also formally dressed, in a suit that seemed out of date but well preserved. His appearance also had a rather stately, aged look, for he wore a bulky tie that had long ago gone out of fashion. Like his suit, he seemed to be of an earlier time—say, the late forties or the early fifties—and he was a man who managed to convey some essential but ineffable quality of a time before.

Together, Mr. Mason and his wife made an elegant though faded couple.

Their son, William, on the other hand, seemed entirely out of place with the elder Masons. Where they were courtly, he was slovenly and unkempt. And there was the disagreeable manner in which he sloppily lounged across a small chair in the corner of that tiny room designed for only a doctor and a patient. We were four grown adults compressed into a small medical cubicle. But William's odd visage seemed to make the situation even more tense, and his introverted behavior forced the rest of us to shift somewhat uncomfortably—and in the opposite direction.

The Masons stared directly at me, anticipating my greeting. Their son, however, gazed downward to the floor, apparently brooding over the current situation. He seemed irritated about being in the ER, and somehow I knew he'd had dealings with people like me before, people who were sent to help him, or the experts who'd counseled his parents about what they might do whenever problems began to surface.

I introduced myself, extending my hand to Mrs. Mason. She took it gently into her own, smiling politely as she did. I moved to greet Mr. Mason, and he stood up as quickly as he could from where he'd been sitting, smoothing his gray suit and clearing his throat. It seemed as though he was about to say something formal. But his standing so abruptly had been a physically demanding task for this seventy-year-old man. He tried to conceal its effects from me, but his breath became more rapid as he began to speak.

"Hello, Doctor," he said, extending his trembling hand. "I'm Elliot Mason, this is my wife Grace. And this is William, our son."

Mr. Mason then stayed standing, since there were only three chairs in the room and he wasn't sure it would be polite for him to sit. He struck me as a man who had typically risen to the occasion in his life, had met things head-on, standing firm. But now his frail appearance made him seem almost propped up there in front of me. I assured him I was perfectly comfortable, as I leaned against the exam table placed up against the wall. So, eventually, he lowered himself slowly back into his chair and sighed with relief.

"Can you tell me what the problem is here?" I asked. "The chart doesn't really say too much, I'm afraid."

"Well, I'm not surprised," Mr. Mason replied, with some irritation in his voice. "When we told them why we were here they just put us in this room and left." He glanced quickly to William in the corner, who was now mumbling something to himself. "I think they were at a loss for what to do with us, at least that was my impression." He looked over to his wife for her opinion, but she sat frozen and offered none. "Maybe we should just go home now," he added meekly.

I felt the need to take the blame for the delay myself.

"They were waiting for me to come down to talk with you," I said. "I'm sorry it took so long. But I am here now and I'd like you to tell me why you've come to the emergency room." I addressed my question to Mr. and Mrs. Mason primarily, but I heard William mumble something in response.

"What was that?" I said, directing my question to the younger man.

"He said I overreacted, Doctor," Mrs. Mason replied, having translated her son's unintelligible remark for me. "To make a long story short," she continued, "we're afraid of our son, Doctor. We're afraid he might hurt us." With these words, William sat up in his chair and bristled with anger.

"You're *afraid* of your son?" I inquired. "Can you tell me more about that?" I quickly scanned both parents for the telltale signs of physical abuse. It seemed the thing to do, since it was something I'd learned to do with the children I'd seen over the years, especially when there was any mention of violence or the fear of it. But I could detect no evidence of abuse. I knew that this was only a cursory evaluation, though, and the consequences of most human violence couldn't be seen at a glance.

"We're getting on in years now, Doctor, and we can't do a lot of the things we used to be able to do," Mr. Mason said. "So it seems like we've needed to rely on William a bit more than before. And I'm not sure he can handle it," he added, now looking to his wife. I could see the pain in both their faces and guessed it was because they were un-accustomed to depending upon their son—or on *anyone* but them-selves.

"We don't like to burden him, Doctor," Mrs. Mason said. "Neither one of us feels that's right. But we have so few choices now. And he *is* living with us."

William remained mute—his eyes fixed upon one particular tile in the floor of that tiny cold exam room. Every now and then I would hear him mumbling to himself, and not at all for my benefit.

His wife having broken the ice, Mr. Mason assumed the role of the leader in our discussion, telling me it was the police who had actually brought them to the hospital. He told me that Mrs. Mason had called 911 when she became afraid that William might harm him, for they'd been arguing back and forth most of that day. William's father had asked him to help him rake the leaves, which had built up in rotting piles, scattered on the lawn around their home. The elder man had told his son he was willing to do the raking, but he needed William to bag the leaves and carry them to the sidewalk for removal.

William had refused—as he'd refused many other requests his parents had made before. But *this* time Mr. Mason persisted, he explained, because of his embarrassment over the unsightly appearance of his home, sinking gradually into disrepair. It was difficult for me to envision Mr. Mason badgering his son in the way he described, for he seemed too feeble and, in some ways, much too civilized a man. But his home must have represented the way things had been long before, when the Masons were in their prime.

The police officers who responded to the call hadn't felt comfortable just leaving all three of them alone. Since it was just another domestic dispute to the investigating officers, and no crime had actually been committed, they couldn't bring the Masons to the police station. Instead, they dropped them off at the hospital emergency room—a magnet for all sorts of cases involving marital and family violence.

Mr. Mason went on to tell me about the problems he and his wife had been having with William during the past three years, since he'd returned to his childhood home. Unmarried and chronically unemployed, this middle-aged man was now completely dependent upon his parents financially and had no real social life of his own. As he listened to his father's words, I could tell that William was growing more irritable. But I also sensed he wouldn't do or say very much while he was there. Not in the hospital, that is, and not while there were other people around.

And, his father told me, William just seemed to *threaten* to do violence when he became upset, or when he was confronted by his parents. Usually he would yell and slam doors, or throw things in the house. Only a few times had he resorted to any sort of physical violence against his parents—once or twice shoving his father out of his way and occasionally grabbing his arm in a threatening manner. But William had managed to control his seemingly explosive temper and hadn't physically abused his parents up until then. Yet for some reason *this* time had been different, for Mrs. Mason had never called the authorities before about William's occasional outbursts. *This* time her son had seriously frightened her in a way he had not in any previous episode.

After getting the sense that William wouldn't talk to me with his parents present, I asked if they could go into the waiting area for a while. They seemed grateful to escape the room, with the four of us in such close quarters, and thankful to put some distance between themselves and their brooding adult son. I situated myself in a chair adjacent to William. He hadn't looked me in the eye during the entire time I'd been speaking with his parents. Even as I sat next to him he chose to stare off into a corner.

"It's your turn to tell me your side of things, William," I said calmly. "You've heard what your mother and father have to say about the problems at home. Do you have anything to say at all?" I paused to give him time to consider my question, and as I did, he fidgeted in his chair, again mumbling something barely audible.

"Do you have anything you'd like to say?" I tried again. "I would really like to hear your view of things."

He raised his head slightly, pointing the side of his head in my direction, his gaze still averted from my own. This motion reminded me of one or two blind children I'd known in the past and the way they would talk to me with a sideways glance, a compensating behavior for their lack of vision. They'd seldom position their head face front and in my direction as we talked. Instead, they would tilt their heads subtly, as if to use their sense of hearing as the primary means for gathering information about the immediate social world.

"I just want to get out of here," he whispered angrily, as though he were trying to convince me he might lose all control at any moment. Somehow, though, I knew he wouldn't, and this was only an attempt to frighten me. I sensed he was much more afraid of me than I could be of him. Indeed, he was like a younger boy, relatively defenseless against me, the more powerful adult figure.

"Before you can go home, William, we have to be sure that no one is going to get hurt at your house," I said. "Do you understand why the police came? And why they brought you here to the hospital?"

"I don't need to be in a hospital!" he said firmly. "Even the other doctors said that. They told my parents that a long time ago." He shifted back and forth in his chair, and his head moved once quickly from left to right, so he could change position without looking at me directly. As he did this, though, our eyes met for just an instant. He looked frightened of me and of the place itself.

"What *other* doctors?" I asked, although I had a feeling I knew what this was about.

"The ones my parents took me to when I was a kid. When I was in high school. They were like you—psychiatrists or something. Shrinks! All you shrinks look alike, you know!" he said, although I wondered how long he'd actually been able to look any of these people directly in the face.

"What did those other doctors say about you," I asked him.

"The same thing all you shrinks say about somebody who doesn't fit in with everybody else," he responded angrily. "They said I was a weirdo."

"What do you think I should tell your parents?" I asked. "They don't seem to know whether or not you're going to do something to them. Do you think you're going to do anything like hurt them, or break anything? Are you planning to do something like that when you get home?"

He looked down at the same tile in the floor, suggesting our brief conversation might be winding down.

"No . . . I'm not going to hurt anyone," he whimpered. "I just want to go back to my house. I want to go in my room and be left alone. None of this would've happened if they'd just let me stay in my room."

He seemed sadder now, less angry, for I think he must have realized I wasn't afraid. He seemed to be trying to convince me now that the problem could be so easily corrected, if only his parents wouldn't place unreasonable demands on him.

Following a brief evaluation of the dangerousness of the situation, and after consultation with the social service workers in the emergency room, I knew there was little we could do about the Masons there and then. No one had actually been hurt, for example, and William was not expressing the active intention or desire to harm his parents or himself. And the "crisis" was judged too minor for immediate or formal attention from the psychiatric emergency services or any of the social agencies that might intervene.

Mr. and Mrs. Mason were both physically able and mentally competent to decide whether or not they would go home with their adult son, which is what they eventually did. As they left, they apologized to the medical staff for the inconvenience. It almost seemed as though they regretted ever calling the police in the first place. After time had passed since Mrs. Mason's feeling that her husband was in some danger and the crisis had subsided, it seemed less important somehow. As though it *had* been an overreaction. But Mrs. Mason's fear had been real and intense at the moment she'd experienced it. I wondered how *this* event had come to be seen as different, for William had threatened them many times before.

A physician friend of mine had once told me that there were very few true medical emergencies and that the majority of the time the things we feel immediately threaten our lives are actually false alarms, or they're things that can easily wait a day or two, despite our sense of urgency. That was the way our initial encounter with the Masons had been handled, as a little crisis embedded within a much larger problem—a problem that would take more time to understand, let alone to change. It was a situation that had taken many years to develop and might take many more to resolve.

And so, like other people with psychosocial problems who are seen in a medical emergency room, the Masons were sent home with several appointment cards. An appointment to see a caseworker at the Department of Social Services, who would investigate the situation. An appointment to meet with the Elders Advocate in their region. And an appointment to see me for a follow-up visit in my outpatient office the following week. I asked if they were willing to come talk with me again, to give me more time to understand the situation. They agreed; at least Mr. and Mrs. Mason said they'd come, and they said they would bring William if he was willing. I had too many unanswered questions just to let them walk out of the ER. And I suspected they had questions that needed answers as well.

■

As I prepared for a follow-up visit with the Masons, I went over what I remembered about their case. My first visit with them in the emergency room—compressed in time and space—had served to point out some of the details of families characterized by the problem of elder abuse.

First, the threat of any real abuse was more likely to derive from the psychological problems of the potential abuser and *not* from the parents' growing dependency on the adult child. In years past, several articles in the professional journals had suggested it was the growing burden on the caretakers that provided the motivation for

abuse and neglect of the elderly. More recently, though, better studies had shown—as in cases of battered women or abused children—
that such abuse was more likely to result from the personal problems
of the perpetrators and not from any qualities peculiar to the victims
themselves. Not, that is, except for the fact that the elderly, women
and children can be easy, convenient targets for their aggressors.

I knew William had a diagnosable psychiatric disorder, and my initial impression was that it would be *characterologic*—the vernacular
term for the fact that he just was the way he was and was not likely to
ever change. My initial evaluation had turned up no real evidence or
history of a psychosis or a marked loss in William's ability to know reality, as is the case with the schizophrenic or paranoid patient, and, my
impression was that he wouldn't be violent at home. At least not yet.

I didn't doubt William's parents would keep their appointment, as
promised. But as I walked toward the waiting area, I wondered if
William would be there as well. At first, when I didn't see him, I assumed he'd stayed at home. But I did notice that Mr. and Mrs. Mason
had arrived on time and were looking intact and in good health. So I
relaxed a bit and reassured myself that I hadn't made a big mistake in
letting them go home after their domestic altercation.

"Hello, Doctor," Mrs. Mason said, as she reached out to gently
shake my hand. "William will be along in a few minutes," she added.
"He didn't want to walk with us. He always likes to go another way."

Mr. Mason sought to explain.

"It's just as well, Doctor, since we'd like to meet with you first, if
that's alright," he said. "William said he'll wait for us to come out. He
says he has something to say to you, too, although I don't know what
he's got on his mind. It's pretty unusual for him, Doctor, let me tell
you. I mean, to want to talk to someone like you."

We settled into my office, and Mr. Mason reached over and
handed me a large faded envelope, stuffed full of papers he'd saved
across the years. Even before I opened it, I knew it must be William's
envelope, for I'd had so many parents do this same thing during initial
visits about their troubled children. I knew it would contain the official story of the Masons and their lives together as parents and child.

"There they are," he said with finality. "There are all of my son's
records for you to read." He handed it over as though he'd released a

huge burden. He even sighed with relief as he sat back in his chair.

The envelope contained various reports and documents collected over many years. There were brief evaluations from William's school days, beginning approximately in the second grade. There were copies of records from his visits to several different kinds of doctors. A neurologist's report, for example, from almost thirty-five years before. And a list of a school psychologist's recommendations made to William's parents in a letter written during William's adolescent years. And there was a psychiatrist's diagnostic summary, composed when William would have been in his twenties. These were ordered chronologically and neatly stacked.

There were even copies of his rejection letters from various branches of the military, received after his physical and mental evaluations prior to induction. His draft board had classified him 4-F, and even his parents' unexpected desire for him to join the service hadn't been enough to get him in.

"He was only out of the house for a few months, really," Mrs. Mason said, as I read through the many papers they'd brought me. "He'd go off for a few weeks or so, to look for a job, or to see some part of the country," she added calmly. "But he'd always come back without any money or a job. He'd just show up one day unannounced and need a place to stay."

"We could never turn him away, Doctor," Mr. Mason interrupted. "After all he *was* our son. Our only child. We'd keep his room just the way it was, you know, in case he came home again. But each time we'd hope it would work out."

Mrs. Mason was glancing around my office, and I could see she was even trying to read some of the titles of the books I had in a bookshelf next to her chair. Finally, she gazed up to the wall beside her, where I kept a photograph of my children.

"Oh . . . you have sons, too, Doctor," she said with genuine delight. I looked up from my reading momentarily to respond.

"Yes, I have two sons," I said.

"Oh, really. Very good, very good. Might I ask how old they are?" she said, smiling sweetly.

"One is seven, and the other is about a year old," I answered proudly.

"It's good you have more than one, you know, Doctor. It's good you have more than one child," she repeated more softly, as she stared intently at the photograph on the wall.

"All kinds of bad things can happen to children, you know," she said, turning to me directly. "They can get sick—they can even die. And they can go bad on you, too," she added almost as an afterthought. Her mood just then seemed to darken. "It's just not wise to have only one child."

I nodded slowly, although I was not prepared to pursue my curiosity about her comment. Instead, I pulled out one particular report about William Mason that had caught my eye before his mother interrupted my reading. It was the psychiatrist's evaluation of William performed decades before. It was written in a language I understood.

"I see that Dr. Johannsen evaluated your son," I said. "Do you remember what he had to say in his note?" They both nodded that they did. I had the feeling they'd probably read these papers many times over the years, in search of some clue or answer that had somehow eluded them before.

"It never really made a lot of sense to us, though," Mr. Mason offered sadly, as his wife nodded in agreement. "Maybe it's because I'm a banker by training, I just can't understand some of that medical gobbledygook you fellows throw around."

"Well, it says here that William has *schizoid tendencies*," I recited from the report. That specific phrase resonated with my own initial impressions of the man I'd met in the emergency room. The man who was their child. "Is that what you mean? Is that one of the terms you don't understand?"

"Yes, Doctor," Mrs. Mason replied instantly. "We've never really understood what that meant. Dr. Johannsen tried to explain it to us, though. It has something to do with William not having any friends, doesn't it? And because he seems so, well, so irregular?" She looked to me sincerely, as if I might now at long last give her some essential understanding she'd been denied by the other experts with whom she'd discussed her son so long before.

"Yes, Mrs. Mason, those are reasons for using that particular term," I said. "This letter is rather old now, though. Did William see Dr. Johannsen at all, I mean, did he see him for treatment after this evaluation was completed?"

"No, I don't think the doctor wanted to see him again, really," she said. "He seemed pretty pessimistic about William's chances. At least, that was my feeling at the time," she added, glancing to her husband.

"That was my understanding, too," Mr. Mason said. "He gave me the notion that William would always be that way. And I suppose he was right, now that I look back. When he was younger we just hoped it would all get better one day . . . one day when he'd be older. You know, when he got out of school and found a job. We hoped he'd just grow out of it. After a while, we stopped going to doctors about William. Just didn't seem much point to it. He didn't get worse, really. He stayed pretty much the same all those years."

"There weren't any times when he was functioning better or worse than usual?" I asked.

"No, not really," Mr. Mason replied. "He wandered around a bit, and we kept hoping he'd call us and say he had a job, or he'd found a place of his own. But we never heard from him. He never really made any friends—none that we knew about anyway. Why, he never even dated a girl during high school, either. He never had any real interest in dating women."

"It *wasn't* supposed to be this way, Doctor," Mrs. Mason said. "It really wasn't supposed to be this way at all." And then she paused and seemed about to cry.

"What do you mean?" I asked. "How *was* it supposed to be?"

She shook her head slowly and began to forage through her pocketbook for a tissue. I handed her the box of Kleenex I kept on the side of my desk. She wiped a tiny tear from the corner of her eye.

"He was supposed to graduate from medical school in the class of '63," Mr. Mason answered for his wife. "He was supposed to be a doctor like yourself. But it just wasn't meant to be, I suppose."

"We saved money for so many years," Mrs. Mason added. "So our William could go to a good college and then to medical school." She wiped away another tear, even as it began to form and glisten. "We wanted him to be happy, to make something of himself. You know, we wanted him to get ahead in this world."

Mr. Mason cleared his throat, the way he'd done that first time I'd met him in the emergency room. It was his cue that he was about to say something important. Something formal.

"Doctor, one of the reasons we so looked forward to coming here today is that we'd like to have some answers," he said. "We don't have too many years left, I mean my wife and I, and we both have a need to make some sense of all of this—our son, and how things went wrong." He paused to look to his wife and then back again to me. "When we're all alone, which isn't too often, my wife and I wonder out loud if it was *our* fault. I mean, was it our fault that William turned out the way he is?"

He looked to me as his wife had done, as though *I* might be the one to have the final answer, some basic insight into their entire lives as William's parents. Lives they had now begun to see largely in terms of failure and through the dark glass of unrealized ambitions for their only child.

"I was a banker here in town for many years, Doctor," he went on. "I was something of a success myself. But nothing was more important than my son. For both of us, my wife and I. We tried to love him and take care of him every way we could think of. At a time when no one was saving for the future, we started a bank account for his college education. He was just a little baby when we started that, but we knew we'd have it for him when he needed it." He seemed dejected. "That money's all gone now, though. We gave it to him in bits and pieces over the years. Each time he'd go away on a trip, we'd give him a certain amount of money. And each time, he'd come back with nothing."

"We figured the money was his, you see," Mrs. Mason interrupted. "We never thought he'd spend it all. We thought he'd settle in and go to school. But he never did."

"Please let me finish what I was saying," Mr. Mason requested politely and gently of his wife.

"Go ahead, dear," she said.

"I was a banker. Now I'm retired, of course, but I still think like a banker thinks," he continued. "This may sound funny, but I think of children as a kind of an investment that parents make. That probably seems harsh and unfeeling. But when Grace and I decided to have children, I know I thought about the pros and the cons. You know, I weighed the advantages and the disadvantages of children. And when I finally decided to go ahead with it, I approached it like everything else then. I made damn sure I did it right." Mr. Mason gestured forcefully with his frail thin arms, pointing to the ceiling with a withered index finger.

"My father always used to say 'Anything worth doing is worth doing right,'" he added. "But I don't know if I would've had the guts to admit it to you then. You know, admit that I saw my son as a long-term investment. Not back then. It just wouldn't be seemly."

"And now you feel you can?" I asked.

"That's right. What do I have to lose now? The fact is, I just want to understand before I die—was it something we didn't do? Or was it something we did? But it all happened so slowly, and sort of, well, sort of spread out over the years. We hardly knew there was a problem until one day there it was, smack dab in front of us."

"You mean to say that William's problems became apparent gradually?"

"It seems that way to us now, Doctor," Mrs. Mason said. "It started with little things, really. Odd things in the way he was when he was very young. They weren't *terrible* things; don't get me wrong. But they were . . . well, they were *different*."

"Such as?"

"He never really seemed to care if he had any friends." She answered immediately and as though she'd already given my question at least a decade of careful thought. "Even when he was a toddler and we'd try to invite other children over to the yard, he'd want to go off by himself, or go in the house. We had to almost force him to play with other children."

"We thought it would improve with time," Mr. Mason added hopefully. "But it stayed that way right on through elementary school. And right into high school, too. By then, it seemed we couldn't do anything to make it better. We couldn't force him to make friends. All he wanted was be alone—to be left alone in his room."

"We never really had a sense of what was wrong," his wife added. "The only person who ever tried to give it a name was Dr. Johannsen. And he couldn't really explain it that well, either."

Something was very upsetting about this elderly couple sitting there with me, agonizing over their child's life, uncertain when or how things had first gone wrong. Wondering how they might be to blame for his situation, which had now become *their* situation again. William was back home, and nothing seemed likely to change the circumstances of their lives. And not just the immediate circumstances of living with what appeared to be a mentally ill, or at least a socially deviant, adult child. The situation seemed hopeless, and it had seemed that way to them for more than a few years. Only now were they actively seeking help again, and primarily because of their concerns over William's uncertain future, a future *without* his parents to care for him any longer. But even more pressing seemed to be their *fear* of William and what he might do to them when they became unable to care for themselves.

"We don't want to throw our own son out of his home, Doctor," Mrs. Mason said sincerely. "He's our flesh and blood! But we're becoming more frightened of him now, and that's a new feeling for us. We're afraid he could hurt us." She trembled visibly as she said her last few words. Her husband reached over, and with his own shaking hand, touched her on the sleeve to reassure her he was there beside her. "We're not as strong as we once were," she added finally.

"He's supposed to care for *us* in our old age," Mr. Mason said. "At least, if he's going to live in our house and eat our food, he should begin to pitch in and help out. But he does nothing. He just lives in that house day in and day out and does nothing at all. We don't talk to him. He doesn't talk to us. He tries to avoid us, even when he has to go to the kitchen or the bathroom. We'll hear him in the middle of the night, creeping down the hall to take a bath."

"And it's usually long overdue," Mrs. Mason added.

"He's supposed to be taking care of *us* now, not the other way around!" Mr. Mason raised his voice. "Did we give him too much? Didn't we love him in the . . . in the right way? He's been the center of our lives for so long, and now we just want to see him go away. We just want him to go away and never come back." Mr. Mason became visibly upset as he said this difficult thing. His wife sobbed silently.

And as things would happen, at that very moment there was a quiet thud outside my door. Not really someone knocking, but just a soft bumping against the door to my office.

"That will be William," Mrs. Mason said, in a more controlled voice. She wrapped her tissue neatly into a square and placed it in her handbag, clicking it shut. Mr. Mason also adjusted himself in his chair, pulling at the hem in his suit coat, removing the wrinkles as he did. This dignified couple resumed their more reserved pose, but not in a cold or calculating way. Rather, they seemed intent on holding themselves together in the presence of their son.

Since our discussion had been abruptly ended by the noise at the door, I rose from my chair and walked toward the unusual sound. The soft bumping noise had continued unabated. As I opened the door, I could see William's shadow move quickly from the threshold. He stood just outside the door, again with his face pointed to the side, his eyes directed toward the floor. I suspected he wouldn't say a word until spoken to, and so I asked him to wait a few minutes more and then it would be his turn to come into my office.

William mumbled something that made me think he understood, and then he walked slowly down the hall.

I sat down again to finish my time with Mr. and Mrs. Mason. I had one final question I wanted to ask at that particular moment.

"What is it you think I might do that could help you in this situation?" Mr. Mason looked to his wife, as if neither one of them knew the answer to my question. It was as though they'd hoped I would tell them everything, without their having to specify any needs. Finally, Mrs. Mason broke the silence.

"Well, for myself, Doctor, I don't know if I think there *is* anything you can do right now. The way I see it, Elliot and I have to decide how much longer we can tolerate this. The policeman told us William would have to hurt someone, or at least threaten to hurt one of us, before we could get any help from the authorities. He pretty much left it up to us, to Elliot and me, to . . . .to *evict* William."

"That's what he told us to do," Mr. Mason blurted. "He told us we should just throw William out."

"It's not easy to evict your own child from the house in which he was raised," Mrs. Mason said sadly. "We *do* love our son, you know. We want him to be taken care of even after we're gone. You see, we gave up on our dreams about his future years ago—about the time he turned thirty. Now it's fear that seems to torture us. Fear about our own future with William."

■

As I paused before going to find William Mason, I thought about what the nature of his problem might be. I was aided by the many reports and opinions of others, the ones who'd seen him before. The most helpful information had been the note from the psychiatrist who, I felt, had correctly diagnosed William's problem from their first meeting. At least, he'd given it a name that conformed with the current psychiatric thinking about William's peculiar pattern of behavior and development.

William could be diagnosed with something psychiatrists now call *schizoid personality disorder*. It is a pattern of behavior characterized by a gradual deterioration in social relationships, although even a very young child can demonstrate an unusually strong and active avoidance of other people, as in William's case. But the more pronounced features of this disorder typically become most apparent during adolescence or early adulthood, at a time when the affected person—perhaps for the *first* time in his or her life—has more freedom to decide whether to mingle with other people or not. When they are finally given more of a choice, individuals with this personality style will select isolation and will generally ban others from their world.

Schizoid adults can also develop what might seem mildly bizarre behavior. They can appear cold and aloof and seem to experience a restricted range of emotion. In social situations they can show little nonverbal communication. They tend to smile very little, for example. And they may not even be able to manage a nod to indicate they understand what someone else has said to them. And yet, they comprehend most of what goes on around them, for they are not mentally incompetent or insane, at least not in the traditional meaning of those terms. Instead, and for whatever reason, they've chosen to retreat into their own personal and very private world. As a result, they can seem more out of touch with reality than most of the people one might meet. Because of this, people who encounter a schizoid person for the first time might think that person must be psychotic or mentally retarded.

Like William, schizoid people will typically show no interest in sexual experiences with another person. And they may not enjoy being with familiar relatives, as is the case in other disorders that seem to be based on a paralyzing fear of *new* people or novel social situations. The better functioning schizoid individual might be employed and able to hold down a job. But typically their work will allow them a good amount of isolation from others—a "niche" the schizoid adult seeks out intentionally—perhaps a job as a night watchman, or a clerk stationed at a lone computer terminal day in and day out. These lucky ones have somehow managed to adapt to the world around them. A world that doesn't look kindly upon those who actively shun social relationships.

But the ones who cannot obtain work to begin with, or who have problems keeping a job, will often be found eking out their existence in skid-row neighborhoods. This particular disorder is thought to be overrepresented among the urban homeless and among "hermits" residing in desolate, rural areas.

Although the most serious cases of schizoid personality disorder are thought to be uncommon, most people will quickly recognize at least one extended family member who shows some characteristics suggestive of such a pattern. The most common practical problems arising from this condition are chronic or intermittent unemployment and difficulties associated with forming and maintaining warm and rewarding social relationships. Adult children with such issues may, from their perspective, wisely, choose to remain at home rather than take their chances elsewhere.

In William's case, he was able to use his childhood home as a base for many years, as he would briefly journey into the outside world, always at the urging of his concerned parents. But he would return soon thereafter, learning he simply couldn't get along in any place that was filled with other people. In the end, his parents had allowed him to return for good, providing him with the necessities of life and the one thing that meant the most to him of all—a room of his own. A room with a door he could close to shut out the world he had no interest in.

Now as I walked from my office to fetch William, I mused over the meaning of his psychiatric diagnosis. I realized it only helped me to put a name to the problem and to devise some sketch of what his past, present and future might be like. I knew that in all likelihood William had showed this pattern of behavior throughout his life, although perhaps it had been more subtle when he was younger. And I knew he would probably always be this way.

He was waiting for me toward the end of the hallway, staring into

the wall and away from the mainstream of people walking just behind him. Because there was no window, no picture for him to look
at, only the bare wall, a few people would pause to glance at William
and wonder what was wrong. But he was oblivious to them and to the
strangeness of the scene he created.

"Hello, William," I greeted him, and he grunted in my direction.
"Would you like to come to my office now? It's your turn to talk with
me." Without making eye contact, he began to shuffle along the side
of the hallway, much as he'd done before when I'd met him. But he
seemed to move with a sense of purpose now, I imagined. He appeared more motivated than when we'd spoken in the emergency
room several days before, though he still seemed a tired and defeated
middle-aged man.

He entered my office and walked straight to a chair in the corner,
without looking at anything else in the room. He turned quickly, still
staring at the floor, and sat down, almost as a robot might. As he did,
he seemed to rock very slightly back and forth, and he mumbled to
himself very softly. If I hadn't known his history, I would have
thought he was blind or autistic.

"So, William," I started, "is there anything you'd like to say to me?"
He ceased his gentle rocking and spoke immediately.

"Yes, I have a lot to say," he announced, surprising me with this
unusually forthright approach. His response made me momentarily
uncertain whether my guess at a diagnosis had been correct. But I
soon remembered that many individuals with schizoid personalities
could rise to certain occasions, if it was in their interest to do so. In
fact, *this* was the inherent mystery of the problem—the fact that they
were people who were mentally and linguistically intact, but chose to
behave as if they weren't.

William began to speak again.

"I came here today because *I* wanted to, you know?" he said. I nodded that I understood.

"Nobody can *make* me do this," he warned me. "No one can make
me go talk to a shrink." His statement made me suspect he'd had this
kind of discussion many times with his parents, as they'd probably
encouraged him to seek professional help. But I was curious as to why
he would agree *now*, after so many years of active and successful re-

sistance. In some ways, both he and his parents projected a sense of desperation. Somehow, something *had* changed, which was why they *all* seemed more motivated now.

"They shouldn't have called the police on me," he told me. "There was no good reason to call the police. My mother is just plain crazy if she thinks I'm gonna hurt Daddy. I wouldn't hurt Daddy." His moderately defiant independence was slipping away now and was being replaced by a sadder, more helpless tone.

"I think she was afraid you might do something to your father," I offered. "What did you do or say that made her feel that way? Do you remember doing anything in particular?" I asked.

"They were bugging me like they always do," he said. "They were trying to make me go outside, and I didn't want to. I don't like going outside in the daytime, it's too bright and there's too many people. I like to go out at night. They know that," he added. "They shouldn't try to make me go outside when I don't want to."

"What did they ask you to do exactly?" I asked.

"They told me to go pick up leaves," he replied. "I had other things to do."

"What other things did you have to do instead of picking up leaves?"

"I was working on a project," he said. "And they interrupted me in the middle of it."

"A project?"

"Yeah, I was studying in my room with my coin collection," he said. "Once a month I go over the whole collection and make sure I know all the coins I have. I have 3,211 coins in my collection, you know?"

"Really," I said, trying to seem sincerely interested in his hobby. "I didn't know that. Your parents didn't mention it to me."

"No, they wouldn't. They think I'm too old to collect coins," he said. "But a lot of famous people do, you know?"

William shifted his head from right to left, as he'd done when I met him in the emergency room. As he did this, he made eye contact with me for just an instant. At that precise moment he looked into my eyes deeply, as he tried to gauge if I was *truly* interested in his coins. If I'd blinked just then, I would have missed it.

"But they don't care about what I'm interested in," he continued.

"All they ever talk about is how I didn't go to medical school and be a doctor." He shook his head slightly and sat back a bit in his chair. "If I hear one more word about the class of '63 I'll just go crazy."

"Can you tell more about that, William?" I asked, surprised at his ability to share this piece of information.

"I'm sure they told you all about it," he said. "They tell anyone who'll listen. About the son who never became a doctor, even though they did everything they could." His anger turned into sadness, as he began to turn it inside out.

"I know I'm a failure. They don't have to tell me. I know I didn't do much, like everybody else. But they don't have to keep bothering me about it, do they?"

We went on like this for several minutes, carrying on what was almost a normal conversation. We discussed his attempts to leave his home, to find a job—and the chain of failures he had encountered. I was surprised at how open and forthcoming William now appeared, despite his long history of refusing any help. Something was somehow different now. Something had changed.

Eventually we returned to more recent events, to the crisis that had led up to our first meeting.

"What happened the other day . . . I mean, when your mother called the police?" I asked. "Did you do something that might have frightened her?"

"It was just talk, that's all, just talk," he said. "When I get mad I just say I'm gonna do things. You know, do things to get them to leave me alone."

"What did you say exactly?"

"I . . . I guess I said I was bigger and stronger than Daddy and Mommy now," he replied meekly. "And if they didn't leave me alone I was gonna beat Daddy up. That's probably what I said."

"You said you say these kinds of things when you're mad," I asked, remembering that schizoid individuals typically do not show intense anger—at least not nearly as frequently as people with personalities in the normal range. I suspected that the anger he claimed to feel might not have been openly expressed in the way that most people might show it. He might have seemed quite calm as he spoke those desperate words of violence to his father.

"What *makes* you feel so mad?" I asked.

"I don't *really* want to be the boss in the house, you know," he said. "I just want them to leave me alone. Just let me do my projects. When they bother me, and I'm working on something important, I feel like I'm their little kid again. I don't like that. That's when I tell them I'm going to hurt them. When they try to come in my room and tell me what to do. When they act like everything is the same as it used to be."

William seemed to wonder why his parents would ever need to bother him at all, as though they should have figured out his likes and dislikes many years before. I suddenly realized he was talking to me now for much the same reason his parents had consulted all the experts about him long ago. He wanted me to change *their* behavior. He wanted me to fix the situation for him, as well.

"But I don't *want* to be the one in charge," he went on. "I don't *want* to be responsible." He shifted in his chair, his upper body remaining rather stiff and protective. "They're sicker now, my parents, I mean. One of them could get real sick and die," he said with apprehension. "And then what am I gonna do?" He fidgeted more anxiously in his chair. "Who's going to take care of me then?" he pleaded.

Our conversation went on like this for about another half hour. We really accomplished little that day, at least in terms of changing the situation, or modifying William's behavior. But my time with him had offered some insight into how the Masons could avoid future crises like the one they'd encountered only a few days before. This part would be easy.

But I had few ideas about how they might solve the *real* dilemma in their lives, or about Mr. and Mrs. Mason's questions as to what had gone wrong in William's life and who was to blame, and what exactly they should do about him now or in the future.

Similarly, I had few easy answers for William's worries over his own later years, after his parents were unable to care for him any longer.

■

Three weeks later, Mrs. Mason called me and asked for another appointment. She told me things were a better now, although William was much the same. My advice about how to prevent his threats of violence appeared to be working, and this had somehow energized the Masons to see me once again. I had advised them against direct confrontation—at least for the near future—and rehearsed with them a basic approach for making their wants known as to a child, a method that still allowed William certain choices. It didn't deny him his seemingly crucial sense of dignity and autonomy, which were the only things he still sought to maintain in his childhood home.

By then, the Masons had also had contact with the Department of Social Services, which had already closed their case. William hadn't actually hurt his parents yet, and in the workings of such large bureaucracies, priorities were often determined by the seriousness and immediacy of each case. The Masons had also met with an advocate for the elderly, a woman who had much experience with parents of adult children living at home. I knew of her excellent reputation, and it made me more comfortable leaving the situation entirely in her hands.

But Mrs. Mason told me on the phone that they still had some things they wanted to discuss. It might only take another session, she thought. And so I agreed to meet with William's parents once more.

Several days before I knew they would arrive to see me, I pulled out an article I'd copied a few years before. It was a theoretical article from a professional journal—about the psychological meaning of children to their parents. The author had studied parents and children under stress and had tried to make sense of what he'd seen. He made a rather provocative claim in his writing about the meaning of the child—made statements that I suspected were largely dismissed by his readers. But I'd saved this article for some reason, perhaps because his words had resonated with at least some of my own experiences.

It was Mr. and Mrs. Mason's comments during the follow-up visit that prompted me to find and reread that essay. For example, Mr. Mason's *banker's* assessment of the meaning of the child. He said he thought of children as "investments."

And there was Mrs. Mason's broad advice for parents to have more than one child, since all kinds of unexpected things could happen. An attitude I thought she must have gleaned from a life of disappointment with her son.

I'd seldom heard such no-nonsense, unromantic and practical views of the child in adult life before. Of course, the parents of my patients were all much younger than William's father and mother, and most were newly immersed in caring for their children. Even Mr. Mason had suggested his comment was one he would never have made as a younger man. But now he intimated that, even as he had contemplated William's conception, his son had been a kind of plan being put into place. A plan that would reap rewards further down the road for both William *and* his parents. And it was only later, as an older man toward the end of his life, that he became able to openly draw his practical banker's comparison. Only as he was forced to look back on the meaning of his child.

The article I found in my files said something very similar. The author had noted that parents, in the face of life's stress, psychologically view their children as something tantamount to a concrete resource, much in the way they would view other assets or investments and even the various objects they might happen to possess. This process, he argued, was largely out of their conscious awareness, and it was only when they were forced to consider the meaning of the child during times of failure—or perhaps in the face of some serious crisis or disappointment—that it might come into clearer view.

Mr. Mason had unabashedly compared his son to a financial investment from the very beginning. And his awareness of this had even been a part of his eventual decision to have a child at all. An investment with some degree of risk, or so it now appeared to him in retrospect. Mrs. Mason seemed more attuned to the emotional wages a parent might be forced to pay when the dream was left unrealized— the dream that *is* the child—and to the damage done when the initial investment of the adult self is somehow rendered worthless. But even her assessment of William's problems had somehow come back to her *own* sense of loss. The loss of what *she* had expected.

"Doctor, we wanted to see you again so we could finish saying some things we didn't have a chance to say last week." Mr. Mason once more began our discussion, taking charge of the situation in a manner faintly reminiscent of his earlier and more dynamic years in the world of finance.

"Yes, Doctor," Mrs. Mason added, "we found it very helpful to get some of these things out into the open last month. After so many years of just talking about it between ourselves." She paused, but then spoke again, before I could manage a reply.

"I'm not a psychologist or anything like that, of course," she said, "but Elliot and I are at that point in our lives when it is very important to us to understand what's happened. I mean, to accept our son and what our lives have come to." She seemed more in control than during our previous meetings. I suspected that the fear of her son had temporarily subsided, and that she'd given her thoughts careful consideration prior to our meeting.

"Yes, that's right, Doctor," Mr. Mason said. "I think we are running out of time . . . well, only a few years left, anyway, where we'll be able to think about these things and come to any real conclusion. You know, a conclusion that will help us to make peace with William. To accept what he is and to finally know that he isn't the son we thought we'd have."

"He *should* be a comfort to us now," Mrs. Mason explained. She had said this same thing during our previous session. "He should reassure us in our old age. The way that nice girl Cynthia is so helpful and supportive to her mother, Mrs. Ponte. She's an elderly woman just down the street from us. Cynthia's not married—just like William—but she seems so much better . . . well, so much better adjusted," she added. "She is such a comfort to her mother now when she needs her most."

Mrs. Mason glanced up again at the photograph of my two sons on the wall. "We should have had more than one child, Elliot. We just should have had more than one."

"For me, Doctor," Mr. Mason began, "it's a matter of coming to grips with how much William's failures have become, well, how they've become my own failure as a man. These days I feel like, well, I feel as though I never really accomplished anything much in my life. I know it doesn't seem too reasonable. I mean, I know I can point to my career, to my home, to my marriage to Grace. You know, I can go down the list of the things I *should* be proud of. The things that should make me happy now."

For the first time, as he began to relax in my presence, I realized Mr. Mason seemed defeated, even moderately depressed.

"But my son turned out to be much more important than I'd ever imagined before. It's as if I will die without leaving anything behind me. Nothing of any *real* value, that is. I have no grandchildren. My son will never be much of anything at all. I know now that William will never change. He'll never be the son I wanted."

As Mr. Mason uttered these words—and in a tone that saddened me immensely—I thought of the psychoanalyst Erik Erikson. Erikson had theorized about the developmental stages of a person's psychological life and had written that the last stage of human development was concerned with the resolution of an essential psychological conflict within the self. He felt it was a conflict that could render one of two possible outcomes. He called the positive outcome a realization of a sense of personal *generativity*. By this he meant the achievement of a psychological task that allows an older person to feel his or her life has contributed to the lives of others, and that his or her own existence somehow fit in with the lives of those who'd come before and with those lifetimes yet to come. The successful realization of this developmental goal, Erikson supposed, was to provide older persons with a calmer, more accepting view toward the gradual and unrelenting deterioration of the self, and he guessed it might allow them the ability to better cope with the prospect of death itself.

The undesirable alternative outcome of this developmental stage, according to Erikson's theory, was to know despair. It was to know a sense of personal failure that a person could only experience toward the *end* of one's life. This could be more intense and powerful than any disappointment or sadness one might have known before, for it was the overwhelming feeling and belief that one's entire life had been for naught. Such an overwhelming sense of defeat could, in turn, set the stage for what one philosopher had called "the sickness unto death."

Mr. and Mrs. Mason were now at this point, locked in the psychological struggle between knowing their lives held some final and lasting value, versus a dark, bottomless despondency implicit in discovering that the meaning of their lives had been illusory.

And, as Mr. Mason had pointed out, nothing else seemed to matter. Not their own personal successes, their happy memories, nor the assets they'd acquired. Their son William—a daily reminder of the child they could never have—now impinged on their personal worlds in ways they'd never imagined. Always hopeful things might

233

change—that he might turn around and make the leap from odd middle-aged man to the son they'd always envisioned—they were only now coming to terms with the likelihood this would never happen. Not in their lifetime, and not in William's lifetime either.

This had proved to be too much to absorb, especially now, as they gradually became less vital and more dependent. If they could help it, they would gladly choose to avoid the ultimate confrontation with personal meaning even a while longer. But their circumstances somehow no longer allowed it.

"What we wanted to ask you, Doctor . . ." Mrs. Mason finally said. "The reason we wanted to see you again is this. Can you help us to resolve this somehow? Will you try to help us find an answer?" Her body trembled slightly as she said this, as a shudder seemed to travel down her spine.

"If we don't come up with an answer soon, then it will all seem to be for nothing. And that's *not* what we bargained for," she added solemnly, gazing up to the photograph of my sons on the wall beside her. Her husband nodded in agreement, as he looked down to the floor. His wife sadly repeated her words again.

"We just never bargained for anything like this when we decided to have a child."

EPILOGUE

I SIT ON THE GENTLY SLOPING HILL that overlooks my home. As the winter's day turns to night, I can see the lights inside my house begin to shine through the windows. My youngest son is running across the lawn in front of me. Since he is relatively new to this world, he clumsily trips over a toy and rolls happily down the hill. He is almost two years old, another boy—his name is Conor.

It seems that sons have become a kind of specialty for me. He is my third child, and he will be the last. Surprisingly, there is some measure of both sadness and perspective in such a realization, in knowing I will have no more children. As I view my son just beneath me on the grassy knoll, I find myself thinking back to the time of his birth and to the joy and anxiety we knew upon his arrival. I remember quite clearly taking him from his mother's embrace and the look in his gentle, frightened eyes. He had emerged whole and intact, the rosy color of his newborn's skin shining in an otherwise uninspiring and sterile delivery room. I recall the relief and celebration in bringing him home to his brothers, and how seemingly well prepared we were for him. Much better prepared than in the early, uncertain days of first parenthood.

I am lost in these thoughts about my son's first few hours of life when suddenly he is sitting on my crossed legs, pointing up toward the darkened sky above us. This time with him becomes a quiet moment with a beloved child that a parent might savor above all others.

"Mooon . . . ," he says in singsong fashion, and with a clear sense of his infant wonder. "Mooon . . . ," he says again, pointing above.

The moon is particularly bright and prominent in the sky tonight, and it seems so close to him that he reaches out as if to touch it. But he soon realizes he cannot.

"Yes, it's the moon," I echo back. He snuggles closer to me against the wintry chill and for reassurance against the darkness that begins to envelop us.

We sit there silently, taking in the broad universe that is spread out before us. From the distance I hear the sounds of the commuters' cars speeding along the nearby highway. I can see the lights of the city just beyond, and they begin to grow brighter. These sights and sounds serve to remind me of the complexities of modern urban life and of the many dangers I know lie hidden there. With this realization—and as my infant son clutches closer to me in the cold night air—I perceive a parental fear rising within me.

"Oh, that you could live forever," I say silently to my little son, although I know this cannot possibly be. And so I revise my parent's prayer.

"At least, I hope you'll be safe and happy and healthy all your life."

The concerns I once had for myself, I now have for my children. My dreams and wishes—and my expectations and fears.

Although I am aware my children cannot *be* my life, it is clear they have become central to what I am as a person. How is it that children become so essential to what we are? What is the exact nature of our relationships with our own children? What are these thoughts and feelings for my sons, and how are they different from the way I think about other people's children?

Slowly my tiny son leans over and rests his head upon my shoulder. In that moment I know an intimate bond that perhaps only a parent can experience—or, anyone, really, who has set aside a substantial part of his or her own life to care for and nurture a child. It is a bond that is simultaneously primary and intense. We both sit in a state of wonder, my infant son and I, focused upon new worlds we have only begun to discover. He, in awe of the sky above, and I in contemplation about the meaning of this child and the essential power he now wields within my adult life.

• • •

This book, a collection of stories about extraordinary children I have known, is my attempt to explore certain aspects of adult-child relations. It is an indirect approach, admittedly—perhaps too oblique a method to provide a clear understanding of such a complicated matter. But I seriously doubt that anyone can write a book that captures the essence of this human relationship in direct or exacting terms.

I do know, for example, that the children I encounter each day in my work, as well as my own children, raise questions and emotions within me that can often be difficult to explain in very precise terms or in any sort of psychological jargon. The special knowledge I gain from them, and from having children in my life, may be knowable only at the level of emotion, and therefore, difficult to share with others in an objective manner. I think of it as a knowledge held deep within my heart, for lack of a more scientific term to explain the process or its nature.

If these stories have made you reflect, if they have somehow made you think more carefully about children and their role in the psychological lives of the adults around them, then I have accomplished what I intended. It is likely that each of us will make sense of these extraordinary young lives in our own way and perhaps find something of personal meaning or value. I do know that these children are a part of my life now, and I have learned much from time spent with them and with their parents.

I have also learned from the other adults who have somehow become important to these children's lives—the doctors and nurses who care for them and provided them solace, for example, and the teachers who help to guide their way. I've learned, too, from the strangers and neighbors whose contact was less intense. Though I haven't actually met most of those people, knowledge does derive from learning of their reactions to such children, from seeing the prejudice and fear in some people's response to the child who is very different, as well as the immense kindness and compassion many adults will gladly offer to the atypical child they encounter—the sick or physically defective child, for example, or the poor child who has known hunger and neglect. The children who, for whatever reason, are thought of as imperfect.

It seems that *these* are the children whose lives serve to tell us the most about ourselves and about the real place of children in the world around us. These extraordinary children, and the manner in which we respond to them, may reveal to us the truth about the meaning and the value of the child. These are the ones whose existence directly and dramatically challenges our deepest beliefs about the sacred status of the child—of *any* child, not just the child who happens to be our own.